three
more
words

ALSO BY ASHLEY RHODES-COURTER

three little words

three

ASHLEY RHODES-COURTER

more

words

atheneum

NEW YORK LONDON TORONTO SYDNEY NEW DELHI

ATHENEUM

An imprint of Simon & Schuster Children's Publishing Division

1230 Avenue of the Americas, New York, New York 10020

For information about special discounts for bulk purchases, please contact Simon & Schuster Special Sales at 1-866-506-1949 or business@simonandschuster.com.

The Simon & Schuster Speakers Bureau can bring authors to your live event. For more information or to book an event, contact the Simon & Schuster Speakers Bureau at 1-866-248-3049 or visit our website at www.simonspeakers.com.

The text for this book is set in Bodoni Twelve ITC.

Manufactured in the United States of America

First Edition

2 4 6 8 10 9 7 5 3 1

Library of Congress Cataloging-in-Publication Data

Rhodes-Courter, Ashley, 1985–

Three more words / Ashley Rhodes-Courter. — First edition.

pages cm

ISBN 978-1-4814-1557-6 (hardcover)

ISBN 978-1-4814-1559-0 (eBook)

1. Rhodes-Courter, Ashley, 1985– 2. Adopted children—United States—Biography.

3. Foster children—United States—Biography. 4. Foster home care—United States.

I. Title.

HV874.R56A3 2015

363.73092—dc23

[B] 2014035385

The palest ink is better than the best memory.
—Chinese proverb

For my husband, Erick,
and for Millie, who never lived
happily ever after

Four cops burst into a condemned home and march every-one out the door with their hands raised high. Two officers wait outside while the others investigate the dwelling. Inside, the walls are crumbling. The smell is so fetid that the first officer gags; the second uses a handkerchief to cover his mouth and nose. The first officer spots what he thinks might be a body in the corner of the room. He bends closer and touches the woman's outstretched arm.

"She's breathing, but unresponsive," he calls to his partner. "She must be high on something."

The second officer stumbles over a coffee table littered with vials containing squarish rocks. "They've got the whole setup." He points to some small glass pipes, a bowl of steel wool, and scattered lighters.

The woman moves. The cop startles and draws his gun. Out from under her, a little boy wiggles himself free and blinks in the light from the open front door.

"Hey, there's a kid here," he shouts. "Call it in. He'll need to be removed immediately."

He carries the docile boy with the wild bush of hair to the patrol car. The child is clutching a bottle of souring milk and a filthy baby blanket with a silken edge that he has worn into tatters. His sodden diaper droops to his knees. When his huge chocolate eyes land on one of the cuffed and shackled men, the boy strains toward him, his arms beseeching. "Eh! Eh!" the boy says, without the language to identify what he wants.

Although neither my husband nor I yet know it, in a few hours this same little boy will be in our foster home. I still have terror-filled memories of the moment I was wrenched from my mother's arms as a young child and placed into the maw of Florida's foster care system, where I did not emerge for the next nine years.

Now I was the foster mother and was determined to give this little boy everything I had been denied. "It's going to be okay," I would murmur to him. Yes, I whisper the promise. It will be okay, both for him . . . and for myself.

1.

three little words

The ones I pity are the ones who never stick out their neck for something they believe, never know the taste of moral struggle, and never have the thrill of victory.
—Jonathan Kozol

A thousand eyes were staring, expectant and ready to listen to me. For some people public speaking triggers a primal fear, arousing the fight-or-flight response, but each time I face an audience I look forward to another chance to be heard. During my almost ten years in Florida's foster care system I had no voice, even when I had something important—possibly lifesaving—to say. Even more, I was branded a liar because nobody wanted to hear the truth. Since everything I did as a kid became a part of my case file, attempts to discredit my word were written up as official documents and could have ruined any chances I had to be adopted or to lead a normal life.

The people who come to hear me speak often have special connections to the foster care system. Among them are parents, judges, legislators, social workers, child welfare executives, and teachers. Sometimes my audience is made up of children or teens who have experienced loss or trauma like I did, or maybe they are young people from more traditional backgrounds and my story shows them what it might be like to grow up without a stable family. Maybe there are people who realize for the first time that children like me are in their midst.

Even if my audiences have read my first memoir, *Three Little Words*, they want to hear me repeat some of the stories and ask me questions. Many are fascinated that someone can be adopted successfully as a young teen. I also defy the stereotypes of former foster youth. I don't have a criminal record. I'd never been homeless or lived in poverty as an adult. I did not become a teen parent.

"I spent almost ten years in foster care, during which time I lived in fourteen different foster placements," I begin. If there are caseworkers or foster youth in the audience, there are often nods of recognition or nervous laughter. My story is hard to hear, I know—and it's also difficult for me to recount over and over.

"Imagine being three years old," I say. "The police put your mother in one car and you and your baby brother in another. A few hours later caseworkers separate you from your brother. Nobody explains anything. That night you are in a shelter home, crying yourself to sleep. The next day you are moved again, and you then enter a world of ever-changing 'placements' and 'beds,' broken promises, confusion, and the overwhelming feeling that everything is your fault or that something is inherently wrong with you."

My audiences are often well intentioned and dedicated to helping children, but my story reminds them of the crushing impact of their decisions. "After seven years, my mother's parental rights were finally severed. Even though this was the only way for me to move on, it felt like she had died. I mourned her then, and in some ways I mourn her still—even though she is now a peripheral part of my life. For several years after the termination of parental rights (TPR), or final legal separation, I remained in foster care, eventually landing in a children's home with a staff that helped me heal. I am one of the lucky ones who finally got out of the system. Even at the awkward age of twelve, the perfect family came forward to adopt me. You would have thought I would have been thrilled, but I had lived in so many hideous homes—including with people who were later convicted of child abuse, molestation, and other felonies—that I didn't trust anyone to be kind to me, let alone keep me more than a few months.

"On my adoption day I was sullen and wary; so when the judge asked if I wanted to be adopted, I mumbled, 'I guess so'—the three little words that were also the title of my first memoir.

"Yet none of the assumptions I made that day turned out to be true. Our family now laughs about the tug-of-war as they tried to welcome me into their fold while I pulled back with all my might. For years, I couldn't admit—even to myself—that I had left an ember burning in my heart for my biological mother, the person who had smothered me with kisses and called me affectionate names when she showed up for the infrequent visits social services arranged.

"My new life with Phil and Gay Courter seemed too good to be true. I had my own room and could have slumber parties. There were no locks on the cabinets or refrigerator. I always had someone to help me with my homework, and they were interested in whatever was happening in my life. I worried that one day they would discover I wasn't perfect and would send me back. To speed the process, I found ways to make my new parents quarrel with each other, and lied indiscriminately to keep them guessing. I tried pushing every button they had. I was admonished, but they did not reject me."

This part of my speech always gets resounding applause—not for me but for my adoptive parents. I've told my story many times, and still the shame of my antics never fades. It's all part of my life. I don't like thinking of a time when I was cruel or withholding to someone who was trying to love me—especially after having been on the other side of the equation while I was growing up. But my honest admissions illustrate a crucial point for me. I had no blueprint for healthy relationships; I had no maps or role models. I had to learn on my own that love means forgiveness at many levels.

"I began to trust in baby steps. When I felt accepted no matter what I did, I started to attach. That attachment led to love."

I had been giving different versions of this speech since I was fourteen, but on this occasion my memorized patter sounded hollow. I wondered if anyone sensed that I felt as though I was standing on a precipice with a few pebbles of loose gravel beginning to fall with faint pings down into a valley so deep that I had no idea where they were landing. I have been to the edge many times before—not knowing if I would finally return home to my mother or be shuffled to yet another temporary home run by people who were paid to house and feed me. This time, it was the summer after my senior year of high school, and I was about to voluntarily leave my first real sanctuary for college. All my friends were more than ready to get out from parental control, but my adoptive home was my first real refuge, and I hadn't really been there that long.

I continued to speak, my mind swirling with the paradox of sounding secure while trying to navigate my way through new complications with boyfriends and my birth family. I took a deep breath. Audiences like to feel closure and hear a happy ending, but the reality was that my story was evolving every day. "I'm thankful to the parents and professionals who dedicate their time to helping young people, especially those who assisted me during critical times. Without strong advocates, so many more would fall through the cracks with no one to speak for us." The audience rose to their feet, clapping. As the sound melted away, the chattering began. The little questions, the small talk, the compliments, and my responses made me seem like I had it all together. If only they knew how nervous I was to be going away to college—or that my biological mother had just emerged from the shadows.

My birth mother, Lorraine, once asked my adoptive mother, "When will Ashley get over it?" "It" refers to everything and anything she did or did not do for me. Lorraine saw the past as a door that could be closed. I felt she wanted to pretend we were distant relatives who had just gotten to know each other for the first time and not have to acknowledge all the ways she broke my heart as a child, or all that I endured because of her actions. The dispensation she seeks is not mine to give. I was the baby, the toddler, the frightened little girl who yearned for her mother and believed her when she told me she would return. She said everything would be all right sometime, somehow, soon. Soon turned into a very long time, and "all right" was far different than either of us ever imagined.

I spoke with Lorraine for the first time in five years when I was thirteen years old and had been living with the Courters for two years. Everyone assumes that after being moved fourteen times, adoption meant that the sun shone golden rays, a double rainbow appeared, and that I opened a magical door into a fairy-tale future. Not only did I distrust Phil and Gay, I had also been wrongly told that adoption meant I would never be able to see my birth mother again. There was a part of me that resented my adoption for taking her away from me—even though she'd never really been there for me in the first place. So it came as a surprise when Gay said, "We have no objection to you communicating with Lorraine."

I called her bluff. "When?"

"You want her phone number?"

"Really?" She handed me her phone.

I passed it back to her. "You dial and ask if she even wants to talk to me."

The call was brief. When I assured Lorraine that I was thriving and was comfortable in my new life, she told me that I sounded like a "stuck-up Valley girl." I threw the phone at Gay and ran out of the room before she saw my tears. Once again I had felt a tug from an invisible umbilical cord; and once again it had been slashed by a callous remark.

Now and then Gay mentioned Lorraine, not realizing that hearing her name felt like a cheese grater scraping a layer of skin. "You could write her a letter," Gay suggested.

I pretended not to care, but I made her a card. Lorraine wrote back saying she had just married again, and she included some pictures. A few months later she announced that she had given birth to Autumn. The news sickened me because my half sister was born a few days before my birthday and had been given my middle name. This was tough news for me to process. I felt like I had been replaced.

Thinking about Lorraine with a new baby reminded me of two other babies that had come after me: the tiny baby who died in infancy and my brother, Luke, whom I endlessly worried about.

A few days later Gay picked me up from school. I found it easier to approach her when her attention was directed at driving. "How can they let Lorraine take care of a new baby when her other children were taken away from her?" I asked.

"You mean social services?" responded Gay, who had been a volunteer Guardian ad Litem—or CASA child advocate—for almost ten years before she met me.

"Yes. Why don't they place her in foster care before somebody hurts her?"

"I see your point," Gay said, "but your mother will be given a fair chance to take care of this baby. After all, she never physically harmed you."

I wanted to shout that I preferred Gay to call her plain "Lorraine," because it stripped my biological mother of any power over me, creating the distance I needed to protect myself from my own raw feelings.

"Shouldn't we tell someone that the baby might not be safe?"

"We would need proof," Gay said. "But don't worry. I'm in touch with your aunt and uncle. They'll let me know if anything goes sour."

"Would you take her?" I asked. "Caseworkers like to place siblings together."

Gay laughed. "How much do you like to change diapers?"

After that, Lorraine faded into the background. When I was a sophomore in high school, Lorraine contacted Gay.

"Lorraine wants to see you," Gay announced without preface.

"Do I have to?"

"It's okay if you are curious," Gay said. "It's also fine if you want to skip it. Either way it won't hurt my feelings. Better the reality than the daydream."

How did she know that I had never stopped having fantasies about living with Lorraine in some alternate universe? "I wouldn't mind meeting my baby sister," I admitted. "She's almost two."

We met at a sandwich restaurant for about an hour. I hadn't seen Lorraine in almost seven years. Autumn didn't look related to me. At least my South Carolina cousins had my vivid red hair, but Autumn's was mud brown like her mother's. Until I met my cousins and uncle, I had never seen other family members who shared so many of my features. I felt no connection to Lorraine's voice, mannerisms, or even her smell. Her laughs were forced, her voice ragged from smoking, and she spent more time shooting worried glances at the friend she'd brought to help with Autumn than being attentive to me.

On our way home, Phil asked, "How was it for you?"

"Weird. Not what I expected."

"Which was?"

"That I would *know* her—that something would have clicked. It was like talking to a total stranger who happened to know a lot about me." I turned from Phil because his tender gaze reminded me of what I had not seen in Lorraine's eyes.

I didn't see or hear from Lorraine for two years after that visit, but as technology changed, she began texting me. I'd given my number to my uncle Sammie—Lorraine's brother—when he brought his family to attend my graduation from high school. He had suggested that we not invite Lorraine because she wasn't sober. "Who's taking care of my sister?" I asked.

"Most of the time she's living with her 'nana'—an old family friend who watches out for her." He promised they were in close touch and would step in if Autumn wasn't safe.

Shortly after that, Lorraine texted me: 1ST RHODES 2 GO 2 COLLEGE!

I simply responded: THX.

By then I'd lived with the Courters more than twice as long as I'd ever lived with her, but maybe, I reasoned, she had been waiting, biding her time until I was an adult to start a relationship. I didn't know what to expect, but I didn't need a mother like I once did. The space in my heart I had once desperately wanted her to fill was by then brimming with the love and support of the Courters. I had a stable home and parents and adoptive brothers, Blake and Josh, who loved me and looked out for me. It was difficult to figure out how Lorraine would fit into my life—and easy to imagine all the ways she wouldn't.

2.

the fishbowl

I am not afraid of storms, for I
am learning to sail my ship.
—Æschylus

"Ashley, you are 'college material,'" my Children's Home counselor used to say.

Before I landed there, I had changed schools at least twice a year due to my frequent moves. Each time I entered a new classroom, I was determined to defy the stereotype of a problem foster child. Teachers also protected me. When I lived in the abusive Moss foster home, teachers called the authorities. Most of those investigations were dropped because the other children were too scared to corroborate, and eventually I was removed for being "a troublemaker." That had been particularly terrifying because my brother, Luke, had remained in that home. By the time I entered sixth grade in Crystal River, where the Courters lived, I had attended ten schools. Each one had been a refuge from the chaos of the rest of my life. When I had to say good-bye to a favorite teacher before one move, she gave me a hug. "No matter what happens, Ashley, nobody can take your education from you."

At The Children's Home I won a scholarship offered to the girl and boy with the best grades. All the Courters had gone to college. "I'm going to college too!" I bragged to them. "I already have a scholarship."

Phil and Gay looked dubious, but they found that there was a small fund from a generous donor in my name. "This will help you pay for books," Gay said, "but don't worry, you'll get to go to any college that accepts you."

I still assumed they would let me down. The only person I could rely on was myself.

When I was fourteen, Gay brought home *USA Today* from her doctor's office. It featured an essay contest called "How the Harry Potter Books Changed My Life." She thought I should enter. I had joked that Harry would have fit right in at The Children's Home because Hogwarts wasn't that different—weird kids and all.

After Gay read my first-draft essay, she said, "You're going to win."

"What makes you say that?" I said snidely to cover my hunger for her to be right.

"Because it is brilliant, that's why!"

I didn't let on that I had marked the announcement day on my calendar and even checked the newspaper in the school library to find out who had won. I couldn't find any mention of it, but that evening the call came telling me that I was one of the ten winners out of more than ten thousand entries. The prize was a trip to New York and breakfast with J. K. Rowling.

From then on I pounced on any opportunity to enter contests. My school counselor had a stack of entry forms from corporations, local clubs, veteran's groups, newspapers, the library, even the nearby mall. It was amazing to be heard and validated for the first time in my life. People were interested in my story, and I loved the flurry of congratulations and encouragement from my parents and teachers. "Why don't I ever win?" one of my friends whined.

"Did you apply?"

"No," she said, laughing.

When I was a junior in high school, we were watching old family videotapes one evening. Phil popped in one taken at my adoption day four years earlier. "I was really a brat that day!" I said after watching it.

"It could have been worse," Phil said. "You could have said no!"

A few days later Gay pointed out that the *New York Times Magazine* was running an essay contest for high school students.

The inspiration came instantaneously. "I know just what to write!" Winning that contest became a pivotal event in my life. It led to writing my memoir *Three Little Words* and many other exciting opportunities. Growing up, I was rarely praised. Foster children are expected to stay out of the way and not make waves. Many kids—like my brother—were so desperate for someone to notice them that they acted out for negative attention. Having my book published finally gave me the approval I'd been seeking for years as a girl, and it reinforced my passion to improve the foster care system and help others like me. In many ways it evened the keel of my ship. I was emerging from the churning seas of my childhood and felt confident for the first time.

I was now a normal teen with friends and a boyfriend, and I was looking forward to college. I had been accepted to Eckerd College in St. Petersburg, Florida, on a full-tuition scholarship. Eckerd has a resort-style campus on a peninsula poking out into the Gulf of Mexico that attracted students from all over the world. Going to college felt like a natural next step, but I had no idea that there were many lessons in store for me both inside and outside the classroom.

I never would have imagined that the dorm would feel homey to me. The smells of the industrial cleaning supplies—from the sharp mint in the bathroom to the lemony floor-polishing wax—were redolent of The Children's Home, where I had lived for several years before I was adopted. In foster care, I had learned to be very protective of my reputation, but here I was shocked at how easily I became swept up in the antics of my peers.

The first official day of college I met my professor mentor, who would guide me for the first year, and I began Marketing Cool, the cross-disciplinary course that would last for the introductory three-week orientation term. Our class was held on an outdoor patio, and we were all sipping water out of recycled bottles.

"First let's examine how our emotions and unconscious are the gatekeepers for attention." We had been asked to bring glossy magazines. "Can anyone find an outrageous photo?" the professor asked.

We started riffling pages. I held up one for Jimmy Choo shoes. "The girl's in the opened car trunk, and the guy is leaning on a huge shovel like he's getting ready to bury her."

"Why use death or violent images toward women to sell expensive shoes?" the professor asked.

The discussion ricocheted around the class. So this was college! I thought jubilantly. We were taking only one class during this orientation period, but we were also engaged in community-service projects, which took us out of the little bubble of our campus to homeless shelters, mentoring programs, and environmental cleanup sites. We replanted sea grass, painted a Habitat for Humanity house, and recycled. There were lectures on campus, trips to local theater groups, even sailing classes. I enjoyed getting to know my new friends better. Sid, who had grown up on a military base in Germany, had an African-American army officer mother and a German father, and he spoke four languages. My roommate Iris's parents were both architects. Scarlett was the classic California girl with long legs and straight blond hair, who also played the cello. Their backgrounds and accomplishments were vastly different from my Crystal River classmates, not to mention the kids with whom I had grown up in foster care.

Most of my high school friends either didn't aspire to college or could only afford to take courses at the community college and eventually enroll in a state university while working to pay for their tuition. I thought it ironic that I would be one of the few in my graduating class to be going to a four-year private college. The odds were even worse for foster children. Since most of my foster friends were never adopted, they had few prospects. Many kids who turn eighteen and age out of the foster care system become homeless; others become teen parents, turn to drugs, are incarcerated—or worse. Without the crucial advantage of a stable family or support system, succeeding in college is often impossible.

※

One caution my parents had given me before going to Eckerd College was that I had a lot of local friends and ties in St. Petersburg. Gay and Phil wanted to be sure I immersed myself in college life and spent my time forming new relationships and experiences on, rather than off, campus. Gay even gave me a long lecture about dating a variety of guys.

In high school my friend Nikki and I loved going to concerts that featured regional bands, so we often traveled to St. Petersburg, which has a thriving arts and music scene. Nikki started hanging around a group called Fat Aggression and flirting with Ian Smith, the bass player.

During one set, Nikki said breathlessly, "Don't you think he's awesome?"

"He's really cool," I said to be nice. "Who's the guy on guitar?"

"What's it with you and guitars?" Nikki laughed because my boyfriend, Gavin, played lead guitar and sung in another band. "That's Ian's brother, Erick."

I caught Erick looking toward us, but he glanced away as if he had been caught doing something he shouldn't. After the show, Nikki and I were invited back to the Smith brothers' home.

Once we arrived, I sank into the corner of a living room sofa that was missing the middle cushion. A guy who I recognized as the band's lead singer said, "Don't believe whatever Nikki has told you about us."

"Yeah, we're not fat and we're not aggressive," the drummer chimed in.

When I didn't laugh, the drummer asked, "Are you feeling okay?"

"Just a headache."

"Must have been my fault," the drummer said, though it took me a few seconds to get the joke. "Want one of these?" He held up an Olde English beer.

"I'm driving."

"Hey, Erick, your girl wants an OJ," the singer said.

Your girl?

Erick arrived with a glass promptly.

"When he saw you coming in with Nikki, he went and combed his hair and shaved," the singer said, laughing. "I mean, sometimes he does one, sometimes the other, but never both at the same time."

I took a sip of the juice, then gagged.

"How many years has that OJ been in the fridge?" the singer asked.

"Sorry," Erick mumbled. "I'll find you something else."

Feeling sick, I hurried to find the bathroom. A few splashes of cool water helped revive me. I looked into the smeary bathroom mirror. My hair, unruly at the best of times, now tumbled around my face. I fished a barrette out of my pocket and pinned it back.

Sighing, I returned to the party, wondering how soon I could pry Nikki away. Erick was waiting for me. "I think the OJ's sell-by date was pre-Civil War."

I cracked a smile.

"Can I get you a soda? I have a secret stash in my room."

He brought me a Coke. "I didn't know if you preferred diet." He spoke as though he had rehearsed the line. "Not that you need diet. I mean, you know diet has a lot of chemicals." He blushed and turned away slightly. An old-fashioned word crossed my mind: bashful. Still, something seemed to pull his glance back to me. I stared into his gentle hazel eyes and felt a connection to a sweet, secret soul.

In the car Nikki said, "Erick's insanely crazy about you."

"He just met me!"

"Don't worry, he wouldn't blow you off all the time like Gavin does."

"Thanks a lot," I said, and unexpectedly started to cry.

I had fallen hard for Gavin Parnell when we met at one of his shows. After that, he asked me to most events, so I assumed there weren't other girls. We maintained a long-distance relationship for almost a year. He was on the road often with his band, but I was completely smitten. A few weeks after I met Erick, Nikki and I were excited about a Battle of the Bands that was taking place in Tampa. When we arrived, I headed to the stage where Gavin was playing. Fawning girls surrounded him. I waited for him to notice me.

"Hey, where've you been?" He pulled me toward him and gave me a light kiss on the forehead.

That small gesture should have made my place in his life clear to the interlopers, but one of them—a girl with black hair that looked like it had been painted with shoe polish and an outfit that was more lingerie than street clothes—curved her high-heeled boots around his calf. "We're going to Ybor tonight, right?" she cooed. Ybor City is an historic neighborhood in Tampa that was once the hub of the cigar industry, but now is filled with trendy nightclubs. Some permitted entrance if you were eighteen and gave you a wristband or stamp on the back of your hand, but many wouldn't admit anyone under twenty-one. Even though Gavin looked like a young college kid, he was almost seven years older than me, so age limits on clubs hadn't been an issue for him in years.

Gavin looked at her and then back at me. "We're supposed to talk to a guy about some club dates," he told me.

"Really? You're doing *business* tonight?"

He extricated himself from the other girl and steered me to a quiet spot. "By any chance do you have a fake ID?"

"Of course not," I said, shocked that he would ask the question.

"How about we go surfing on Sunday?"

"You know I don't surf!"

"What do you want to do? Drag me around a mall or see a PG movie?"

I backed away from him. "Besides, I'm not available next week. I have a speech in Santa Barbara."

"You'd better update your hair and makeup for California," he said as a painful put-down. And after that, he never called me again.

After I returned from California, Nikki wanted me to go with her to St. Pete to see Ian and hang out with their bandmates again. I was still moping over Gavin.

"Come to the beach with us," Nikki begged.

"I burn to a crisp in fifteen minutes."

"You can stay back with Erick and then we'll grill later," she suggested.

I agreed because at least their house was shady and cool. Erick made me a sandwich and put on some CDs. One of them was Hoobastank.

"I love that song!" I said when "The Reason" came on.

Erick sat beside me and was so silent I became aware of his soft breaths. At the second chorus, he whispered, "Me too." Erick's arm had been leaning on the sofa behind me. It slowly slipped around my shoulders, and he pulled me closer. "There are reasons," he murmured before his lips brushed against mine.

Erick pulled back to see my expression, then kissed me again, longer. At that moment I realized there was a reason for everything. Gavin was history.

That evening I drove back humming along to a CD that Erick had loaned me. For the rest of that summer before college, Erick and I saw each other every week and spent hours on the phone chatting. But I wasn't sure if I liked him as much as he liked me. Finally, just before I moved into the dorm, I had the talk many couples have before one of them goes away to college. I told Erick that he should feel free to see other people.

"May I still call you?"

"Sure. We don't have to be strangers, but we're not going to be together, either."

"Okay, I guess." He had the good sense to know that if he wanted to see me, he had to let me go.

Maybe I shouldn't have been so quick to pull away from Erick, who was actually a rather good influence on me. Being in college, I was so eager to fit in, and I was overwhelmed with my new sense of freedom and adventure. My usually cautious, introverted personality was replaced by a social butterfly that I sometimes didn't recognize.

As it turned out, many of my new college friends went to

Ybor to party as well. I had wanted to see what these places were like ever since I had been with Gavin. I remembered feeling left out because I wasn't old enough to go to clubs where he played or if I *could* get in, I felt out of place as his friends ordered drinks when I couldn't.

One Friday night a group of us carpooled to a club that admitted eighteen and over. When we got to the second floor of the trendy refurbished warehouse, Scarlett and I ordered Cokes, and her boyfriend Carter asked for a beer. He was carded, and then was served.

"Let me see that." I reached for his ID. "Is that . . . ah . . . new?"

"A senior who lives off campus makes them," he said.

Scarlett and I glanced at each other, and I knew she wanted one too. Maybe if I had had one when I dated Gavin, things would have been different. I wasn't about to alienate myself from friends or feel left out again. So I ordered one.

Unfortunately, I had forgotten one of the first lessons I had learned at The Children's Home: On a small campus it is impossible to remain anonymous. Even worse, it is more like living in a fishbowl, with the curve of the glass magnifying your comings and goings. Someone knows if you did not sleep in your bed, and someone else knows where you slept. Someone will see you at a bar or club. Someone saw you smoking a joint and with whom. Yet once I had settled into college life, I felt secure and invincible.

I was walking across campus when the assistant dean waved me over. I hurried to where she stood under a covered walkway. I had just applied to be a resident adviser the following year, and because she was in charge of the program, I assumed she was going tell me something about the process.

"Ms. Rhodes-Courter," she said in a clipped voice. "Please turn in your fake ID." She stared and gave an impatient grunt.

I leaned against a pillar, and in a mix of panic and shock I did what she asked. "I only used it to get into dance clubs," I said in a tremulous voice.

"Ashley," she said more gently, "as far as the school is concerned, this is an internal matter."

"I guess I won't qualify to be an RA."

"On the contrary. You can impart the consequences of this sort of foolishness to your freshmen."

"Stupid, stupid, stupid!" I muttered to myself as I hurried back to my dorm. Drinking was an unimportant part of my life. I didn't like the taste, didn't crave it, and instead of helping me relax and enjoy myself more, it usually made me feel sleepy or sick. I had risked my reputation for something I didn't even care about just to feel a part of the crowd. I thought I had dodged a bullet, but I had to then face another round of consequences—this time on the home front.

Mother's Day was more important to me than it was to Gay, who scoffed at "Hallmark Holidays." I loved honoring her as my true mother and planned to go home that weekend to be with her.

I was already on the road when she called me. "Do you know anyone named D. A. Warner?" Gay's voice seethed through the phone.

I clutched the steering wheel. Had the dean alerted my parents? "What do you mean?"

"This person sent me some, ah . . . disturbing links to pictures of you on the Internet."

My hands began to sweat. "Hey, you're breaking up. I'll be there in about an hour."

I dialed Sid. "Are you near a computer?" I asked in a panic.

"What's wrong?"

"I'm not sure. Someone sent my mother social media links, and she's furious."

"Okay." There was a very long pause.

"What did you find?" My voice was verging on hysteria.

"There's one that looks like it was taken in a tattoo parlor. You got some ink I don't know about?"

"No! I only went to that place because Scarlett was getting her belly button pierced." I was choking on my angry tears.

"Hey, calm down, it's not the end of the world."

"Maybe not your world. My family has already seen this crap, and I'm freaked."

Gay was sitting at her desk, her face reflecting the glow from the computer display, when I got home. I came over to her like a child summoned by the principal. She handed me a printout of the e-mail.

"Who do you think sent this?"

I read it to myself: *You think your daughter is so amazing; it's time you saw what she's really like.* Below it were links to several online pages.

"Anyone have it in for you?" Phil asked.

As Gay clicked through the photos, Phil draped his arm across my shoulder to show his support. "These photos could be easily misinterpreted, and some are pretty bad, Ash," he said.

"But not *that* bad," Gay said, surprising me.

The first picture was a dorm party in the common room taken just before Christmas. Two guys wore boxers and two girls were in scanty bikinis decorated with tinsel. I wore a tube top, and tights under a short skirt, with a fair amount of cleavage showing. I was pretending to guzzle a bottle of vodka. My expression was dopey—with half-closed eyes and my tongue to one side. "I had a couple of wine coolers, but I wasn't as wasted as I look. We were kidding around."

"Yeah," Gay said softly at first, "college kids party. No big deal. But do you want to know what is wrong with this picture?" She waited two long beats. "It's on the friggin' Internet!" she screeched. "What did I tell you? Don't do anything that you don't want to see printed on the front page of the newspaper the next day!"

"I didn't post it," I croaked.

"You posed for it."

"Where does this person get off sending your mother pictures like this—for Mother's Day, for heaven's sake!" Phil snarled.

"I already wrote this Warner person and warned *them*," Gay said.

"What did you say?"

"They had no right to duplicate and distribute your image, and that it was slanderous, libelous, whatever."

My parents' reaction was completely different from what I had feared. They weren't happy to see me looking slutty or drunk, but they were directing their wrath at the messenger.

"Do you know what 'schadenfreude' means?" Gay asked. I shook my head. "It's the sick satisfaction some people feel when they hear of someone else's misfortune. People love to see those on a pedestal fall from grace—like a politician caught in a sex scandal or a movie star getting arrested. The tabloids bank on this unpleasant human trait."

"What Gay is trying to say is that the more well-known you are, the more pleasure someone will get from seeing you brought up short," Phil said. "No matter what you were doing or not doing, these photos give the *perception* you were naughty."

"I'll deal with it," I promised.

As it turned out, cleaning all my accounts and adding layers of privacy settings was more difficult than I had anticipated. We were the naive pioneers of social media. Nobody expected that parents, old boyfriends, stalkers, potential employers, school administrators, and law enforcement would scrutinize our web presence. When I was in foster care, any misbehavior was written into my permanent record, and childish mistakes as well as official inaccuracies haunted me for years to come. This was the adult version of the same curse.

Early in my sophomore year, I was helping Sid serve refreshments in the theater lobby.

"Hi, Sid," a rail-thin professor said.

"This is Professor Wydell," Sid said. "I'm in his religious philosophy class."

"What are you doing for Winter Term?" he asked Sid.

Eckerd closes the campus in January for Winter Term, which is an intensive study of one subject or community service, including college-sponsored courses worldwide.

"My parents want me to do a project near our home in Germany."

"What about you?" The professor stared at me with electric-blue eyes. "I'm leading the one in South Africa."

"I'd love to go."

"We'd love to have you," the professor said so warmly that I assumed my reputation wasn't as bad as I thought.

During the second semester of my freshman year, I had joined the women's rugby team. I knew from the first scrum that I had found my sport! Running, tackling, and grabbing the ball were outlets for any pent-up frustrations or annoyances—even ancient angers that lingered in my bones. I gained respect for being both fast and tough, and was nicknamed "Chainsaw" for my fierce tackling.

The Courters came to the first match of my sophomore year, and Phil filmed my game-winning try. Running toward the ball, I turned one direction and my knee went another. My leg buckled under me. I had to be carried off the pitch, and the searing pain did not subside despite icing. I had torn my ACL and needed replacement surgery.

"But I'm going to South Africa in January!" I complained to the surgeon.

The doctor consulted his calendar. "If I operate within the next two weeks, you can get your rehab done over the holidays and go on the trip—as long as you promise not to go out for one of the rugby teams over there."

After the surgery, Phil and Gay took turns nursing me. My leg was wrapped with a clumsy apparatus that pumped cool water around my knee to prevent swelling. It had to be refilled with ice every few hours.

The second day I was home, Erick showed up unannounced. I was camped out on the living room sofa because I couldn't make it upstairs to my room. I opened my eyes and tried to focus, but his features broke into fragments, then re-formed in the light glinting off the bay. I started to sweat. Erick brought me a wet washcloth and wiped my face. "Here, drink some ginger ale," he said, guiding the cup to my lips.

That night he slept on the other side of the U-shaped couch and got up to refill the ice compartment. The next day he said, "I'll take care of Ashley in St. Pete."

"That's a lot for you to take on," Gay said. "She should stay here for a few more days."

"I have to get back to class," I insisted. "He can stay in my dorm room." One benefit to being an RA is that you get a private room, and mine had a comfy thrift-store couch.

My residents brought me food from the caf, but Erick added fresh ice through the night and rearranged pillows when I moaned.

Getting around on crutches was harder than I expected, but nobody minded when I stumbled into class a few minutes late. I was taking extra courses because I had decided to major in both theater and communications and had added two minors in psychology as well as political science and couldn't afford to get behind. Immediately after New Year's, my doctor cleared me for the trip to Africa.

By the time we arrived in the hostel in the Observatory section of Cape Town, my knee was throbbing from being in the cramped airline seat for more than twenty-four hours.

I had also slept through breakfast on the plane, and when I got to the hostel, I was starving and bought a hot dog from a street vendor. I woke in the middle of the night with stabbing stomach pains and started retching in the sink.

Professor Wydell checked in on me when I missed the orientation meeting. "Take it easy on the booze. I know it is legal for you to drink here, but obviously you're not used to it."

"I have food poisoning."

"That's one way of describing it."

Perhaps some other students had already gotten drunk, but the strongest beverage I'd had so far had been a Coke. I dragged myself to the hostel's common room for the next lecture, which was a short course on the history of South Africa.

The next day we were to start the volunteer portion of the program, but the bus never arrived, so we were on our own. There wasn't much to do where we were in the Observatory section of town except go to restaurants or bars. The closest place was an English-speaking bar patronized by students from all over the world. When I first hobbled in, the waiter sat me in a booth where I could rest my leg. "How'd ya manage that?" he asked when he saw the still-livid scar.

"Rugby."

"Bring this one a springbok on the house!" he said.

I took a sip. It was minty and tasty. Best of all, I wasn't breaking a law by drinking.

That afternoon I had several springboks. The first relaxed me, the second masked my knee pain, and by the third I was finally having a marvelous time. I stumbled back to the hostel, but I don't remember much more than the ceiling spinning when I lay down and not waking up until morning.

The next day we began our service projects, and the final week we toured Table Mountain, the Cape of Good Hope, Robben Island, and the seal and penguin colonies. The group even took a wine-tasting tour. Wherever we went I ordered a springbok—or two—to help ease the pain of walking. Except for my sickness, I enjoyed the trip and received full credit.

A few months later, I exited the campus post office and saw Professor Wydell and a student soliciting donations to send mosquito nets to malarial villages. He waved me over. "Want to contribute?"

I paused a bit too long. The professor hissed, "Ashley, if you donated half as much as you spent on your bar tab, we could outfit a whole village."

I reeled. Since the trip, I hadn't had a single alcoholic beverage. I was angry that he was so mean-spirited and worried that someone might have overheard the nasty remark. I made a quick donation, then turned and walked to the far side of the campus with my face burning in a combination of rage and embarrassment. Why did I have to keep learning some lessons over and over? Apparently, once you blow your reputation, it is almost impossible to restore it. Professor Wydell thought I had been wasted, even though I'd had food poisoning. When he later saw me drunk on the springboks, his suspicions were confirmed. He had moved his mental index card on me from "dependable" to "unreliable"—or maybe something worse.

Someday I hoped to change his mind.

3.

family matters

Biology is the least of what makes someone a mother.
—Oprah Winfrey

Once Lorraine knew I was in college, she started to text me on a regular basis. Seeing her name on my screen flooded me with conflicting emotions. Sometimes I gave quick responses; sometimes I ignored her. The Courters said I should "make peace with my past," and "integrate all facets of my life," and that "you cannot have too many people who love you." Even so, I worried that there was an imaginary line with them, and I didn't want to cross it. Also, I knew enough to worry that I could get ensnared in the spidery web of drama that spun around Lorraine.

At the end of October of my freshman year, Lorraine called three times, leaving messages to phone her back. The fourth time she caught me rushing to class, and I answered without looking first at the name on the screen.

"Hey, it's me," Lorraine said. "We're having a Halloween carnival at church, and it would mean so much to Autumn if you could make it."

Scarlett was holding the door for me, but I waved her to go ahead. "I want you to meet Rex." Lorraine paused, then added, "He's the one who got me into this church—and sober."

"Okay," I said, surprising myself. I was curious to see my sister again. Besides, maybe I needed to form a relationship with Autumn in case Lorraine crashed.

I wasn't comfortable going alone. I asked my roommate Iris.

"I need the weekend to finish my paper on Japanese pottery," she said. "Maybe Aiden will go."

Aiden was majoring in political science, and he made even the most boring topics sound interesting. He had a wonderful smile and hair a bit more strawberry than mine. "We gingers have to stick together" was his pickup line. You couldn't call it dating, since there were few planned meet-ups. We just were . . . together . . . a lot. It felt wrong to even suggest the trip to him. Nikki would have been the best—she knew my life story—but she was working full-time and going to community college in Citrus County. Most weekends she stayed in St. Pete with Ian, and I didn't want to drag her away from him. That left Erick. He didn't seem surprised by my call and responded enthusiastically.

"I just need to tell my dad I'll help him with the roofing work on Sunday instead of Saturday."

When Iris heard that I'd called him, she snapped, "You rarely even take his calls, so how can you ask him to be your emotional air bag?"

"We're still friends. We help each other out," I said, as much to convince myself as her.

Iris looked at me challengingly. "Does he think of you the same way?"

I shrugged. How could I explain our bond when I was so conflicted? I compared every guy I met to him and somehow expected that Erick would always be there if nothing else worked out. I knew this reflected poorly on me, so all I said was, "Either way, Erick has excellent intuition. He'll help me figure out if she's drinking and how her kid is doing."

People in stable families have no understanding of chaotic ones. The stronger members feel compelled to protect the weaker ones. Sometimes children parent their siblings or even take charge of their parents to keep them out of trouble and prevent the family from being split by authorities. Nobody from an upper-middle-class, intact family could imagine the terror of never knowing whether you will live under the same roof as the rest of your family the next day. I had done an abysmal job with my brother, Luke, who was never out of trouble. I wanted to protect Autumn—who had already lived with Lorraine two years more than I had—from the same fate, even though I hardly knew her.

"So what's the deal?" Erick asked as he drove my car toward the Sunshine Skyway Bridge.

It was one of those clear October days when Florida is the sapphire jewel on the earth's ring. Behind us, St. Pete's cluster of office towers and the dome from Tropicana Field baseball stadium formed a sculptural background as we headed higher and higher onto the causeway. The Gulf's glassy surface was too bright to look at without sunglasses.

"Just don't leave me alone with Lorraine, okay?" I said, cracking the car window and taking some deep breaths of salty air. I have a tendency to get motion sick, and my anxiety caused a sour taste in the back of my throat.

"What are you so worried about?"

I swallowed hard to suck down the bile. "You don't know how she can be."

I was relieved to see that we were turning into a nice neighborhood. Rex's house was freshly painted a sunny yellow. The open garage door revealed several Harleys in various stages of repair.

"Cool," Erick said.

Autumn was almost six and already in costume. She ran out the kitchen door that led into the garage. "Ashley's here!" she shouted as Lorraine followed behind.

"Wow!" I said. "Which princess are you?"

"She's Aurora from *Sleeping Beauty*," Lorraine answered for her.

"This is my friend Erick," I said formally. He stepped closer to shake Lorraine's hand.

"I'm a hugger." She reached around him for a squeeze, but I backed away. "We need to head over to the church in about twenty minutes. Did you bring costumes?"

"I did," I said. Erick had leant me an Elvis costume he'd worn for a Halloween party the year before, which came with a black wig. I added gold chains and large sunglasses.

Lorraine looked to Erick, who shrugged. He hadn't brought anything.

"How about one of Rex's motorcycle outfits?" Lorraine showed him how to pull the studded motorcycle chaps up over his jeans. "Hottie!" she giggled, making me wonder if she was trying to flirt with him. "We can't all fit in my truck. You want to follow me?"

The fair was bigger than I expected, with many booths and crafts for sale, including Bible covers and Christmas items. There was a biblical petting zoo, pony rides, freshly squeezed lemonade, and tables filled with homemade baked goods.

Lorraine bought a stack of tickets so Autumn could try the games. Erick helped her throw balls for prizes, while Lorraine and I lingered in the background.

Out of the blue Lorraine said, "I would have gone to college if I hadn't had you." She squinted into the distance. "At least I finished high school, even though I was pregnant—a real diploma, not a GED."

Erick stepped forward. "Is it okay if Autumn has her face painted?"

"Do you have enough tickets?" Lorraine asked.

"Yep!"

She waved to a friend. "Everyone was so excited to hear that my firstborn was coming. No one can believe I have a daughter old enough for college."

I shifted uncomfortably, wondering how she described her relationship with me. Was I the taken-away-by-the-cruel-state-who-refused-to-give-her-a-helping-hand daughter or the one she lost because of her illegal and irresponsible actions? Well, maybe some higher being forgave all if she was saved, but that didn't mean I had to absolve her as well.

She watched Erick lead Autumn by the hand. "I like your guy. He's *very* handsome! Does Gay like Erick?"

I bristled. "She doesn't really know him."

"What did Gay say about you coming to spend the weekend with me?"

"I don't tell Gay everything I do."

"Did Sammie let you know that I'm divorcing Autumn's father?" I shook my head. "He was a bad influence. Now I'm clean, and so is Rex. He's been sober for ten years this Thanksgiving." I nodded. "You've been happy with those people, right?" she probed. I recognized her jealous tone. Envy is one of my flaws too.

In the car on the way back to the house, I said to Erick, "Let's come up with an excuse to go back tonight."

"Okay," Erick agreed, but we couldn't come up with a plan, and Erick is a terrible liar. Then Rex offered to take him on one of his fanciest motorcycles. We were staying.

After Erick's ride, Lorraine said, "Hope you like lasagna." I saw one defrosting on the counter. "I make mine with low-fat ricotta, and nobody can tell the difference." I'm very particular about food—it was like I hadn't yet grown out of that picky-food stage that toddlers go through. I still disliked combination foods, even if the individual parts like cheese, noodles, and tomato sauce were fine, but I didn't say anything. Now it really would have been rude to leave, since she already had prepared dinner.

I picked at the noodles while Autumn gobbled hers messily, then put her head down on the table.

"You finished?" Lorraine asked in a sharp tone. Autumn startled. "Get ready for bed, and don't slop up the bathroom."

"Want me to help?" I asked Autumn.

As I waited for her to put on her nightgown and brush

her teeth, I was imagining my counselor at The Children's Home supervising my bedtime routine.

"I fall asleep in Mommy's bed, then she moves me."

The smell of the perfume in the master bedroom was cloying. Tomato sauce rose in my esophagus, burning my throat. I had no memory of my mother ever tucking me in. "Night," I said, and backed away from the bed.

"Night-night kiss?"

I blew one from the door.

"I had a better time than I expected," Erick said as we drove back. I insisted on leaving before breakfast, blaming a ton of homework, which was true.

"Really? I found most of what Lorraine said irritating. She pretended everything between us was normal—when it was bizarre."

Erick stopped and bought bagels to eat in the car. "Lorraine seemed to like me."

"Yeah, maybe too much," I said, then laughed.

Erick paused for a few seconds, then said, "She is more accepting than Phil or Gay."

I glanced at him, suddenly tense. "Why do you say that?"

"They want you to date guys who are going to be doctors or engineers or dot-com millionaires," he said. "Your mother didn't ask me a single question about school or jobs or even where I lived. At the Courters, it's like the Spanish Inquisition."

"It's not that she didn't ask you about your future— she didn't care, because she only thinks of herself. If you listened, she was all 'me, me, me.' She had no interest in my courses, or my friends, either. I was just an ornament for her to show off."

"That's harsh."

I felt a river of lava rushing through my veins. "She may look like mother of the year to my sister, but she was never there for me!" I exploded. "She left us in foster care because she'd rather hang out with drug dealers—or worse. How hard would it have been to get a job and an apartment, and take a free parenting class? Why couldn't she stay off the streets and out of jail when she had two kids who needed her?"

"Okay, okay." He lifted both hands from the steering wheel in surrender. "But you have to admit she's trying to do better for Autumn, and she's reaching out to you."

"It's way too late for that," I seethed.

Erick opened his mouth to respond, but I ended the discussion. "You can't understand it, because you didn't live it."

A few weeks later Lorraine called again. "Hey!" she began, as if I heard from her all the time. "Can you come for Thanksgiving? My brother Sammie will be in town."

I had first met my uncle and his family when I had attended a drama camp at Duke University and visited them on the way home. I liked them so much I invited them to my high school graduation, but I wasn't about to miss the Courters' feast and traditions.

"Thanksgiving is a major deal at our house."

"Autumn keeps asking for you."

"I'll get back to you."

Every few years my birthday falls on or near Thanksgiving, and we celebrate with cake and gifts while everyone is already gathered for the holiday meal. If I went with Lorraine, this would be the first Thanksgiving away from the Courters, and I would miss seeing the whole family. Impulsively I dialed Erick. He had called several times since the trip, but I hadn't replied to his messages. Iris even asked me why I was avoiding him, and I told her to tell him that I'd been slammed. But now that I had a decision to make, I wanted his opinion. Was that using him? We had our deal, and I figured I was showing him that I respected his judgment. Okay, so I felt a little guilty because I sensed our feelings for each other were lopsided. But were they really? Maybe he was dating other people too. I had convinced myself that I wasn't taking advantage of him by the time he said hello.

"Sorry, I have several papers due and I've been studying for exams," I said before telling him about my Thanksgiving dilemma. "I feel torn."

Erick hesitated before saying, "Why are you willing to bend over backward to please Lorraine, who was never there for you when you needed her most?"

"I thought you liked her," I said, surprised.

"I simply said she wasn't as bad as you made her out to be."

"When I asked Gay, she made it sound like she didn't care if I went to Lorraine's or not."

"That does sound like Gay to me," Erick said with a chuckle. "She knows that if she pulls you in one direction, you'll run in the other."

I laughed. Just because he stood by quietly didn't mean

he didn't understand the undercurrents around him. "Gay's just trying to support your choices," Erick added. "You could compromise."

"How? I'm not King Solomon's baby."

"You could have Thanksgiving with my family!" He laughed. "Just kidding." He lowered his voice. "Why don't you do what you *want* to do—not what you think you *should* do?"

"Isn't that selfish?"

"Whose birthday is it?"

Erick's perceptive points cleared my head. I made my excuses to Lorraine.

And when Lorraine's inevitable Christmas invite came, I had a ready answer. There was no way I was going to miss decorating our huge tree, hanging with my friends and brothers on Christmas Eve, eating cinnamon rolls and bacon in the morning, having the fun of seeing everyone open the gifts I'd sweated over, and enjoying my haul of perfectly picked and handmade gifts.

Erick agreed to come to our house after his family's Christmas lunch. When Blake, Josh, and Phil started playing bluegrass, he picked up an extra guitar and joined in. To my delight they played harmoniously together.

"Why don't you play one of your band's songs?" Phil suggested.

"Can you plug this thing in?" Erick quipped.

For the first time he seemed to fit into our family, and he seemed less tense. I was suffused with warm feelings and began imagining him at the house more and inviting him to events on campus. Then I felt my cell phone vibrate in my pocket and glanced at it. It was a text from Aiden. I flushed as I read: WHEN MOST I WINK, THEN DO MINE EYES BEST SEE. He had just taken a Shakespeare course—was that from a sonnet? With Aiden everything was a game, which was fine, except it left me unsure if he felt as drawn to me as I did to him. I looked over to where Erick was fixing the capo on the guitar. I adored the way a lock of hair fell over his eyes and his shy, sideways glances. I was never confused about how he felt about me. I realized it wouldn't be fair to get more involved with Erick when I was so attracted to Aiden.

Yet how could I be excited by this simple text when Erick was only a few feet away, and he had made the effort to actually be present with me? I'd also been intrigued by other guys during the first few weeks of the fall semester, although most didn't have an iota of Erick's integrity. I tried to take Gay's advice and date the kinds of guys I thought would impress her and Phil. But none of them were as kind, doting, patient, or uncritical as Erick. Was I just too worried about what other people thought? Now Aiden . . . I could see myself with him way into the future, possibly moving to DC, each of us working on our own political causes. Like Gavin, Aiden also loved the spotlight. He would be one to run for political office rather than just support a candidate. Erick, on the other hand, preferred to let me shine.

I felt warm and safe with Erick, yet I didn't have the same zingy thrill that I'd had every time Gavin touched me; I also didn't have the same churning anxiety as when Aiden was seen someplace and he hadn't invited me along. I didn't try to interpret Erick's double meanings, because there were none. Erick's words were simple and his affection as encompassing as his smile. Cleverness was Aiden's calling card. He loved to leave people—particularly me—wondering exactly what he meant. Being with him was like walking the deck on a ship. You were never sure if you would find firm footing with the next step and had to keep reestablishing balance. That was exciting, but also unnerving, because when I was with Erick, I couldn't shed a nagging feeling—imagined or created—that I should be with an altogether different "type" of person. Someone who wasn't just kind and comfortable: someone who was immediately impressive. Trying to focus on the long tunnel that led to the future, I wondered whether a life with sure-and-steady Erick would become boring.

my brother's keeper

There is a little boy inside the man who is my brother. . . .
Oh, how I hated that little boy.
And how I love him too.
—Anna Quindlen

Some people fall in love almost instantly. The Courters knew they were meant for each other after only three days; my brother Josh saw his wife, Giulia, walking toward him across a warehouse, and they made an instant connection. With Erick, my love for him grew like a seed slowly sprouting underground, where I wasn't even conscious of its first tender roots. It was more like the love Gay described to me after the adoption: one that wasn't instantaneous, but would come with shared experiences, both good and bad.

Erick was very family oriented. He and his brother Ian, who were two years apart, had grown up as best friends, then bandmates, and finally housemates. He'd never been separated from his brother for any real stretch of time until he was an adult, while I had lived on and off with mine throughout foster care until I was adopted.

Most families cannot imagine splitting a brother and sister for a few weeks, let alone for a lifetime. There are even foster care laws against doing it, although there are all sorts of exceptions ranging from bed capacity to how the siblings get along. The first rift came the day our mother was arrested, when I was three and he was an infant. Luke and I were placed together six times and separated seven. There were "reasons" for each change, but you don't have to be a psychologist to know any child would be wounded by having the bond between brother and sister so regularly disrupted.

Luke, being younger, needed me far more than I did him. He clung to me the way Harlow's infant monkeys held on to fake wire monkey mothers in his attachment experiments. I felt an obligation to protect my brother—from callous foster parents, from bullies, and from his own reckless ways. Our worst time together had been at the Moss home. There, he received the most sadistic punishments. Mrs. Moss slopped hot sauce down his throat and held him underwater in the bath—letting him breathe at the last second in her version of waterboarding.

By the time Luke was seven, he was deeply disturbed and needed the therapeutic environment The Children's Home provided. Our Guardian ad Litem, Mary Miller, insisted we be reunited there with the goal of being adopted together. However, families who wanted me were unwilling to take my brother. While the adoption counselors had approved of the Courters for me, my parents did not feel they had the energy or skills to take on Luke. Then a younger couple who lived in the same county became interested in Luke, and both families agreed to facilitate our relationship. I was relieved that we could have a connection without worrying that he would ensnare me in his troubles. Unfortunately,

Luke was viciously mean to his pre-adoptive mother. When he tortured her miniature poodle, they realized they weren't equipped to raise him.

After Luke moved back to The Children's Home, the Courters insisted we visit him at least once a month. "Do we have to?" I complained.

"He is so lonely for you," Gay said.

"But he's always clinging and jumping on me. When I lived at the cottage, he bit my arm and it bled!"

My feelings about Luke were like foul-tasting soup. The basic broth was my love and deep affection, but every time I saw him he added some rotten ingredient that repelled me.

"Luke hungers for someone to nurture him like a mother—but that's not your job," Gay said. "Don't feel guilty. You're not the one who let him down."

Five years after my adoption and after Luke had lived in Florida's foster care system for fourteen out of his fifteen years, I learned that someone wanted to adopt Luke. Ed Kemper had served in the military and taught handicapped children—both seemed ideal training for Luke. By then I was driving and made the routine monthly visits, now to Ed's, on my own. Luke was more obnoxious and more physical than ever. He pretended to playfully poke, punch, and squeeze me—but his jabs hurt; he was not a little kid anymore.

"Maybe I shouldn't continue to visit so much," I said to Ed privately. "It's a long trip, and I have a tough schedule at school this year."

"That's fine with me," Ed said. "We need more father-son bonding time."

Luke had a trust fund from our lawsuits against the

Moss family and the State of Florida. While my passage through foster care had been horrible, his had been far worse, and he received a much larger settlement that could help pay for his special needs, especially to continue his psychological counseling. Ed enrolled Luke in a horseback-riding program that proved to be therapeutic. He showed off his ribbons for jumping and loved taking care of the big, majestic horses. "I'm getting my own horse, just like the king!" Luke announced when I visited after he came back from a summer birthday trip to England with Ed, where Luke turned seventeen.

"England has a queen," I corrected. "I can't wait to see you ride."

The first time I went to the stables, Luke was wearing the traditional jodhpurs and riding cap. Sitting up straight in the saddle, he looked like he had been born to an aristocratic family in a grand home.

"Watch this!" he called from the ring. He trotted to an outer circle, spurred his horse, and easily made it over a jump. I clapped enthusiastically, as he patted the horse's neck. "My trustee said I can buy a horse," Luke said.

"He has to keep his grades up," Ed added.

When I left the stables to go home that day, Luke was too busy in the ring to even wave good-bye. For the first time since I had been adopted, I didn't feel as though I was abandoning him.

※

The summer after my sophomore year, I was headed to England for an extension of a Shakespeare class that I had taken that semester. Erick joined me in Scotland after my course, and he turned out to be the perfect travel companion. We were gone for almost a month and never became annoyed with each other—even under stressful circumstances when we were hungry, soaking wet, lost, or exhausted. When we returned, I was to start work at a Tampa television station for the rest of the summer. Erick and Ian had just moved into a small three-bedroom house only ten minutes away from my job, along with Ian's puppy. Erick suggested I move in with them. We had gotten along so well on our trip; I'd agreed to try it until it was time to go back to the dorm.

My relationship with Luke had dwindled to visits on his birthday in July and at Christmas, but it included random phone calls and texts from him, almost always complaining about Ed's unfair rules, being dumped by a girl, or hating school.

On the Fourth of July, Erick and Ian were busy, so Nikki and I drove up to Crystal River to be with our families.

"I tried to get Ian to come up later for the fireworks, but apparently the Smith family picnic is some big-deal tradition," Nikki said.

I didn't contradict her, although Erick had said something about going out with the band members that evening. I wasn't worried about Erick, but Ian had a more flirtatious nature.

Nikki began humming along to a rock song about romance on the radio. "Ashley, are you in love with Erick?"

"Good question. I really can't tell," I said honestly.

"How can you be so cold? Erick is so good to you."

"I'm not sure I'll ever be able to love a guy the way you love Ian. Sometimes I think that the whole foster care thing damaged some crucial love circuit. I'll probably never get married."

"Never say never," Nikki said.

Nikki and I had invited some of our friends to come to my house to swim in the pool, eat barbecue, and climb onto our roof to watch the display being blasted from the fireworks barges. The last of my guests left at midnight, and I was on my way to my room when my phone rang. It was another one of Luke's late-night calls. I decided to ignore it. In a few seconds it rang again. "Why do you always call so—" I started to say, answering.

Luke was screaming, "I'm gonna kill myself if you get any closer! No! Stop it! Don't hit me! No!"

I rushed downstairs. Phil was brushing his teeth, and Gay was sitting in their bed reading a book. I put the phone on speaker. "Luke, it's me, Ashley. Luke! Do you hear me?"

"Yeah!" His breathing sounded like he was running.

"What's happening, Luke?"

"He's going to kill me!"

"Who?"

"Ed and me were fistfighting, and I grabbed a knife to get him to back off."

"Where are you?"

"Down the street from my house."

I heard sirens. "Are there cops?" His next words were covered over by a crunching sound. "Luke! Where are you?"

"Behind some bushes," he whispered. "I can't live like this. I'm going to slit my throat."

"No, Luke, that's crazy talk." I heard a whirring sound. "What's that?"

"Wow, a chopper!"

Phil was standing by me and listening to what could have been the soundtrack for *Law & Order*. He gestured for me to keep talking.

"Luke, listen to me, you know I love you, right?"

"Then why don't you ever visit me?"

"I've been busy, but I'm coming for your birthday in a couple of weeks, or I could come sooner if you want."

Luke began sobbing.

"What happened, Lukie?"

"Ed sold my horse! He sold my friggin' horse! I hate his guts."

I heard shouting coming closer. "Hold on, Luke. You'll be eighteen in three weeks! Ed won't be in control any longer."

"But my horse!"

"Come out of the bushes, son!" The voice sounded like it came from a megaphone.

"Luke, we'll talk about that later, but you've got to do what the cop says." Tears were running down my cheeks now. Phil handed me his handkerchief.

Gay held up a notepad. She had printed: PUT HIS CELL PHONE ON SPEAKER!

I said, "Lukie, put your cell phone on speaker." He didn't respond. "Please, Luke, please." No response. I looked helplessly at Gay. She mimicked holding up two hands high in the air.

"Luke, here's what you are going to do. You're going to put your cell phone on speaker and hold it up in the air. Okay?" I heard Luke panting. "Are your hands in the air?"

"Uh-huh." He sounded more frightened.

Gay waved another note: THROW THE KNIFE AWAY FROM YOURSELF.

"Luke, listen! I need you to throw the knife as far away from yourself as possible—and away from the cops." I could actually hear the *plink* as it landed on the pavement.

Phil whispered in my ear. "Tell him to sit down with his arms up."

"Luke, sit down wherever you are and put your hands up."

We heard a scuffling sound, then, "Got him!"

I started shuddering, and my phone slipped from my hand. Phil picked it up and shouted, "Whoever is there, may I please speak to an officer?"

"Deputy Baragona. Who's this?" came a bass voice on Luke's end of the line.

"This is his sister's father," Phil said, confusing the deputy further. "What's happening to Luke?"

"We're taking him into custody."

"This is complicated, Officer, but Luke is a very troubled former foster child with mental health issues. He needs psychological help."

"That's not my call," he said, and hung up.

"Ash, you talked Luke down!" Gay said.

"And probably saved your brother's life," Phil added. "Some cops shoot first and ask questions later."

A bitter taste rose in my throat as I imagined Luke lying on the pavement covered in blood from a fatal wound. "If I hadn't answered my phone or if Luke had run or—"

"You can't take responsibility for any of this," Gay said. "Besides, he's fine."

But it wasn't a bizarre fantasy for me to think that something like that could happen to my brother. Our grandfather Rhodes had been shot and survived; his grandfather had killed Luke's paternal great-grandfather. Luke seemed genetically wired to attract trouble and plunge into danger.

I looked toward Phil for answers. "He went crazy because Ed sold his horse. Why would Ed do that?"

"Ed probably reached the end of his rope," Phil said, because he knew how Luke loved to escalate conflict.

"What's going to happen to him next?"

"Maybe he'll get the help he needs," Gay said, "but at least he's safe."

Two days later, Ed called. "Your loser brother is being released from jail tomorrow. He's either going to your house or he'll be out on the street."

"Ed, I'm staying with some friends for a few more weeks, and then I have to be back at college."

"He can live in your dorm room."

"That's not possible," I said. "He's your son."

"He's your blood," Ed said, "not mine."

For a moment I considered asking the Courters to take him on for a few weeks, but then I remembered that they were going on vacation. Besides, the only person Luke listened to was me.

"I wouldn't ask this if there was any other choice," I said to Erick. "Luke will be eighteen at the end of the month, and then I can help him get out on his own."

"What grade is he in?"

"He dropped out, which is why Ed sold the horse. I'll get him back in school and find him a job to keep him busy."

My voice became more tentative. "Would you do it—for me?"

"No," Erick said, "*with* you."

⁂

The next morning Ed's car turned into the semicircular driveway in front of Erick and Ian's house. Ed popped open the trunk. "Get your crap out of my backseat," he barked at Luke. As soon as Erick slammed the trunk shut, Ed gunned the motor and drove off.

"Good-bye, asshole!" Luke cursed, then spit, splattering Erick's Pumas. He left his bags in the driveway and marched inside. "I'm starving!" He opened the refrigerator, pulled out the orange juice, and gulped from the carton.

"Hey, Lukie, that's disgusting," I said.

"Don't call me that stupid baby name."

"Then stop acting like a child."

He gulped, belched, and tossed the empty carton—which had been half-full—in the sink.

"The garbage is over there," I said, indicating the trash can. "And maybe someone else wanted some."

"So, buy more." He opened the refrigerator again. "Where's the beer?"

I was seething but didn't respond. Thinking ahead, Ian had removed all the beer and booze from the house. He even cleaned out some empty bottles from under his bed and found a few swallows of cheap rum, which he poured into a Coke and finished off before kissing the bottle—with a real smack of a kiss—good-bye.

Most of Luke's laundry was clean—or could pass the sniff test—and I placed it in baskets in the third bedroom.

Luke seemed content to let me do the arranging. One of my biggest fears—of Luke ending up in jail like his birth father—had come true. I hoped he had learned his lesson and would not do anything worse.

The next day I took Luke to a supermarket to apply for a job. "Show me the money!" Luke crowed when he was handed the application.

"Keep it down," I hissed. "You work on that while I do some shopping."

I brought home pork chops, canned green beans, bagged salad, and ranch dressing.

"How do you cook your pork chops?" I asked the guys.

"Our mom fries them," Ian said.

I checked the cabinets only to find the boys were out of oil.

"Luke, would you please go buy some vegetable oil?"

"Do I have to?" he whined.

"You can get it at the convenience store across the street."

After half an hour I began to fret—there were four lanes of traffic to cross to get to the store. I opened the front door and looked in the direction of the store. Luke was leaning against the fence of the house, smoking.

"Where did you get those?" I yelled.

"Where do you think?"

"Put that out and come inside." I grabbed the bag. "Where's my change?"

"I'll pay you back."

"With what?"

"Ed gets a ton of money from my lawsuit trust fund and the state—that's the only reason he wanted me. He sold my horse and will keep that money too."

"Well, right now I'm supporting you, and you can't buy cigarettes or anything else illegal on my dime."

"Ed lets me drink beer."

Maybe he did and maybe he didn't. With Luke I never knew what was true. "That's not going to happen here."

"That's not going to happen here," he repeated in a mocking tone.

For a moment I actually felt sorry for Ed.

All my life I had wanted my brother to be safe and happy—and loved. The truth was that I wasn't always able to be there for him because of the separations; and even when we had been together in foster care, I had to keep pushing him away like a pesky puppy that wouldn't stop jumping or scratching. We were now off to a rocky start because neither of us knew how to negotiate this new dynamic. I didn't want to be an authority figure like Ed, but I also couldn't let him do anything he wanted, especially in a home that wasn't mine. For years I had been lectured by foster mothers and counselors who told me that I wasn't my brother's mother, it wasn't my job to discipline or care for him, and I needed to "know my place" and just "be his sister." My therapist called my overwhelming feelings of responsibility "being parentified." Supposedly this hindered my development. No matter what I was told, though, I still worried about Luke whether I was four or fourteen. Finally, with no other volunteers in sight, I had to be his mother again.

While we were eating the pork chops, Erick told Luke about some of his own problems in high school. "I hated being ordered around," he said, "and I was terrified to speak up in class. Also I didn't fit in with the snobs who were headed to college or losers who couldn't wait to just sit around all day."

Luke nodded. "Yeah!"

"So I transferred to another school right here in St. Pete where they treated me like an adult." Luke didn't have a smart retort. "I'd like to show you around the place."

Erick took him the next day, before he could lose interest. When they returned, I asked Luke how he'd liked it, but he merely shrugged.

A few days later, the grocery store called and said Luke had the job. He was to report the next morning. "The hell I will," he said. "I don't need to work. I'm rich."

Late the next evening two guys wearing ragged hoodies, who I'd never met, knocked on the door, and Luke answered it. "Hey, man!" he said, and started to invite them in.

"I don't think so," I said with my arms outstretched to bar the door.

"Sorry, guys. My sister can be a real bitch."

"That's it!" I said to Erick when we were alone. "He invites creeps to the house in the middle of the night and then calls *me* names!"

"Here's the part I don't understand," Erick said. "Your brother went into foster care when he was less than a year old. I thought people lined up to adopt babies."

"They kept giving our mother chances to get us back."

Erick thought about that. "Poor kid," he finally said. "I can hang in there if you can."

Two days before Luke's eighteenth birthday, Ed Kemper called. "How's my son?" He sounded ablaze with loving-kindness.

"Okay," I said warily. "Do you want to talk to him?"

"No, just tell him I'll be there later to bring him home. We need to be together for his big birthday." Ed was crying. "He'll always be my son."

The next day Luke disappeared with Ed as fast as he had arrived.

Cleaning out Luke's room, I found two mysterious pills that Ian thought might be Ecstasy, rolling papers, and an empty bottle of Jägermeister. I felt as if I had been slapped in the face. What if a deputy had come for him, searched Erick's house, and found the drugs? It wasn't fair to have put any of us in jeopardy. I was amazed that Erick had been willing to take in my brother and assume these risks. His generous heart and optimistic outlook were inspiring and made me feel closer to him than ever. He didn't look down on me for having such a complicated family, and he could see the best in even Luke, even if my brother was determined to be his own worst enemy. We had weathered this together.

At the same time, my childhood dream of being the perfect big sister was shattered. Luke still had his golden hair and cute, crooked smile, but he was wrestling demons that were far too powerful for me. Knowing this freed me from responsibility, but I would never regret trying. If I hadn't, I would have always wondered if I could have diverted his destructive course.

5.

get-out-of-jail card

Children begin by loving their parents; as they grow older they judge them; sometimes they forgive them.
—Oscar Wilde

After those crazy weeks with my brother, I was relieved for school to start. As a theater major, I was in many plays on campus. I invited both Lorraine and the Courters to see me—on separate nights—acting in our class's version of *Alice in Wonderland* with Alice as a psychiatric inmate surrounded by her imaginary acquaintances. The Courters arrived opening night and sat in the first row.

I was the Cheshire cat, and my scene took place high on the catwalk of the black box theater. "How arrrre you doing?" I said, rolling the *r*'s. At the end of my main scene, I exited the stage by sliding down a pole before scampering offstage.

After the performance, Phil said, "I thought you might *really* break a leg sliding down that pole so fast."

Sid joked, "Come back next week for *Cheshire Cat on a Hot Tin Roof* with Ashley singing 'What's New, Pussycat?'"

Gay and I groaned. "On that note—" Phil said, and waved

good-bye. I walked them to their car and thanked them for coming so far.

"Wouldn't have missed seeing my little kitty cat," Phil said so kindly my eyes watered.

The next evening, Lorraine and Rex roared up on separate Harleys. Both wore black leather jackets and German-style motorcycle helmets. They took seats in the last row and leaned against the back wall. When I made my entrance, Rex whistled, but Lorraine kept him quiet for the rest of the performance. I left the dressing room with my makeup still on to say good-bye.

"I didn't get it," Rex said. Lorraine shot him a warning glance. "But I loved that pole trick."

"Glad we came," Lorraine said.

"Who were they?" the director asked when I returned.

"My mom and her boyfriend."

"Weren't your parents here last night?" the girl playing Alice asked.

"Yes, but—"

Sid filled in. "Ashley's family is complicated."

I gave him a grateful smile. "To say the least."

The Courters wanted to have an elegant dinner the night before my college graduation. "I think we should invite the Hecklers," Gay said. Lou Heckler was my speech mentor. "And the Gaffneys, who gave you your first college scholarship when you were still at The Children's Home. Who else?"

"Erick." I was now living off-campus with Nikki and another friend. Ian was always around, and inevitably Erick and I were seeing more and more of each other. "His parents have me over so often I'd like to invite them, too."

"Okay," Gay agreed. "It's your special night. What about your mother and sister?"

"Not at the dinner at the Vinoy!"

"No, sorry. I was thinking of the actual ceremony and the luncheon after."

"Why would she want to come?"

"You're the first person in the family to graduate college. Maybe this will help inspire Autumn."

"Are you sure this is a good idea?"

Gay shrugged. "They'll be in the audience with us, and I'll make it memorable for them."

Eckerd College graduations are held in a shaded tent very early in the morning to avoid the cruel May heat. Gay brought three bouquets of flowers. She gave the roses to Lorraine and handed a smaller nosegay to Autumn with a note that read: *You'll get a bigger one on your graduation day.* Mine was an enormous bunch of sunflowers—my favorite— interspersed with a riot of yellow and white daisies. Phil took photos of various family groups and then had Lorraine take one of me with Gay and Phil. To an outsider, nothing about the scene would have suggested how odd it really was.

At the restaurant Lorraine and Autumn sat across from Ms. Sandnes, my primary counselor from The Children's Home. Her only information about Lorraine had come from my files, and I wondered what she thought about this unusual reunion. Thankfully, lunch went smoothly and everyone left in good spirits. I returned to my apartment, flung myself on the couch, tossed off my heels, and felt a merciful relief that classes, exams, rituals, and the co-mingling of people from my past and present was over.

Life after graduation was much the same as it had been before—without all the studying. Ian had moved to Pennsylvania with his dog, but not Nikki, who was taking their breakup so badly that Erick preferred not to come to the apartment. Erick and I had agreed to try an exclusive relationship—no more seeing other people—but living apart. Some part of me still wanted freedom . . . just in case.

I became a full-time motivational speaker, which meant traveling for keynotes, seminars, and fund-raising appearances. My bookings increased considerably when *Three Little Words* was published, and I did several publicity tours and national television appearances, including *Good Morning America* with Diane Sawyer. I was on the road almost every week and exhausted when I was home. I had volunteered to become a Guardian ad Litem (or CASA), following in the footsteps of both Gay and Mary Miller, the woman who helped get me released from foster care so I could be adopted. I decided to specialize in teen girls, thinking that they might be more willing to talk to me since I was only a few years older and had been through the system too.

One weekend when I went to Crystal River for Gay's birthday, she handed me a packet of recent mail. I was about to toss a postcard that looked like an advertisement. On one side was the Monopoly Get-Out-of-Jail card. As I tipped it to the trash can, I saw that it was an invitation to Uncle Perry's release-from-prison party in South Carolina. He had served more than twenty years for second-degree murder. At the age of five I had visited him in prison when I lived with Grandpa Rhodes—his father.

A few days later Lorraine called and offered to pay for airfare and a hotel for both Erick and me. At the graduation lunch she had taken me aside and said, "I'm happy to see Erick is still around."

"Do you want to go?" I asked him later that day.

"I wouldn't mind meeting more of your family."

"I've only been there once before—and it was . . . awkward."

"Don't forget I have twelve aunts and uncles—I'm used to wild and crazy reunions."

"Maybe not like mine. The first thing they showed me was a photo album with the picture of a dead baby brother who I never knew existed. Then they took me to the grave of my brother's grandfather, who was murdered by his father over a card game." Erick's eyes widened. "Oh, and that's not all. Lorraine, who wasn't all cozy with her family at that point, heard I was going to be there, and so she started driving up from Florida. On the way she was arrested for speeding, and Uncle Sammie had to drive a hundred miles to bail her out."

"Are you trying to scare me or talk *yourself* out of it?"

"A little of both."

"It's a holiday weekend and we have a free trip, so why not?" he said, but his voice sounded more worried than his words.

"Okay," I answered, "but don't say I didn't warn you about where I *really* come from."

☀

Erick drove the car Lorraine had rented for us down rough roads lined by cotton and tobacco fields. "Look, the cotton is in full puff!" I said.

Erick laughed. "I love your expressions."

"What would you call it?"

"Full ball? I'm sure there's an agriculturally-correct term."

I laughed. Everything with Erick seemed so easy, so natural, especially since the trip to England. I used to think I was using Erick when I called him for advice or to travel with me; now I realized I asked him because I trusted him the most. I had never expected to still be involved with Erick after all this time—but here we were, closer than ever.

"There it is." I pointed to Uncle Sammie's driveway.

Erick sighed audibly when I pointed out the blue house with white trimming, dormer windows, and a wraparound front porch. Uncle Sammie's machine shop must have been doing well, because there was a new addition on the house. "Oh wow, this place is really nice," he said.

The weather was mild for the Veteran's Day holiday in November, and it was also Erick's birthday that week. Autumn's would be the following week and mine the week after that, and so Lorraine and Aunt Courtney had planned a joint celebration along with Uncle Perry's party.

"Got big plans for today," Lorraine said in a giddy voice, when she ran out to the car to greet us. I felt a twinge of memory—a time when she had been sparkling and silly and happily doting on me.

She drove us to Walmart and insisted on buying us both camouflage boots and four-wheeler gear. When we got home, Aunt Courtney handed us extra-large T-shirts and goggles. Lorraine helped Autumn into her dirt-bike outfit while Aunt Courtney did the same for Travis, the oldest of the three cousins, and Tina, the youngest. Each kid had boots and matching slacks and jackets with racing patterns on them. Travis wore blue and Tina green. The colors set off their coppery hair and brown eyes—exactly the same shades as mine. Tina's freckles even formed the same pattern over her nose as mine did after too much sun.

"We're like sisters!" Tina crowed.

"She's *my* sister," Autumn said.

I couldn't say I felt that same bond for Autumn. Just like with Luke, I would feel a responsibility for her if something were to happen, but I didn't sense any innate closeness. We had never lived together or shared a familial experience. It didn't help that I was more than a decade older. If anything, I retained a tinge of resentment toward Autumn that I worried I'd never be able to shake. I knew it wasn't fair to begrudge a child, but in some dark place it hurt that she was getting what I had been denied.

"Ever been on a four-wheeler before?" Uncle Sammie asked Erick. He shook his head, so Sammie demonstrated the controls. Then he turned to me. "Hop on back and hold on tight!"

There was a wild whoop as the little kids took off on their own mini dirt bikes. Travis cut in front of Sammie. I couldn't believe how fast they were going—even Tina zoomed past at what had to be thirty miles per hour. We bumped through the almost leafless woods and followed their tracks across a sloppy field.

"Rained on Wednesday," Sammie yipped. I guessed that was a good thing for muddin', as I later learned our escapade was called. When we came out into a clearing, the three kids were circling an archipelago of puddles that reflected blustery clouds. Lorraine purposely slammed her front wheels into a manure-colored pit. A curl of mud splashed

Erick full in the face. Just as he shook it off, she slid into the mud from another angle and slimed his legs. Uncle Sammie was not going to be out-mudded—or whatever they called it—so he revved the engine and did almost a 360, drenching me in slimy gook. I had been caught so unaware that my mouth had been open. I coughed and spit a mouthful of what tasted like rotten mushroom soup.

Lorraine zoomed from the side and directed her splatter on us. "Gotcha!" she crowed.

I reached up and touched my hair, which now was a dripping helmet of sludge. *Helmet!* I suddenly thought with horror. None of the adults had helmets on. If Gay could see me now, she'd have heart failure. She called guys who ride motorcycles without helmets "organ donors."

I heard a sucking sound as Sammie's wheels spun but we didn't move. I lifted my goggles enough to see that we were stuck in the deepest part of the mud hole. My uncle stood up and rocked the four-wheeler back and forth violently. Lorraine and Erick laughed raucously. When we were free, we headed to the dry edge. Rex arrived on a dirt bike and offered to trade it with Lorraine. She gunned it deftly, climbed a small mound, and did a trick jump as the bike came off the top. After another turn around the muddy pond, she stopped in front of me.

"Wanna try?"

I was aching to wash up. Were mud critters already burrowing into my skin? Could I get ringworm or gastrointestinal disease?

"Come on!" Erick coaxed.

"Okay," I said reluctantly. "Show me how."

After a few minutes of basic instruction and a couple of

false starts, I took off down the trail far enough that nobody could see me practicing stopping, getting on and off, and riding at various speeds. Strangely, I was most stable at a fast speed, and—holy cow—it was fun! Trees whizzed past, stones flew out from under my wheels. I turned around in a clearing and rushed back to the group full speed ahead. I had seen the spot where Lorraine had entered the mud-hole and plowed straight in—closing my eyes at the last second. There was a sound like a giant belch, and the bike stalled in the muck. I opened my eyes.

Sammie came over in his four-wheeler and nudged my bike onto the bank. He spit brown slobber into the grass. "Yep, you're a Rhodes all right."

Back at the house, Aunt Courtney and Uncle Perry's wife, Marlene, were wearing plastic rain ponchos. The kids knew the drill. They stood against the garage wall while the women hosed them down. Then they rushed to the back deck, tossed off their outer layers, and hurried into the house to change. Erick and I shivered while we waited our turn. I shrieked louder than the kids when the cold water pummeled me.

Erick and I hustled our way to the bathroom, dripping grimy water through the hall and kitchen. Once in the shower, I tilted my head to rinse my ears, then shook my head like a dog to clear them.

It looked like coffee was running out of Erick's nose. "That's so gross!" I said.

"But it was worth it!"

"Yeah, that was a blast!"

As we were toweling off, Erick said, "I like these folks."

"Really?"

"They're easy. They don't expect anything from me."

I had a list of goals, and I was checking them off one by one. Erick had a comfortable job managing rental properties for a family friend. Although he could make his own hours, it was unfulfilling. He needed much more, but he also needed to want more. His excuse was that nobody in his family had really pushed him in high school or set expectations for him or his siblings. I argued that even before I was adopted, I had plans for myself and knew I wanted to go to college. The Courters had the same values and made certain I was well prepared and kept me on track with my academic objectives. While I didn't want to be annoying, I hoped I could give Erick the self-confidence he needed to go to college and find a more rewarding career. I wondered if then he'd feel more accepted by my family.

When we came out dressed in dry jeans and sweaters, the kids were snuggled under crocheted blankets on the sofa, drinking cocoa and watching television. Through the living room window we could see Lorraine and Rex in the hot tub. We joined Uncle Sammie in the kitchen and sat on the bar stools. He handed Erick a beer.

"Cocoa for me," I said.

He poured me a mug and started recounting the muddin' blow by muddy blow. Soon the rest of the family gathered around us. Aunt Courtney shooed the kids to follow her. "Party time!" Uncle Sammie led us into the old garage, which had been converted into a rec room. Some neighbors and other family members must have arrived and gone directly there, because lots of people we hadn't yet met were milling about. A party banner read: HAPPY BIRTHDAY ERICK, AUTUMN, AND ASHLEY. Underneath, another read: WELCOME HOME PERRY.

Uncle Perry carried in aluminum platters filled with take-out Carolina barbecue. There were hot chicken wings, beef and pork ribs, beans, slaw, a few salads, snowflake rolls, and cut-up chickens. A giant cooler was filled with ice, sodas, and beer. Travis put some country music CDs in the player. The kids sat cross-legged on futons, while Erick and I were offered canvas chairs with drink holders.

To me the scene was as foreign as if it had been in a Parisian café. I tried to fix the tableau in my mind. Here was the only half of my biological family that I knew—including my cousins, half sister, birth mother, aunts, and uncles, plus some of the neighbors who had known me at the age of five when I had lived nearby during one placement that had ended abruptly when my grandfather had almost died after a gunfight. If I hadn't already been in Florida's foster care system, I might have grown up with these people. Even though I had no sense of belonging, I felt comforted in having some kinship on one side of the family tree.

"Mommy!" Autumn said. She had her mouth open like a baby bird and was enjoying being hand-fed pieces of chicken. Both of them were giggling. For someone who was turning nine, she was too big for that, but Lorraine seemed to enjoy indulging her. I took a mental pulse of my emotions. Was I envious? No. I leaned into Erick, who hadn't left my side. My feelings for him were ten times stronger than for anyone else in this room—maternal figure included. Lorraine had paid for our trip, but somehow the whole relationship felt like a transaction. We were all politely playing our parts, yet there had been no moments of shared insight, apologies for past mistakes, or promises of a renewed future connection.

Whenever I returned home to the Courters, it was like coming out of the cold and sitting beside a comforting fire. I got to thinking: What would I be like if I had never moved away from the Rhodes clan in the first place? I would never have gone to college and would probably have a kid or two of my own by now. Erick mistook the shiver that went through me for a chill and began to rub my back. Once I had yearned for Lorraine's doting care; now that I was almost twenty-three, my gut rejected it.

Tina sweetly singing "Happy Birthday" interrupted my reverie. Everyone else had finished eating and joined in raucously. Aunt Courtney carried a cookie sheet filled with cupcakes with lighted candles. She stopped in front of Erick, who tried—but failed—to blow them all out. Autumn—in a maneuver reminiscent of Luke—jumped in and blew spit across the pan. There were pats on the back, jokes about me dating an old man because Erick is four years older than me. Perry and Sammie then crept behind Erick and creamed his face with two cupcakes.

"Whoa!" cried Travis, and landed one on his sister's forehead when she ducked.

Then Sammie handed me one and directed my arm into Erick's nose. The leftover food went flying: potato salad, carrot sticks, even an empty beer can.

Tina yelled at Autumn, "Don't get it on my fleece!"

Travis banged into the door as he headed outside to avoid a full-on face of icing.

I was doubled over laughing. "Oh, Erick!" I sputtered. "Can you imagine this happening at the Courters?"

"No way," he said.

6.

my splashy wedding

We come to love not by finding a perfect person, but by learning to see an imperfect person perfectly.
—*Sam Keen*

For six years Erick had been my touchstone—I tested the worth of other men by comparing them to him. And for six years he had put up with my insistence on dating others, my trips without him, my moods, my insecurities and meltdowns, not to mention letting Luke live with us for those few disastrous weeks. That experience had been a crucial one for me, because it showed he was as willing to commit to helping Luke in any way he could as I was.

"Luke respected him more than me," I told Gay during a visit.

"Erick is a good role model for your brother."

"I think those are the first positive words you've ever said about Erick," I said, munching on potato chips. "Does that mean you finally like him?"

"I've never *not* liked him," Gay insisted. "We wanted you to have more experiences with different guys, that's all."

"I have, and none of them compare." I tilted the bag and

ate the last chip crumbs. Gay's disapproving expression made me feel defensive, because after my knee injury, I was no longer as active, and my weight reached the highest it had ever been. "He's been my rock."

"Through thick and thin," Gay said.

"That was rude!"

"Sorry, Freudian slip, hon, but all those carbs and salt don't help."

"At least Erick isn't critical like you are. He would never call me fat."

"We should ask Doc Rollins about it." Dr. Rollins had taken care of me since I moved to Crystal River. "Maybe there is a metabolic reason for your sudden gain. And Erick does love you, which is why he deserves more than being your fallback position."

I had now been out of school for more than a year and was busy on the road with my speaking engagements. Erick was keeping me sane while I traveled alone, and it was nice to have someone to check in with and entertain me from random hotels and airports.

When I got home from my last trip of the year that December, he asked if we could share Christmas with his family. "I know you like to be with the Courters on Christmas morning, so I was thinking we could stay over Christmas Eve and then come back to St. Pete and have dinner with my parents."

I was about to object until I saw a glimmer in his eyes that showed that this was very important to him. "Sure," I said.

The Courters were welcoming, and they made sure he had an overstuffed Christmas stocking. It was almost lunchtime by the time Erick handed me the final present of the day—a huge blue box with golden ribbons. It nested six more boxes, each one smaller and smaller. I should have caught on, but I was too busy with the tiny ribbons and distracted by the loud holiday music blaring on the stereo. As I approached the smallest box, Erick dropped to one knee, and the family fell silent. Josh muted the stereo with the remote, causing Erick's voice to fall to a raspy whisper as he asked me to marry him. After the initial shock, I jokingly said, "I guess so."

Everyone laughed knowingly. They were the same three little words I'd used to approve my adoption, and we all knew how that turned out. Finding a husband hadn't been on my to-do list. I loved Erick's company and how secure he made me feel, but was this the man I wanted to spend the rest of my life with? Just as I had tried to imagine how my adoption might fail, I thought of all the ways a marriage could crumble. Most of all I wondered if I was worth loving forever. I looked around to see my whole family smiling and nodding. My brothers and father each gave Erick a bear hug. I had no way of knowing what my future with Erick might hold, but in that moment I felt loved on every level.

⁂

"When?" asked Gay a few hours later, looking at a calendar on her computer.

I glanced at Erick. "As soon as possible," he said giddily.

"I'm totally booked in April, because it's National Child Abuse Prevention Month," I said.

"Giulia and I are filming in Ethiopia in June and then are spending a month with her family in Rome," Josh said.

"We have trips in May and October," Phil chimed in.

"September won't work for me," Blake said.

"Anyone have a problem with March?" Gay asked.

"That's less than three months!" I exclaimed.

"We arranged ours in six weeks," Phil said. "What sort of a wedding do you have in mind?"

"It would be nice to do something unusual that everyone would enjoy," I ventured. "I've always thought a destination wedding would be a blast."

"You want the whole family on your honeymoon?" Blake chortled.

Gay looked up from her computer. "A cruise would be a very reasonable option. Let's see if we can find a date that works."

※

"Do you think we should invite any of my birth family?" I asked my parents.

"Do you want them there?" Gay asked evenly.

"Wouldn't Tina be an adorable flower girl?" I said to Erick.

"And there's Autumn, of course," Gay said.

"She and Lorraine would be a package deal," Phil said in a tense tone.

"She's been stable lately. I think Rex has been good for her."

Gay waited a beat. "It's a very large ship."

Lorraine was thrilled to be included and offered to help out with the rehearsal dinner financially. The Courters were surprised but didn't object.

Gay e-mailed Ed for his new address. He wrote back that

Luke was going through an angry phase and couldn't be trusted not to make a scene. With a heavy heart—because once again my dream of including my brother in my life had been dashed—I decided not to take any chances, never expecting that someone else would misbehave onboard.

Erick and I decided to get married on a cruise ship sailing from Tampa to Cozumel. About a hundred guests would embark for the ceremony and luncheon. Then those who were not sailing with us would leave the ship, but sixty friends and family members were able to stay on for the four-day cruise.

The night before the wedding we had a rehearsal dinner that included some people who couldn't attend the actual wedding. Right away I noticed that Lorraine seemed rattled, although I assumed being surrounded by so many Courters and strangers had to be stressful. There were some awkward moments when I introduced her to the other guests as Lorraine, without explaining our relationship. Some already knew, but more remote friends did not need to be clued in.

The next day our guests arrived at the pier. Everyone was squinting in the bright morning sun. I ducked into the terminal to protect my upswept hairdo from the brisk wind. Lorraine came up to me and opened her coat. "I don't think I wore the right dress."

"You look perfect!" Her long champagne gown was simple and classy.

"I'm so nervous!"

"Me too."

"I never had a big wedding like this."

"Neither have I!" I laughed, but she did not get the joke.

"My sister gave me a pill to calm me down. I hope I don't keel over."

Uncle Sammie, Aunt Courtney, and their children greeted me. "Thank you so much for having us," Aunt Courtney said. Lorraine's sister, Leanne, walked over and introduced me to two people who had been anxious to come, but who I didn't remember. Clara had been my babysitter when my mother worked when I was a baby; and I had lived with Marcy after Luke was born prematurely.

"We've always cared about you," Marcy said in a timid voice.

"You look gorgeous!" Clara added.

All together there were ten people representing my birth family and their friends. It felt odd to have people I did not remember at my wedding, but even more peculiar to have family that were strangers too. I backed away to greet some of the other guests gathering in the embarkation area. Loving people from my past including Mary Miller, my Guardian ad Litem; and Ms. Sandnes and Mr. Todd from The Children's Home. My literary agent, Joëlle Delbourgo, made the trip from New York, along with several of Gay's cousins. Her sister's whole family had come from Maryland, and friends of the Courters had traveled from France. This was really going to happen!

If I was nervous on my wedding day, Phil was even shakier. From the moment he saw me in my gown, his eyes filled with tears. "Never expected to be walking a daughter down the aisle." He swallowed after the last words.

"Don't you dare cry," I warned, "or you'll set me off." We were standing in the hallway leading to the Candlelight Lounge in the aft of the ship.

Phil wiped his brow. "I'm a bit rocky."

"Think of something silly."

"Oh, honey . . ." His voice broke.

"Think of puppy farts."

I laughed so hard I almost burst my back zipper. Then the processional music started. Erick's father, Rob, led his mother down the aisle. Josh and Blake escorted Gay to her seat in the front row. Uncle Sammie walked Lorraine to one beside Gay.

Next came my flower girls, Tina and Autumn, wearing matching white dresses. Their curls were tied back with white ribbons. Erick's friend Brenda wore a tux and stood with the groomsmen, while my friend Aaron was in my bridal party and wore a teal cummerbund that matched my bridesmaids' dresses. I was overwhelmed with happiness that I was in a room full of people from both my present and past. For better or worse, each person had impacted my life in a powerful way. Then I looked at Erick and realized that he was standing there, ready to help carry my heavy baggage and create new memories. The ship shifted slightly—just enough to remind us we were not on solid ground. I held on to Phil's arm. I had never been much for clichés, but at that moment I realized I was being married on a ship, ready to sail off into the sunset to live happily ever after.

At the end of the service, Gay's sister Robin held up a wineglass wrapped in a linen napkin. Knowing that most of the guests would not have seen this ritual before, she said, "As is the custom in our family—which is Jewish—the groom is going to break the glass. The shattered glass reminds us that relationships are fragile and we must treat them with special care. On a lighter note, some say it will be the last time the groom gets to put his foot down."

Everybody laughed as she placed it beneath Erick's feet. He crunched it, and the audience yelled, "Mazel tov!" We kissed. Then we kissed again.

In the most gallant of gestures, Phil escorted both Gay and Lorraine out of the lounge right after Erick and me. For a brief moment in time I felt that my minuscule corner of the world was a peaceable kingdom.

The luncheon was held in one of the ship's grand dining rooms. Just like on a cruise, there was almost a waiter for every table, and the meal was going to be served promptly—because the ship was going to sail away that afternoon. When everyone was seated, Erick and I made a grand entrance down a curved staircase and walked around, greeting our guests.

Lorraine was sitting at one of the first tables with her family members. "Where's Rex?" Erick asked.

"He couldn't get out of work."

"Will he still be able to sail?" I asked, before I noticed Sammie shaking his head.

I nodded and we moved on to another guest. Little did I know that Rex had dumped Lorraine just before they reached the rehearsal dinner. Nikki had witnessed them arguing over the car keys in the restaurant's parking lot, and Lorraine pitched them into the bushes before marching off. It wasn't until after the cruise that I learned that Lorraine had joined the younger crowd at an Ybor nightclub after the rehearsal dinner and danced on a table. She ripped a guy's button-down shirt while dirty dancing, and then whipped off the guy's belt and held it up like a trophy. When the club's security approached, Josh and Blake had to wrestle her into a taxi.

I had no idea that Lorraine's sobriety had ended just as she embarked on a cruise where there's a server around every corner who can't wait to give you a cocktail in exchange for a swipe of your cruise card.

Meanwhile, I glided through the motions of being a bride, loving every minute of the lunch, and saying farewell to the guests who were disembarking. Then Erick and I posed for our wedding photographs on various outside decks, curving staircases, balconies, and theaters. Every time I caught a glance of myself in a mirror, though, I was reminded that I was overweight. Erick, however, kept grinning and telling me how beautiful I looked.

As soon as possible, I hurried to our honeymoon suite to get out of the tight dress and into something loose so we could help the Courters unpack. Their luggage was more suited to a royal entourage than a short cruise. They'd brought duffels full of party favors, swag bags, contest prizes, and glow-in-the-dark flashing rings.

Gay had packed a computer and printer and produced a newsletter for the guests that included the times for ping-pong tournaments, pool parties, face painting, predinner cocktails, and afternoon tea. My bridesmaids had organized themes for each dinner and had suggested that guests pack tropical shirts, black-and-white for formal night, and fancy hats for a contest.

Whether we felt like being alone or were battling seasickness, Erick and I ended up spending much of our time in our suite. When we wanted to socialize, our best friends and extended family were there; when we desired privacy, it was easy to slip away.

On the first day at sea, Gay organized a Ladies-Only Tea in the Piano Bar, which I didn't attend but heard about later. On her way there, Gay found Lorraine and my aunts lingering in the corridor. "Are you coming to the tea?" she'd asked.

"Not sure we'll fit in," Aunt Courtney had said.

"Sure you will. They have delicious biscuits called scones. You'll love them." And she swept them along.

Gay made sure everyone was introduced. "This is Ashley's birth mom, Lorraine, and her sister Leanne and sister-in-law Courtney," she began. "This is my younger sister, Robin, and my cousins Sandy and Esther— they're sisters." Finally she said, "This is one of my closest friends, Ruth—she's a midwife, who I hope will come in handy one of these days." Everyone laughed.

After the tea was served, Lorraine said, "You want to hear something crazy? Ashley was married on the twenty-fifth anniversary of my mother's death."

"That must be hard for you," Aunt Robin said with sympathy.

"Yeah, but that's not the weird part. See, I think I conceived Ashley that night, and so it's like she got married on the date she was made."

Supposedly her remark silenced the chatter. Ruth, the midwife, fumbled in her handbag and pulled out a wheel. "That means Ashley was born around November twentieth."

"The twenty-second," Gay and Lorraine replied in unison.

Lorraine rambled on with some inappropriate speculation about my paternity, while the Courter side of the party gulped their tea in silence.

The next day Gay's cousin Sandy said to her, "I can't believe that you insulted Lorraine."

"How?"

"You told her that she was dressed like a hooker."

Gay's jaw dropped. "Did Lorraine tell you that?"

Sandy nodded.

"First of all, I never said that—and never would. Besides, her clothes have been completely proper."

"Well, that didn't sound like something you would say." Her cousin gave a sarcastic laugh. "You know what she said next?" She waited a long beat. "She said, 'Even when I was a hooker, I didn't dress like one.'"

A short while later Aunt Courtney confronted Gay. "Was that tea party of yours some sort of a setup?"

"In what way?"

"Lorraine thinks it was a trap to get her DNA."

Gay, who wears hearing aids, thought she missed something. "I don't understand."

Courtney sighed. "Lorraine thinks that you persuaded us to attend the tea to get some of her hair for DNA."

"Courtney, you're a nurse! Nobody doubts that Lorraine is Ashley's birth mother, which is the only thing that her DNA would prove."

"I know," Aunt Courtney said. "Lorraine has a conspiracy theory for everything."

The troubles escalated, or so I learned. The next day, Josh's fiesty Italian wife, Giulia, was doing face painting poolside. Autumn and Tina asked for matching butterflies, while Travis was running around in his mustache and pirate patch shouting, "Argh!" Giulia had just finished painting my bridesmaid Jill with flowers that matched her sundress.

"C'mon, Mommy, you're next!" Autumn said.

Lorraine held back. "I'll do it if Gay does."

"I'll go first if you want me to." Gay asked her daughter-in-law for birds and vine leaves.

"Butterflies to match Autumn's" was Lorraine's request. "Oh, that's so awesome!" she said when Giulia showed her the painting in a mirror. "I'll hate to wash it off."

"I'm going to wear mine to dinner," Gay announced.

Lorraine looked at her dubiously. "Really? Will you pinky swear?" Gay laughed and offered her pinky.

Erick and I went back to our suite and ordered sand-wiches and didn't show up again until the meet-up in the Café des Artistes Lounge, where Phil was hosting pre-dinner cocktails.

Gay spent the afternoon socializing with her relatives. The deck they were on was shaded, but still, her cousin Esther said, "Don't look now, but your bird is running."

"Huh?" Esther pointed to her cheek. Gay touched the spot and her finger blotted the color. "How bad is it?"

"Depends whether you like abstract art," Esther said.

"I'll get Giulia to redo it before dinner," she said.

When the time came, Giulia and Josh weren't in their room. "Phil, you have to find Giulia or Lorraine will be furious."

"Just clean the rest off your face," Phil said. "You look better without it."

"That's not the point."

"Hers probably melted too."

Lorraine wasn't at the cocktail hour, but Gay walked right up to her as soon as she entered the dining room. The restaurant was alive with clinking glasses, rattling silverware, service carts, and the excited chatter of cheerful cruisers. I was sitting with my back to Lorraine's table and with all the clatter didn't notice the interaction. Later I learned that before Gay got a word out, Lorraine began cursing. "You friggin' lied to me!"

"The humidity ruined it, and—"

"I knew you were setting me up to look like a fool."

"I tried to find Giulia, but—"

"The hell you did!"

"Mommy," Autumn had begged, "stop it!" She put her hands over her ears and burst into tears.

Aunt Courtney jumped up and hustled Autumn out of the restaurant. Josh did the same with Lorraine.

Before dessert, Erick and I walked around and chatted with our guests. I asked Uncle Sammie where Lorraine and Autumn were. "Lorraine took her down to the cabin because she was feeling iffy," he replied smoothly.

The next day we docked in Cozumel, Mexico, and everyone had different plans for going ashore. Our bridal party went out together. Autumn and her cousins had a beach day. Erick and I went back to the ship early and brought a snack to have on our balcony, which faced the harbor. Exhausted by all the walking in town and bartering for souvenirs, we tried to nap. Erick crashed quickly, but my mind whirled. I got up and took an icy water bottle from the mini-fridge and went out on our balcony. Even though the sun was shining, it was drizzling, but the overhead balcony covered me. I watched the droplets pinging into the water several feet from one another. Each one made a discrete circle that widened slowly until it impinged on the next one. I was mesmerized by the designs—so random, and yet they seemed to have an organizing pattern when viewed from afar. Erick grunted and turned over into his deep-sleep position. So this was where all the random circles of my life had led: to this room on a ship in the harbor of a Mexican island, with many of the people I cared most about in the world. Even Lorraine was here. I had once been told I would never see her again. Nobody could have predicted she would be at my wedding. I found myself aching for Luke, even though I knew Ed was right. There were so many ways he could have gotten in trouble, particularly since he couldn't legally drink onboard. He also had not made peace with any of our family, and I had no way of knowing how he would react to everyone. He still held a lot of anger and resentment that he couldn't channel properly.

During that moment of optimistic serenity, I had missed all the signs that Lorraine was no longer sober. Later I heard about all the beers she'd had at the rehearsal dinner, the mixed drinks at the Ybor club, and the serial cocktails at various bars all around the ship with people unconnected to our wedding guests. While my mind was drifting with naive thoughts, Lorraine, wearing a bikini, was cackling uproariously with some strange men on the adults-only deck. I heard about it later from Erick's father, who commented: "She wasn't feeling any pain."

We planned a group photo on the grand staircase, with everyone dressed in black and white. I had brought along a second, more casual wedding dress, but when Erick zipped it, the seam burst. I dissolved into tears. "I'm fat!"

"No, this fabric is flimsy."

My heart swelled at his lovable lie. "What will I wear?"

"How about your real wedding dress?"

"I'm not up for that corset, pantyhose, girdle, and the double Spanx. And I don't want the other passengers staring at me."

"They'll stare anyway, because you are the most beautiful girl on the ship."

"Thanks," I said, wiping my tears, "but that's laying it on a bit thick." I went to the closet. "The only other dressy one is red!"

"Bellissima!" Giulia said, approving my "decision" to wear the red dress. "You are the rose in the garden."

As the photographer was lining everyone up for the photo, I asked where Autumn was.

Aunt Courtney told me that she and Lorraine had gotten too much sun.

The photographer was getting impatient, so I hid my disappointment that all my guests would not be in the picture.

Later I learned that when Gay and Phil returned to their cabin after dinner that night, there was a flashing light on their phone with a message to call Uncle Sammie's cabin. "You've got to help us," Aunt Courtney cried hysterically when Gay reached her. "They're arresting Sammie."

"Whoa," Gay said. "Who's arresting Sammie?"

"The ship's police."

"Why?"

"He got into a fight with Lorraine."

"I'll be right there."

Gay later described the scene to me. "There were two Filipino guards in the room and one in the corridor. Apparently Lorraine asked Courtney to check in on Autumn while she went back on deck to party with some guys she'd met. But Sammie knew when his sister was over her limit—and Lorraine was *way* over—so he told her to call it a night. She said, 'The hell I will' and headed for the door. Then it gets confusing. Your uncle grabbed her arm. Lorraine shoved him away, but then lost her balance and hit her head on the edge of the bunk. After that she ran to her room, called security, and claimed that Sammie had assaulted her."

"What did you do when you arrived?"

"I explained the situation—about the two mothers and one feeling so guilty for not raising her own child, the only way she could cope was to get drunk."

"Who would buy that?"

"Well, it *is* the real story. Anyway, he called his supervisor." Gay grinned. "You should have seen this guy. He had the fiendish smile of the good guy who comes in right before the interrogator with the electric gadgets. When I pointed out that that Lorraine was drunk while Sammie was sober, he agreed that Lorraine was the troublemaker.

"They put Lorraine on cabin arrest, which meant posting a guard outside her door. When they cleared her to leave the cabin the next day, they blocked her cruise charge card, which meant she couldn't purchase drinks."

"That was smart."

"Too bad it didn't stop her," Gay said. "Phil saw her in the Violins Bar with a couple of guys who seemed happy to buy her whatever she wanted."

As far as Erick and I were concerned, our group honeymoon was a huge success. Autumn and her cousins said it was the best time ever. Our friends urged us to repeat it for every anniversary. Gay's father, then ninety-four, zoomed everywhere in his power wheelchair. Erick's grandmother reveled in every new experience. The Smiths and the Courters bonded, and Gay and Erick's mother, Sharon, dreamed about grandchildren.

We never knew until much later how close Uncle Sammie had come to being detained on the ship and possibly turned over to Florida authorities when we returned. Nobody told us that one of Erick's cousins, who is a deputy sheriff, took it upon herself to monitor Lorraine's behavior. In the area where pictures taken by the ship's photographers were displayed, Phil noticed risqué photos of Lorraine with strangers and tucked them out of sight.

"Everyone protected us," Erick said right after we heard various versions of Lorraine's antics, "and I'm grateful."

So much for those overlapping circles blooming from the drizzling droplets! While I had been fantasizing, Lorraine had been splintering. "Poor Autumn. Where will they live now?"

"Seems to me that she always lands on her feet," Erick said. "Lorraine's still attractive, and apparently she had plenty of admirers onboard. Maybe she just wanted to prove that Rex isn't the only fish in the sea."

"Oh, that's not it!" I gulped, unable to find words to explain how the woman who had given me life had found yet another way to undermine something good.

7.

divorcing my mother

Life can only be understood backward;
but it must be lived forward.
—*Søren Kierkegaard*

Even after I heard about Lorraine's misbehavior at my wedding, I wasn't angry, mostly because it hadn't affected the joy Erick and I felt at the festivities. Besides, I think Lorraine was embarrassed, since she avoided me for a few months.

"Hey," she said when she finally phoned in June. "Still married?"

"Yes," I said with a laugh, hoping she was joking. "We're very happy."

"Still in St. Pete?" she asked.

"Yes," I said without elaborating. I'd moved into the house Erick had shared with Ian before Ian left for his job in Pennsylvania, and I had begun making decorative improvements.

"That's nice," she replied in a dismissive tone. "Just wanted you to know that everything's great here. I'm in touch with an old friend from high school who has a connection to NASCAR."

"Cool. Erick's younger cousin is a NASCAR freak."

"How old is he?"

"Jasper just turned twelve."

"Autumn will be eleven this fall, so they should get on fine."

Jasper and his older sister Penelope were the children of Erick's cousin Tasha. After Tasha was arrested for possession of drugs, the Department of Children and Families had placed her children with Tasha's mom, Erick's aunt Liz, who had a demanding job as an X-ray technician. When she had to work overtime, friends and family took turns babysitting. Erick and I had volunteered to pitch in too.

"Why don't you guys join us in Daytona for the Fourth?" Lorraine asked.

"Erick's cousin will be with us then." Penelope had plans with friends, and we were taking Jasper to the Courters' to watch the fireworks from their boat.

"He's welcome too. Wes has a big house right on the beach."

I agreed to discuss it with Erick, and when I did, I admitted that the whole idea didn't thrill me. "Jasper would flip out," Erick said, "and it sounds like a hoot to me."

During the drive from St. Petersburg to Daytona Beach, Jasper prattled nonstop about his hero, Dale Earnhardt, Jr. "I hope he does better tomorrow than he did in the Daytona 500," he said.

"What's the difference between the Daytona 400 and 500?" I asked.

Jasper laughed uproariously. "A hundred miles!"

"I have to watch them driving around and around for four hundred miles?"

"Vroom!" Jasper said, doubling over. "Vroom, vroom, vroom!"

Jasper was a smart, kind, polite preteen whose mother was too lost in her own problems to care for him. If anyone could understand his confusion, it was me.

"Grandma Liz said Daytona is right on the ocean. Now I'll finally get to see real waves!"

"Yes, so will you," I said as we passed the speedway and headed toward the beach.

"Are you sure this is the street?" Erick asked.

Although Lorraine had billed Wes's house as "beach-front," the address was actually across a highway from the surf. I knocked tentatively on the door, half expecting to be at the wrong place, but Lorraine opened it. Autumn popped out and pulled on my arm. "Come see my room!"

"Give her a minute," Lorraine said in an exasperated voice. She introduced us to Wes, who was watching some NASCAR news on the television. He raised his beer bottle in salute but didn't get up. "Okay, now you can show them their room—and yours."

As soon as our bags were unpacked, we headed into the kitchen.

"How can I help?" I asked. Lorraine handed me some cold pieces of white toast. "Put those on that baking dish, then put a slice of cheese on top of each." When I was finished, she put the dish in the oven.

When they were done, Lorraine scooped hot chili into bowls and placed a piece of cheesy toast on top of each. "You can add your own chopped onions or more cheese," she said. "The sodas are on a shelf in the fridge."

I piled extra cheese into my bowl and we took our dinners to the dinette area. Jasper looked longingly at the speed trials on television, but I was afraid he'd slop sauce on the sofa and pointed to the kitchen chair. Just then Erick's cell phone rang. "You told them we were coming here, didn't you?" he said. "I'm sorry, Aunt Liz, but there's no way we are turning around and bringing him back tonight. It's over a three-hour drive." He stared at the ceiling as if looking for divine intervention. "Yes, you can give her this number. We'll figure something out."

Jasper looked upset. "What did I do?"

"Nothing. Your caseworker never did her June visit and wants to see you today."

"But it's July," Jasper griped.

Erick's phone rang again. "Hi, Clover," he said. "Yes, I heard. But you knew about Daytona. Who said we needed a court order to take him to another county?" Erick rolled his eyes at me.

I whispered, "That's only necessary if he goes out of state."

"Look, Clover, we're having dinner, and tomorrow we're going to the races. There's no time to drive back and forth, but you are welcome to come here." He held the phone away from his ear as she blasted him about bogus rules and regulations. "Okay," he said. "You have to do what you have to do."

"Do I have to leave?" Jasper asked.

"No, she's calling the local police for a child well-being check."

"What the hell?" Lorraine screeched.

"They just have to verify that Jasper is okay," I said gently.

"What will the neighbors think?"

Autumn burst into tears. "Everything's ruined!"

"You guys can go to a hotel and the cops can meet you there," Lorraine said.

Wes clicked off the television and strode over to the table with his hands on his hips. "There isn't a hotel room available within fifty miles of here."

"You'd be crazy to let them come here," she argued.

Wes turned to Erick. "The kid can go stand in the driveway and they can flash a light in his face. Without a warrant, nobody is coming inside. Got that?"

"No problem," Erick said. He pushed away from the table. "We'll wait outside."

"It could take hours," I said.

"We could use the fresh air," Erick said, seething.

Wes poured bourbons over ice for Lorraine and himself and went back to the sofa. She joined him, and they whispered together. I started cleaning off the table, and before I was even finished, I saw a patrol car pull up in front of the house.

"Good thing Jasper had his school ID card with him," Erick said when they came back in the house. He turned to Jasper. "Big day tomorrow. How about getting ready for bed?"

"Sure," Jasper said, anxious to get away from our angry hosts.

Wes topped off their drinks but didn't offer us any. He held up his and Lorraine's high school yearbook and flipped through the pages. "Your mom was so hot back then!"

Lorraine looked me in the eye and slurred, "I'd be in a

lot more photos, except I got pregnant with you. You ruined my life."

Before I could absorb her harsh words, Jasper came out in pajama pants and a Dale Earnhardt Jr. T-shirt. "Wow, you came prepared!" I said, forcing enthusiasm to cover my fury at Lorraine's stinging words.

"Maybe you'll get to see him in person," Erick said.

"I'm sure I will! Tomorrow's going to be the greatest day of my life."

The race wasn't until the following evening. Lorraine was planning to work on her tan during the day—a preoccupation I never understood.

"What shall we do?" Erick asked the kids.

"There's a chocolate factory on the boardwalk, and you get free samples on the tour," Autumn said.

"Cool!" Jasper said. "I want to see the candy-making machines."

Unfortunately, the tour wasn't running on the holiday weekend. "It's no big deal," Autumn assured us. "This is the best part." She showed us where we could help ourselves to samples of the different types.

She ate a chocolate-covered potato chip. "These are my favorite!" She reached for another. I pushed her hand down and pointed to a sign that read: ONE PER PERSON PLEASE. She pouted. "What can I buy?"

"You can fill one of those small sacks with whatever you choose," I said.

Jasper picked chocolate-covered pretzels. "The potato chips are better," Autumn told him.

There were also gift boxes we could fill with hand-dipped chocolates. Erick selected some for Aunt Liz and Penelope, while I did the same as a thank-you for Erick's parents, who were watching our dogs and house-sitting. The bill was almost a hundred dollars, but we were stuck because we couldn't put the boxes with our personal selections back on the shelf.

"Pretty slick marketing," Erick commented.

Lorraine had pizzas reheating in their oven in the cardboard boxes for lunch, but the chocolate samples had ruined my appetite. Keeping up with the kids running along the boardwalk on the steamy July day had exhausted us. Erick and I slipped away for a nap.

When we awoke in the late afternoon, the kids were watching television.

"Where are Wes and your mom?" I asked Autumn.

"She's your mom too! How come you call her Lorraine?"

"It's complicated," I said, not knowing how much she had been told. "So where are they?"

"Mom went for a swim, and Wes is helping someone move a boat."

I took out a pitcher of iced tea and placed two insulated glasses on the counter. One of the gift boxes of candy was open, and it was almost empty. I held it up. "Who ate all of this?" Jasper looked at his feet. Jasper's background was almost as unstable as mine, and in foster care my knee-jerk reaction was to avoid the truth. What nobody understood was that it's not about the *lie*—it's about the *why*. Lies were my way of controlling what I wanted people to know. Was he headed in the same direction?

"Well?" I asked him more harshly.

Jasper held his head in his hands.

"It was me," Autumn admitted. Her face pinched into a defiant mask.

Erick came into the room and saw the standoff. "What's going on?"

I pointed to the box. "Autumn ate most of this box."

"Is that the one we got for my parents?" Erick asked.

"I dunno," Autumn snapped. "I got it from your suitcase."

"While we were sleeping?" I kept my voice steady, but my hands were trembling. "You snuck into our room and went through our bags?"

"T-that's s-stealing!" Jasper stuttered.

"Is not!"

"What do you call taking something that does not belong to you without permission?" I asked her, my voice steely.

I heard the sliding door on the back deck scrunching open. "What's going on?" Lorraine asked, looking from Autumn to me. Her hair was wrapped in a towel like a turban.

Autumn burst into tears.

"You're not going to blubber your way out of this one!" I exclaimed. "What you did was wrong and rude!"

"What the hell did you do to her?" Lorraine asked me.

"She took these chocolates from our room." I tilted the almost-empty box.

"Are you so stingy you can't even give a little girl some candy?"

"She had her own bag. Not only that, she snuck into our

room while we were asleep and rummaged through our suitcase."

"Mom-my!" Autumn wailed, sounding more like five than ten years old. She batted her puppy eyes and encouraged more tears to flow.

"I can't believe you are so self-centered and insensitive," Lorraine yelled at me. "Between this and the cops, you've destroyed our weekend." She reached for her purse on the counter, pulled out her wallet, and tossed two five-dollar bills at me. "That should cover it."

All my life I had been able to repress strong emotions. Although a chain of child therapists had prodded me to identify sensations of fear or sadness or joy, I dampened feelings to keep myself from flipping out. But I could not restrain this volcano of rage. I could feel the spumes heating my neck, my face, tingling my fingertips. My core was ablaze. As I opened my mouth to let out the flames, the only sound was a hissing gasp.

I pushed the money back at her. Erick put his arm around me. "The money's not the point," he told Lorraine before propelling his exploding wife back to our room.

"I can't believe Lorraine's defending sneaking and stealing!" I tossed cosmetics into my makeup bag.

"That woman is a piece of work," Erick said in an uncharacteristically incensed tone.

"What the hell are we doing here, anyway? Last night she tells me I ruined her life; now I've destroyed her weekend!" I grabbed the clothes on a chair and tossed them toward our suitcase. "She's the one who never did what she promised. And now she's blaming me for her rotten life choices and excusing bratty behavior."

Erick encircled me with his arms. "Not your fault," he murmured. "You have every reason to be upset with your—" He stopped himself before saying the M-word.

"Let's just pack up and go home!" I sighed into his shoulder.

He held my chin up slightly. "What about Jasper? He'll be so disappointed."

"I just can't stand being here a second longer."

He kissed me lightly on the cheek. "We'll be going to the races soon, and then we'll leave first thing in the morning. Okay?"

After the cops and the drama, I couldn't let Jasper down. "I sure hope he sees Gale Earmark or whatever."

"Dale Earnhardt Junior," Erick said with a chuckle, and kissed me again.

We all crammed into Wes's quad-cab pickup truck. Everyone was in a sour mood except for Jasper and Wes. "Did you know Dale's going to drive the Number Three Chevy, painted blue and yellow like his father's car?" Jasper blurted.

Wes grinned. "Right!"

The Daytona International Speedway lit up the night sky. Seeing the huge grin on Jasper's face, I was glad we had stayed.

Lorraine handed me four tickets. "You guys are sitting together, and Wes and I will be in the VIP section."

Autumn protested. "I wanna sit with you, Mommy!"

Lorraine gave her twenty dollars. "Here's something for popcorn and sodas." She turned to me. "Text me if there are any problems. When the race is over, meet us at this entrance."

Wes tugged her hand. "C'mon, woman!"

Without another word they were off, leaving us with the two kids. "Now I get it," I said to Erick. "She only invited us to babysit so she could party!"

"Did you see that?" Jasper said. His mouth stayed open. A woman loaded with pirate beads flashed a guy sitting below her.

"That's inappropriate," I said, pushing his head in the other direction.

"Not going to kill him to see some boobs." Erick winked. "Chill, babe. Let's have some fun."

We had to climb to the nosebleed section to get to our seats. From that vantage the cars going around the track were hardly more than a blur.

"Look!" Jasper shouted. Dale Earnhardt Jr.'s car had pulled up close to the stands. He jumped out, took off his helmet, and waved to the crowd. Jasper jumped on his seat and yelled, "Eighty-eight, eighty-eight!" He pumped his arms in the air and joined the crowd chanting, "Dale! Dale!" The kid was so happy; I wasn't going to begrudge him this evening.

"I don't think I have enough testosterone to appreciate any of this," I said after half an hour of the same cars going around the same track. For a moment I thought about how much Luke would have loved and wondered if Lorraine had thought of including him in the weekend.

I stood up. "What can I get you guys?" I volunteered to do the fetching as a break from the screaming people and screeching engines.

"Popcorn, Coke, a hot dog, and candy," Autumn said. I put my hand out for the twenty her mother had given her. For a second she pretended not to know what I wanted.

As I walked away to get snacks, I continued to fume about Lorraine's defense of Autumn and lack of respect for me. When I got back, the race was temporarily stopped.

"This is bor-ing!" Autumn complained. She was fading and getting cranky.

I rooted for Earnhardt, who led in many of the laps. Finally he did win. While the guys cheered, I gathered up our possessions and held Autumn's limp hand so she wouldn't fall down the bleachers. More than half the speedway had emptied out by the time we slithered through the crowds. Nobody was at the meeting point, and Lorraine didn't answer our texts or calls.

A security guard said, "We're closing the gate. You have to go outside."

"We're supposed to meet someone from the VIP section," I explained. "Where's that?"

He pointed toward the track. "They're all gone."

An hour later Autumn was sobbing from exhaustion. "Let's call a taxi," Erick said.

Suddenly Lorraine yelled from inside the fence. "Where the hell have you kids been?"

"I told you that's where we said we'd meet them!" Wes told her. "Sorry, guys, this one managed to sneak into the pit, and the guard wouldn't let me go in to drag her out."

"You shouldn't have followed me in the first place," she shot back. It was clear to me—and probably everyone else— that she was intoxicated.

"Cut the bull," Wes said. "I'm here all the time, and you

insulting my friends and jumping security makes me look bad."

We followed them back to his truck. Even though we were practically the last to leave, we were still stuck in a long line of traffic. Both kids fell asleep before we reached the house, despite all the name-calling and yelling from Wes and Lorraine in the front seat. Erick sleep-walked Jasper to our room and took off his shoes. I made up a bed for him on the floor of our room instead of the sofa so he wouldn't be in the middle of their fight, which continued nonstop for hours.

Because of all the shouting and slamming doors, I slept fitfully. Around seven I woke Erick. "Let's just get out of here. We can have breakfast on the road."

While I packed, Erick helped Jasper get going.

Wes was sitting at the kitchen counter, sipping a mug of coffee. "You leaving?"

"Yes. Thanks for everything," I muttered awkwardly.

"Is that an apology for all the trouble you caused?"

I sucked in a breath. "I'll call Lorraine to say good-bye later."

"Oh, she and the kid are long gone." He grunted at my surprise. "She doesn't want to have anything more to do with you than you want to do with her." He ran his fingers through his thick black hair. "I don't know why either of you bother. Lorraine thinks you are the biggest stuck-up piece of crap, and you hate her guts for what she supposedly did to you and your brother. None of it was her fault. The state took you away and wouldn't give you back."

He poured a swig of bourbon into his coffee and took

a gulp. "I knew your mother way back when. She went through hell with that crazy daddy of hers, and finally her mother dumped all those kids at that orphanage. Just when she was getting back with her family, her mama died—your grandma wasn't much more than thirty—and then you came along nine months later. Nobody gave your mother a nickel to help care for you, but she struggled for years to try to get you back. And what do you do? You not only throw it in her face every chance you get, you go out of your way to be mean to your little sister, who worships you."

Erick had come back inside to find out what was taking me so long and heard Wes spewing out more ugliness.

"Let's go," Erick said with a squeeze on my elbow. I followed him without another word to Wes. I was mute for almost an hour in the car as my mind swirled with the retorts I should have said. When Jasper had dozed off, I finally spoke. "That's it. I'm done."

Erick nodded. "I know."

"No more chances, no more visits. She's nothing to me."

"You're right."

We drove on in silence for another half an hour. "Crystal River isn't too far out of our way, is it?"

"No."

"Do you mind if we go there for the Fourth?"

"Of course not."

"Jasper can see the fireworks on our river." I exhaled. "I just need . . . I just need to go home."

8.

the hungry hormone

You have to give to the world the thing that you want the most, in order to fix the broken parts inside you.
—*Eve Ensler*

I had hidden my wedding pictures. They were concrete proof that I was overweight. At least Erick loved me for my true self and wasn't hung up on some perfect female image. I had promised myself I would go on a strict diet after the wedding. Erick agreed to help me make healthier eating choices.

Trying to figure out why I couldn't control how much I ate, I thought about my relationship with food before and after my adoption. In foster care I was anxious about where my next meal was coming from, and sometimes food was withheld as a punishment. Cheap canned, boxed, or pre-packaged meals were the staples of our diet, so fast food was used as a reward. In group homes, we had limited time to eat, so I would cram as much as I could in case I would be hungry later. I mounded large portions of potatoes and other starchy foods on my plate, rarely choosing salad or fresh fruit. There were never snacks or ways to acquire my own food.

The first time in my life I had free access to food was at the Courters' home. On one of my early visits, I had pointed to the fruit on the kitchen counter. "What are the rules about eating that?"

"You can have fruit anytime you want," Phil had said. He showed me a bowl of nuts in their shells. "You can have nuts, too."

I picked up a walnut and twirled it in my hand. I had never seen anything besides a shelled peanut. Phil cracked one for me. I tried it, but the taste made my tongue curl. I spit it into my hand.

Gay handed me a tissue and a banana. "Everyone likes these."

The skin on the outside was mottled. "No, thanks."

"I'll try to get some that aren't quite as ripe," Gay said.

I soon discovered that the Courters had food everywhere! The main refrigerator was stocked with fresh milk, orange and grapefruit juice, homemade iced tea, apple cider, and lemonade. A food pantry held mac-and-cheese, spaghetti and sauces, canned veggies and fruits, peanut butter, and several flavors of jelly. One shelf was loaded with crackers, cookies, pretzels, and chips—even three flavors of chewing gum! They kept a supply of fruit juices; cans of salmon, tuna, and sardines; cake, brownie, muffin, and bread mixes. They had an extra refrigerator in the laundry room for cold beverages and fresh vegetables. The two freezers contained frozen vegetables, meats, and homemade soups and casseroles, and several flavors of ice cream—with chocolate and butterscotch toppings in the fridge. Another cabinet was filled with cereals, coffees, and teas.

The kitchen looked as industrial as the one in The

Children's Home—all stainless steel and granite, with a gas cooktop that whooshed out scary tongues of flame. Pots hung like Spanish moss from the rack over the sink, and a clutter of gadgets dangled from hooks on the wall along with a magnetic strip that displayed sharp knives. I made a mental note to make certain these were hidden when Luke visited. Best of all, the kitchen was just down the hall from my bedroom, so I could help myself anytime I wanted. I knew certain snacks were only put out for picnics and visitors, but I couldn't help myself. When I craved potato chips, I devoured the whole bag. Fortunately, nobody noticed they were missing.

When most people think of hunger, they imagine starving children in developing countries. It's true that each year 2.6 million children die of hunger-related causes, but far more are food insecure, a term that defines how I had felt until well after I was adopted. Some of my first memories are about wandering through a trailer park, begging neighbors to fill Luke's bottle and give me a cookie. For the next nine years the idea of food shimmered in the back of my mind, and I often became distracted by cravings that would never be fulfilled. I salivated at commercials for fast food and decided that I would eat at Wendy's or Pizza Hut every day when I grew up. At The Children's Home, good behavior was rewarded with ice cream or a pizza. Now I realize that one of the most insidious results of my time in foster care was a lifelong struggle to separate my moods from foods.

I've been told that heavier people lack self-control, that they are lazy, indulgent, sedentary, and make unhealthy choices. Although Gay never said any of those things, and she tried to make me feel food secure in her home, we squared off almost from day one as I tested her willingness to let me eat anything I wanted versus her ideas of a balanced diet. Children who don't feel safe have trouble eating. The universal comfort food for American foster children is Kraft mac-and-cheese—and only that brand in the blue box with the neon-yellow cheese—because no matter where you are, it tastes exactly the same.

I'd learned to make mac-and-cheese in another foster home and asked Gay if she would keep some on hand in case I didn't like what she cooked. Once, I rejected meat loaf and made myself two boxes. When it was ready, I stood at the counter, eating it from the pot.

"Ashley, serve some onto a plate and join us at the table."

I went back three times and ate it all. As we cleaned up, Gay said, "Two boxes have far too many calories."

Phil shrugged. "She'll learn to self-regulate."

Gay lectured me on nutrition to the point of disgust. "You need protein in the morning to keep your blood sugar stable," she said, then drew a chart showing the difference between having eggs and milk versus a Pop-Tart and OJ. "Girls need extra calcium to prepare their bodies for having children and becoming older," she said, pushing yogurt. When I came home from school, I was usually famished. She put out carrot sticks and celery along with little squares of cheese and fresh fruit. She also urged me to take lima-bean-size vitamins. She baked chicken nuggets in wheat germ and tried to convince me it was as good as KFC.

I, on the other hand, pranced around chomping on chips to see how Gay would react. Some days she would do her best to ignore me, but other times—like when I asked Phil to make me five grilled cheese sandwiches—she would explode.

"I don't think she should ever again worry she won't get enough to eat," Phil insisted.

"She can have as much *good* food as she wants," Gay replied. "Her body doesn't need junk that will expand her fat cells and ruin her figure."

"Would you rather she be anorexic?"

"No. I want her to have a positive body image and a sensible diet."

"She's not overweight," Phil pointed out.

"Not yet," Gay said ominously.

My brothers jumped on Gay for allowing me to eat foods that had been forbidden when they lived there. "You have sodas in the house?" Blake exclaimed one day shortly after I was adopted at the age of twelve.

"Ashley is limited to one a day."

"We were limited to one every *holiday*!" he replied.

Josh found Fruity Pebbles and Cap'n Crunch in the cabinet. "Ash, this crap is sheer poison," he said. "Read the label. The second ingredient is sugar, and check out the list of toxic chemicals and artificial coloring."

"And since when are you buying junk bread?" Blake tossed a package of plain white bread to Gay.

"We're slowly introducing Ashley to better decisions."

I reluctantly tasted a few new foods and found I liked broccoli (with cheese sauce), cauliflower (with cheese sauce), and creamed spinach.

But no matter how much food was available, my hunger was like an itch that couldn't be scratched. I had to feed the beast that roared through my gut, demanding mounds of buttery mashed potatoes, multiple packages of ramen noodles, white, no-crust bread slathered with peanut butter and grape jelly, a stack of warm brownies, blueberry muffins melting with butter, bagels and cream cheese, a slab of crispy bacon, a bag of pretzels with spears of sour pickles on the side. Take me to a buffet restaurant and I would fill two plates for the first round—one piled high with yeast rolls and the second with every carb offered. Of course I couldn't eat it all, but I had to have it—had to! Even when I felt bloated and ill, I still wanted something . . . something else—although I couldn't have articulated what it was.

At the same time, the more apprehensive I felt about getting perfect grades or how my friends felt about me or when the Courters might reject me, the more active I needed to be. I begged Phil to jump on the trampoline or play volleyball with me in the pool. I skated and biked with neighborhood friends. I had played softball in Tampa while I was at The Children's Home, and I joined a Crystal River team after I moved. I even took a scuba course at the dive shop directly across the bay from our house.

"We had to adopt a girl to get a jock," Phil said with pride, since neither of their sons had shown much interest in sports.

My freshman year of high school, I was recruited to play varsity basketball as a point guard because I was considered an extremely tough and energetic player. I had played basketball and won many medals running track in middle school. I had a sport for every season and no matter how many calories I consumed at the dinner table—or in secret—I never actually put on too much weight.

Early in my freshman year of high school I was having severe knee pains, and the orthopedist diagnosed Osgood-Schlatter disease, which causes a throbbing lump below the kneecap that occurs mostly in kids and teens—especially those who are in sports. The doctor told me to modify my training routine. "No laps or squats. You can warm up on a stationary bike."

"Your doctor is not going to dictate my program," the basketball coach said, and I was relegated to the bench. I ultimately traded varsity sports for drama club.

In a few months I needed a larger size of jeans. I stayed active—but it was nothing like conditioning for sports. In college I kept weight off with my brief stint playing rugby, until I required knee surgery. After that, I was more cautious . . . then I was helping coach some new players. I was explaining a tackling drill, but the girls weren't getting it. "Here, let me show you what I mean." I dove at one of the players. My knee rotated in the wrong direction, and I collapsed in agony. I had torn my knee graft and was faced with having another complex surgery. After considering all my options, my doctor agreed that I could go without another operation only if I retired from sports.

Without thinking about it, I had maintained a weight of around 135 pounds during high school. I'm just over five feet six inches, with a large but proportioned frame. After my knee injury, I gained the "freshman fifteen"—and then some. One visit home during college, Gay had looked me up and down. "Ashley! What do you weigh?"

Phil glared at her.

She stared at my feet. "Your poor ankles are swollen, and your face is bloated."

I went upstairs and pulled out my rarely used scale. I weighed 175 pounds, by far the most ever. The next weekend Erick came for Sunday dinner. I took my usual huge helping of mashed potatoes and a big chunk of brisket. Gay reached over and scooped most of the potatoes back in the bowl. "That's a proper serving size."

I was mortified she had done this in front of Erick, but she was unfazed. "Ash, I also would stop you if you were taking drugs or drinking excessively. Obesity leads to diabetes and numerous health problems."

"Gay, this is not—" Phil began.

"I may have been out of line taking food off your plate, but it was my protective instinct. Let's stop pretending that you don't have a problem."

"So what do you want me to do?"

"Go see Doc. Maybe he'll figure out why you are packing on the pounds."

Dr. Rollins looked at his chart, then at me, and back at his chart—with my weight of 181 pounds recorded and circled. "Honestly, Ashley, I didn't recognize you when you came in. What's been going on? Your blood pressure is high—especially for someone your age. Are you ever short of breath?"

"I had trouble hiking recently," I admitted.

"We're always concerned when someone either gains or loses weight rapidly," he said, "so we're going to run some tests."

A few days later he asked me to return for the results.

"Bring someone with you, if you are comfortable doing so," he said.

A few hours later Gay and I were sitting in Dr. Rollins's examining room. "Ashley, your cortisol levels are through the roof," he said. "That's the stress hormone. Elevated levels can cause rapid, unexplained weight gain, moodiness, irritability, or depression."

"What causes it?" I asked.

"It's a malfunction in either the pituitary or adrenal glands," he said. "We have to eliminate more worrisome causes like tumors—but those are rare."

I almost hoped I had a disease that could be cured and then my weight would melt away. But when I returned after more testing, Dr. Rollins, in his gentle, heartfelt way, said, "You don't have anything serious, but you do have the first signs of metabolic syndrome. I see it all the time . . . in people thirty years older than you." He tried to educate me about my body-mass index and scare me with statistics about diabetes and heart disease. I knew he was right—just like Gay had been—but how was I going to lose forty or fifty pounds?

Gay offered to pay for Weight Watchers and a gym membership. "I lost seven pounds!" I crowed to her after the first week.

I stocked up on raw veggies and melons and started counting points. I spent two hours a day at the gym. I was hungry all the time and I also ached all over, but I lost almost twenty pounds. My friends who hadn't seen me all summer definitely noticed. I appreciated the compliments, but it also made me self-conscious, because I hadn't realized I'd looked fat to them before. And the moment I stopped exercising daily and went back to cafeteria food, I gained again.

A friend suggested a weight-loss clinic to help jump-start the diet again. Not only did the appetite suppressant they prescribed for me cause my heart to race and my face to burn in the sun, I felt so agitated that it wasn't worth the few pounds I lost. The plan was also expensive, and I found it hard to fit weekly injections and doctor visits into my work, travel, and school schedule.

I couldn't avoid Gay's birthday party the first week of October, and I knew she would notice I had gained back my summer losses. Later that evening, she said, "I found this article—it's about foster children who exhibit higher rates of atypical neuroendocrine and have problems with weight control."

"You mean gaining weight isn't completely my fault?" was my first comment as I scanned the words Gay had highlighted. *Childhood abuse or neglect could take a lasting toll on physical health . . . may trigger long-term hormone problems that increase the risk of obesity . . . places stress on the endocrine system, leading to impairment of important hormones that can contribute to abdominal obesity.*

"So, no matter how much I diet or exercise, I'm doomed." I paused to consider my predicament.

"Dieting will still work," Gay said. "It just will be harder for you."

"There must be another way. Maybe I need my hormones recalibrated or something. I don't want dieting to consume my life."

"You're not the only one looking for the magic pill," Gay said. "At least this gives you more information."

Here is a recipe for sure-fire weight gain: travel for work. After graduating college, *Three Little Words* had become a bestseller, and I was in high demand for speeches. That meant quick airport food or expensive room service. A late arrival reduced me to peanuts, candy, and a soda from the minibar. Then there were the embarrassing moments. The person with whom I had made arrangements for a speaking engagement greeted me at the airport. "Are you Ashley?" she asked in a voice that sounded disappointed. I nodded. "You look very different from your poster," she said before realizing her gaffe.

I tried to divert attention away from my body with large flowers pinned in my hair and baby-doll dresses. More than one person asked when the baby was due. Humiliation suffused me. My bookings were getting further apart, and I wondered if my looks had anything to do with it. My size had begun to rule my life and now threatened my livelihood. In this society weight is the elephant in the room, the great bulk that tips the scale, thus you plunge to the bottom while the lightweights float to the top. If it was true that my metabolism had been altered when my mother fed me to the wolves in the foster forest, how could I dial it back?

"We'd like you to consider being an ambassador for our international women's empowerment campaign," said a woman who identified herself as a public relations executive for Levi's. "I read your book," she continued in a chirpy voice. "It's so compelling . . . and inspiring. We're selecting young women who are leaders in nonprofit, fashion, and youth advocacy. Obviously you would represent the latter group."

A few weeks later I was in Chicago, meeting with the firm and the other ambassadors—all of whom were slender to skinny women. Worse, we had to be fitted for jeans, which we would wear when representing the company. While I squeezed my now 240 pounds of blubber into one of only two pairs of jeans in the entire store that I could zip up, the other ladies fussed about which of the many styles accentuated their perky butts or nonexistent hips.

The executives tried to make me feel better, saying that Levi's is for everyone's shape. Still, I was mortified. I attended the TEDWomen Conference, where I felt like a whale next to my tiny and trendy teammates—most conspicuously on camera and during interviews. One of my responsibilities was to produce a short weekly video update for viewers and fans. Now, to my horror, cyberspace is filled with video evidence of me at my chunkiest. I just hoped that people would see beyond my size and listen to my social action message. Still, I was miserable.

On the way back from the conference, I caught a magazine headline: IS YOUR WEIGHT OVER? juxtaposed with a luscious fudge cake. I hated the way the media messed with women's psyches by stimulating their yearning for a high-calorie fix while simultaneously dangling a remedy for the consequences. This time I was far more interested in a permanent solution than a sugar hit. I bought the magazine to read the article on the plane. After years of trying every diet, the writer had had LAP-BAND surgery and lost a hundred pounds, and even her diabetes was reversed.

I had heard about gastric bypass surgery, which is

a permanent choice. It reduces stomach size to a tiny pouch, which makes it uncomfortable to overeat, and then reattaches that pouch to an area where food isn't absorbed as easily. Since Erick and I were planning to have children, I worried that this might not be a safe option for a pregnancy; and I had also heard about the many people who overeat and stretch their pouch back out, leaving them right back where they started. The band, I read, is a different procedure. It cinches the stomach like a belt, creating a small pouch limiting the flow of food from the smaller section of the stomach above the band to the larger section below. One can have the band loosened or tightened in a quick in-office procedure, and the surgery is completely reversible. Driving home from the airport, I saw a billboard with before-and-after shots of an overweight, then slender woman. Again the words LAP-BAND jumped out at me. In the next weeks I caught references to LAP-BAND in a doctor's office, in a full-page newspaper ad, and on television talk shows.

I handed my new husband, Erick, a brochure. "What do you think of this?"

"It seems a little drastic. You don't want to have a risky surgery."

"If I lose a hundred pounds, my risk of death goes down fifty percent."

Erick's face scrunched into a doubtful expression. "Death from what?"

"All the complications from being obese."

"I think you need to get a lot more information."

I started researching the surgery and joined an online support group. The more I heard, the more I thought that this could be a good solution for me. I believed that my cortisol levels were driving my hunger. When I had been deprived of food as a child, I became panicky, and that sensation had never left my body. With this surgery, overeating wouldn't be an option, and it would be physically impossible for me to ingest as much as I craved. The cost, though, was prohibitive, and my insurance did not cover it. I had to set the idea aside.

Only a few weeks later, an ad in the newspaper caught my eye. "Hey, look at this!" I called to Erick. "It's a contest for free LAP-BAND surgery."

"What would you have to do?"

I chuckled. "Write an essay!"

There was a bit more to it. I had to attend an information seminar and then medically qualify with a certain BMI and have various comorbidities. My BMI was almost forty, with high blood pressure, shortness of breath, and swollen feet and ankles. The meeting room was filled with men and women who weighed much more than me. As they talked, I realized that—like them—I also had started limiting my social life, steered clear of mirrors and cameras, and avoided my family, because I either expected their criticism or saw it in their expressions.

Dr. Tiffany Jessee, the bariatric surgeon sponsoring the contest, asked the group, "How much can you eat at one sitting?"

"Five burgers and a half of a pie," said a woman in a pink caftan.

"I usually eat the whole pie," a man who straddled two seats added.

To myself I admitted that I could down two burgers, two foot-long sandwiches, or three packs of ramen noodles.

"This is all about taking control," the doctor said, and went on to describe that they would select six winning essays—three by men and three by women. The finalists would be featured online, and then two winners would be chosen through social media votes.

As I'd hoped, my essay won me a spot as a finalist. I asked Gay if she would come when I was photographed for the web page and had a medical checkup. We had to watch a video about the procedure. I saw her flinch as the video spelled out the complications. "Mortality rate . . . one in two thousand . . . band slipping or eroding into the stomach . . . mechanical malfunction . . . infection, bleeding, pain."

When the video ended, Gay said, "There are some scary complications, and you'll have to change your eating style forever."

"I'll do what I have to do."

The nurse answered Gay's barrage of questions about traveling, problems while in another city, and having a baby.

"We loosen the band during pregnancy," the nurse said to that question, "and tighten it afterward."

In the elevator, I turned to Gay. "Doesn't it sound like the right solution for me?"

Gay waited a long beat. Her penetrating stare put me on edge. "I wouldn't do it."

I gasped. I felt like I was falling off the cliff I had spent weeks climbing. "You are always hassling me about my weight, and now that I am willing to do something, you reject it. This option isn't even remotely as dangerous or complicated as other types of surgeries."

"Ash," Gay said gently, "I didn't say you shouldn't do it, I just said that *I* wouldn't. All those side effects—well, I couldn't tolerate them. It's your decision, because you are the one who will have to live with the result."

I stopped short in the parking lot just as a car was coming too fast toward us. Gay pulled me back. "So it's okay if I have the surgery?" I asked.

"First, you don't need my permission or my approval, and I don't want to give either, because I don't want to take the responsibility if this doesn't work. But Ash, I will support you completely and help you in any way I can."

"Will you ask people to vote for me online?"

"Of course I will."

⁂

I did not win the contest.

"You can't win everything," Erick said.

"Some of our friends refused to vote for me," I fumed. One of Erick's former band members said that if I just had more willpower, I could lose the weight without expensive surgery.

"He probably voted for you anyway." Erick always believed the best of everybody, while I was more cynical.

"Maybe we can figure out a way to pay for it in a few years."

"Don't worry, I love you just the way you are."

Just after our first wedding anniversary, Dr. Jessee called. "I think there is a way I can do your surgery," she said. She explained that she was using a new operative procedure, and it was going to be filmed for educational purposes. "I need a patient who won't mind being on camera."

I would be responsible for some of the hospital expenses but not her fee, the band itself, or the aftercare. The amount was now manageable, and so I agreed.

On the day of the surgery, one of the nurses prepping me said, "You are so smart to do this when you're twenty-five, instead of waiting until you get debilitated by your weight."

I smiled at the slender woman, who looked stylish even in her scrubs. "What do you think of Dr. Jessee?"

"Don't worry, hon, she's the best." The nurse winked. "She did mine!"

My recovery was remarkably smooth, and I had far less pain than I had expected. Three weeks after the surgery Erick went with me to a conference in Nevada. "Are you up for a hike?" he asked, and was surprised that I agreed. Physically I was healing quickly—what took longer was adapting to a whole new approach toward food. Eating too much too quickly could cause me to vomit or experience a lump or pain in my chest. This would have been unpleasant in itself, but excessive vomiting can also cause the band to slip, requiring a surgical repair. This further inspired me to chew food more carefully and eat slowly so my meals could settle. It takes about twenty minutes from the time you start eating for the brain to signal your body that you are full. Just being forced to slow down resulted in my consuming less.

I also learned what foods I could tolerate. At an airport I grabbed my usual fast-food burger while running to a tight connection. I didn't give a second thought to my band, and after a few bites I was terribly uncomfortable for the rest of the flight. I ultimately wasted most of the overpriced sandwich. A few weeks later Erick was joining me for a speech in Italy, and I told the doctor about my worries about the long flight and the tempting food. She loosened my band to make sure I didn't have any problems overseas. Band adjustments are a painless office procedure where saline is either added or withdrawn from the band through a permanent port just under the skin in my belly. When I returned from our trip, I had the band tightened again.

"Everyone goes through a series of fills and extractions," the nurse said. "Eventually we'll find your 'sweet spot'— that's the point where you are consistently losing weight while feeling satisfied when you eat."

When I figured out how often I had to eat and the right portion size, food was no longer the most important item on my plate. I didn't have to think about what I could and couldn't eat. I wasn't deprived, and I barely missed the huge pasta dishes or heavy breads I'd once craved.

At my midyear checkup, Dr. Jessee's staff was complimentary. "Look at you, girl!" the receptionist said.

She pointed to the scale. I closed my eyes. "You're down almost fifty pounds!"

I was more than halfway to my goal, and it had been so easy. I was confident that the surgery had been the right choice for me.

9.

all about albert

Nothing you do for children is ever wasted.
—Garrison Keillor

The events that unfolded during the Daytona trip still bothered me. I felt terrible that Jasper was exposed to such an explosive environment. "Jasper was so humiliated by that caseworker," Erick said. "How can we prevent any more problems like that?"

"Right now Jasper and Penelope are placed under kinship care status, which is basically foster care with a relative," I explained. "All the same rules can apply. But in this instance I felt like we were being punished because the caseworker didn't see him on time that month."

"The rules are absurd!" Erick was furious. "He's my relative, we are volunteers with the Guardian ad Litem program, we already had a background check, and have been fingerprinted. What more do they want?"

"If we had a foster care license, we could travel with them more easily, and if something happened to your aunt Liz, we could take over. Maybe we should get licensed. The foster classes are free, and it would give me another perspective for my studies and work."

In a few months I would begin a master's of social work program through the University of Southern California's virtual academic center, attending live class in real time, interacting with the professors and students, and having supervised field instruction in my community. I could still take classes when I traveled by logging on from my laptop anywhere in the world, which was essential with my schedule. No local universities offered the same academic rigor and flexibility.

"Will you have time?" Erick asked.

"It's only one evening a week, and the foster classes end before my semester starts. Besides, it's not as if we're going to become full-time foster parents."

More than thirty people crowded into the orientation session. "I am thrilled to see so many of you stepping up to the plate to become foster parents in Pinellas County," said Annabelle, the leader. "This marks our first class in a new era where foster parents will team with birth parents to protect their children and enable faster reunification."

There was a buzz in the room. I wondered whether Luke and I might have been able to live with Lorraine again if she had had one of my better foster families helping her.

"Feel free to go if this isn't the right fit for your family," Annabelle said. Two couples left the room.

A few hands shot up. "What if we don't want to have anything to do with the parents who had hurt the children in our care?" asked a Latina woman with hoop earrings.

"You will have our full support to determine the family's strengths and needs."

A woman in a suit and chunky heels stood up. "How soon after we get a baby could we adopt him or her?"

"Foster care is not a path to adoption," the speaker said. "If that's your goal, then this isn't the right place for you."

"But I heard—"

"Can foster parenting lead to adoption? Yes. Do we get babies? Tons of them, particularly right now with the pill mill crisis."

Another hand shot up in the audience. "What's a pill mill?" a gentleman wearing a bow tie asked.

"Some irresponsible doctors prescribe and sell narcotics from semilegal clinics. Right now we have an epidemic of addicted parents. More and more babies are born with drugs in their systems, and they go straight from the hospital into foster care." She sighed. "In our area we have more babies than foster homes who will accept them. However, the vast majority are either going back to rehabilitated parents or their relatives. In the rare cases when a child has nobody or the parent does not complete a case plan, adoption is considered, and the foster parents have the right of first refusal. But if you go into foster parenting hoping to adopt every child, your heart will be broken many times over."

Only six couples and two single women returned for the first official class. We were given a thick packet of forms to fill out at home. "The approval process is tiresome," Annabelle said. "I'm sure you've read the headlines about bad foster homes, but we do everything possible to prevent this."

Erick whispered to me, "Wait till she finds out that you were the child in some of those headlines."

"Before we get into the nuts and bolts of the approval process, let me tell you about some current situations and see if you can wrap your minds around how you might help." The group was riveted as Annabelle gave an example. "Two days ago we had a six-month-old baby come into care when the mother was arrested after a traffic accident. The baby was lying across the front seat in a filthy diaper. She had a blanket, a pacifier, and nothing else—not even a bottle. The impaired mother had driven through a park and was stopped by a light pole."

Annabelle made a passionate plea. "While there is always a huge need to house older kids—chiefly our teens—we are looking for families to consider taking care of babies and toddlers during this crisis until a possible relative can be found. We also need respite homes in case the regular foster parents have an emergency or go on vacation."

Brian, a tall, lanky guy who looked to be about the same age as Erick said, "That's definitely something we can do." His wife, Beth, who had a beatific smile, nodded.

Annabelle pumped her fist. "Great! We'll talk more about the details next week."

On the way home I said, "Are you thinking what I'm thinking?"

We'd been together for so many years that we were already finishing each other's sentences. "That we could do babies on a temporary basis too?" Erick asked.

"Neither of us has nine-to-five schedules. Besides, it would be good practice."

"Are you really up for diapers and barf?" he asked.

"Can't be worse than cleaning up after the pets." We had three dogs, a cat, and a fish tank—and all required scooping, mopping, and scrubbing.

Plus, we had just bought our first house and had extra bedrooms. "We could put a crib in the smaller upstairs bedroom," Erick said. He had a grin on his face that made me want to kiss him at the next traffic light.

By the time we attended the next class, we had started a notebook of lists. After class we had coffee with Brian and Beth.

"We sent out an e-mail asking if anyone has old baby furniture, and I know all the best thrift and consignment shops locally," Beth told us. "I'm excited, aren't you?"

"We're a little nervous," Erick admitted.

"We can help each other out with babysitting and respite," Brian offered.

I glanced at Beth, and we read each other's minds. The guys were bonding, and we were going to be great friends as well.

The licensing process took a couple of months from start to finish, and we didn't even know our license had been officially approved when Erick received a midnight call asking if it might be convenient for them to deliver our first foster child. She was supposed to go to another couple we met in our classes, but they were out of town for the weekend.

Erick put the placement coordinator on hold. "It's pretty inconvenient," he said to me. "We're supposed to go to my grandmother's house tomorrow."

"This child has nowhere to go," I reminded him. And that was it—the start of a new way of life for us.

We made up the crib and waited for our first foster child. A trembling two-and-a-half-year-old toddler arrived wrapped in a blanket. Erick went over the paperwork with the caseworker while I unwrapped LaJanna. She was wearing only a thin shirt and a bulging, putrid diaper. I couldn't remove all the caked-on feces, and so I filled a bathtub with warm water. LaJanna sobbed, gulped, and moaned as I cleaned her.

Erick brought a bottle of warm milk upstairs and helped me dress the limp little girl. She clung to the bottle with all her might and sucked it dry. "Should we give her another one?" he asked.

"I'm not sure."

"We can't let her go to sleep hungry."

As I lowered LaJanna into the crib, she punched and screamed. "I know, I know . . . ," I whispered, and tried again. This time she kicked me in the belly as she arched her back away from me. Erick reached for one of the stuffed teddies we had bought in case we got a child. LaJanna pressed it to her chest with one hand and accepted the second bottle with the other. Erick helped me lower her into the crib.

I dimmed the light and we tiptoed out. "Do you think she'll fall asleep?" I asked.

"How am I supposed to know?" he said. "You usually get nine months to prepare to be parents. It happened to us with one phone call."

I got up several times to check our first charge, but we were really lucky, because LaJanna slept the rest of the night. But she woke at dawn crying inconsolably. I knew that cry—at least the feeling behind the cry: *Where's mommy . . . where's my bed, my house? How do I get back there? I want my mommy!*

While I held LaJanna, stroking her wiry, beaded curls and silky arms, Erick read me notes from her file. "Mom

has a long history of mental illness . . . just decompensated . . . child has only eaten cigarettes and beer for last
several days, perhaps longer." He gagged. "Her mother fed
her cigarettes and beer! That's crazy."

"That's what decompensated means," I said. "She
flipped out."

Erick scanned the paperwork again. "She's supposed
to go to the Sandersons, but they are out of town for a few
days."

"Oh, I remember him— I think he was the youth pastor
who always wore a tie."

"Yesterday I was worried about LaJanna coming at an
inconvenient time." Erick rubbed his temples. "Just think,
she could still be eating cigarette butts!"

LaJanna was glued to me for the next three days. At first
Erick tried to cheer her by playing songs on his guitar and
making funny faces, but LaJanna just pressed herself into
my chest.

"She needs to be sad," I said.

"They talked about children and grieving in class,"
Erick said. "I guess this is what they meant."

I sent Erick to the store for diapers, socks, a pair of
sneakers, several frilly T-shirts, and long pants, since it was
January. She also needed pajamas, a hoodie jacket, and her
own blanket. The agency provides a small clothing stipend
for children when they first enter care, and we had become
members of our local foster and adoptive parent association, where parents often shared items, donations, and supplies.

"Get some Cheerios, bananas, and more milk," I said.
"And fresh bottles. I'm going to toss out her cruddy one."

During her first bath I had concentrated on carefully cleaning LaJanna's filthy body. This morning I tackled her beaded and braided hair, which was more of a challenge. I worked shampoo in between her cornrows as gently as I could while holding a washcloth to her forehead to prevent the suds from stinging her eyes. After lunch, she seemed ready for a nap. Once again she fought being put in the crib, and this time the bottle and teddy didn't help.

"Okay, okay, you win, baby," I said. I carried her downstairs and flopped on the couch. She curled into my lap. I kissed her forehead and inhaled her sweet baby smell. She clutched at the long necklace around my neck with one hand and her bottle with the other and fell asleep. I closed my eyes and rested too.

I woke in about an hour. LaJanna's hands had relaxed, but when I tried to roll her onto a cushion, my necklace pulled toward her. It had become entangled with her hair beads, and I could not extricate myself. I lay back and rearranged LaJanna as best I could and waited for Erick to return from running errands.

The door slammed. LaJanna startled awake, and her head snapped forward, pulling me along with her.

"What happened?" Erick asked as he surveyed my twisted position.

"Just hurry and get my nail scissors."

He looked at where her beads intersected with my necklace. "We're going to have to cut her hair."

"That's against foster rules. Just cut my necklace."

"My mother made that for your birthday."

"She'll just have to remake it," I said as Erick snipped it into pieces and untangled it from the child's hair.

After several days, we packed up LaJanna to go to her intended foster home.

"We were just getting to know her," Erick said wistfully.

"We knew this was going to happen and that she's going to a good place. If none of her birth family are suitable, they are ready to adopt her."

LaJanna had been with us such a short time that I hadn't become attached to her. Besides, I was used to the comings and goings of foster care and was more comfortable with the process—one that seemed cruel to Erick, who was born and raised in the same home by parents who were still married and in love. While I understood the rules, goals, and purpose of fostering, I now wondered if Erick was going to suffer because he loves and attaches so easily.

I was vacuuming the cracker crumbs out of the couch—and finding more necklace beads—when the phone rang asking whether we could take another emergency placement. This time it was even more inconvenient. Contractors were coming the next day to tear out ceilings and install ductwork for a new air-conditioning system. We couldn't have a child in a home with all the dust and construction happening.

"What's the situation?" I asked the placement counselor.

"He's been living in a crack house. They found him under his unconscious mother in an abandoned home."

"Sure, we'll take him," I said.

We had planned to stay with my parents during construction, and I asked Gay if I could bring the new child.

"Of course, I'll get the crib that's at my dad's house," Gay said without a pause.

A few hours later, Juanita, the caseworker, came to the door carrying Albert, a small, thin two-year-old boy who looked younger. Loki, our husky, came to greet the newcomer, followed by Bella, our chubby Chihuahua. "Ahhh!" Albert screamed. He shook so violently I feared it was the start of a seizure.

Erick corralled the dogs into the backyard. The terrified boy hadn't made it a foot into our home yet. "Has he eaten dinner?" I asked.

"I was going to get him a burger," Juanita said, "but he was too hysterical to eat. It was a pretty bad scene when they took him. Crack house . . . lots of people crashing . . . arrests . . . swarming with deputies . . . the father didn't speak or respond. Kid might be retarded or mute or something. The child protective worker thought the mom might have recently overdosed." Juanita nonchalantly rambled on with what little she knew and wasn't very tactful with her words.

"How long will this placement last?" Erick asked.

"A few days to a week. He's from Pasco County, but they didn't have any shelter beds."

Waiting for Albert's arrival, I had made a plate of snacks and fruits. I patted a stool by our kitchen counter. "Place him here. Maybe he's hungry."

He kept clinging to Juanita until I popped a banana slice in his mouth. He chewed it quickly. After a few more, he sat on the stool and let me feed him. Juanita handed me his moldy bottle, which had to go right into the trash. I gave him a sippy cup, which he knocked to the floor.

"He probably needs babying," Erick said, and made up a fresh bottle.

Albert grunted. His plate was clean, but he wanted more. I made a small cheese sandwich for him. He shoved several pieces into his mouth at once and started choking. I fished some out with my finger and let him suck on his bottle to wash the rest down.

Juanita handed a packet of papers to me and headed for the door.

"Time for a bath," Erick said.

Albert took his hand tentatively, and the guys went upstairs. I followed to help start the bath.

Erick waved me away. "Just head on out to the drugstore," he said. "We've got a nest of lice here."

I scratched my head all the way to the pharmacy and back.

Albert seemed comfortable with Erick, but when he put the boy in the crib, Albert became agitated. He crawled out and ran out the door crying, "Eh! Eh! Eh!"

"Let him go," Erick suggested.

We followed him down the stairs as he frantically looked for something. When he arrived, he'd been clutching his bottle and a rag. He zoomed over to the front door and saw that his rag had slipped under the dining table. Erick fished it out and handed it to him. Albert gave a satisfied grunt and allowed Erick to tuck him in with a new teddy bear and the wretched smelly rag of a blanket.

"Lice?" I mouthed. Erick gestured to let him have the rag anyway.

Once again we stood in the doorway, waiting to see if this forlorn child would be able to fall asleep. Soon we heard his raspy breathing. His nose had been running and he had a mild cough. I wondered whether this little one had ever seen a doctor. How many people lived in or visited the crack house? Why didn't he speak any words?

Erick and I went downstairs and made ourselves sandwiches for dinner. There was a loud bumping sound. Erick jumped up, thinking Albert had fallen out of bed. We both stood in the nursery doorway watching Albert—still asleep—smacking his head against the wall.

Erick ran to our bedroom and took the pillows from our bed to pad the wall. Albert had banging episodes all night. A few times he cried out in his sleep, and one of us went to comfort him. He was up for good at six, and the contractors were expected to start tearing apart the ceilings at eight.

Groggily, I packed for myself and planned to shop for Albert on the way to Crystal River. I kissed Erick good-bye. "I don't know who's going to have the toughest weekend," I said.

"Be safe and take it easy. Besides, he might only be with us for a few days."

Those few days turned into more than a year.

Albert was a puzzle. He was far behind in every measurable skill, although we refused to believe that he lacked potential even though most days it was two steps backward for every one forward. Yet he had a purity, a sweetness, and a desire to please. His first response to everything was to nod his head in agreement; he smiled more than he fussed, and when he wanted something, he tucked his little hand in mine and led me to what he desired. He reacted to sounds, and so his hearing was fine, but for some reason he only grunted.

Both Gay and Phil pitched in those first few days while we stayed at their house during the construction. But after a short time Albert always drifted back to me, pressing against my body for physical comfort. "He's attaching to you," Gay said. "That's a great sign, although I'm worried about the head banging. You might have to get him a helmet."

"In my abnormal psych class we're studying the case of 'Genie'—she was a feral child who was locked in her room for more than ten years," I said. "Like Albert, she only grunted, smeared her food, hit her head, and rocked aggressively at night."

"At least he was rescued early," Gay said.

In the morning Phil made him scrambled eggs and buttered squares of toast. He held out his plate for more. He had three pieces of toast, a bottle of milk, and applesauce. A few hours later he ate six meatballs, carrot sticks, and two bananas.

"Poor thing was starved," Gay said.

At naptime we set up a cot in the middle of the bedroom and placed pillows on either side on the floor in case he rocked himself out of bed. While he slept, Gay pried the rag from his fingers and did a quick wash and dry, then tucked it beside him again.

Later, Gay patted Albert's fluffy curls. "I've never seen a reddish, relaxed Afro. I wonder where his parents are from."

"Looks like he's an interesting combo of Latino, European, and African-American," Phil said.

"His father has a Hispanic last name," I said.

"Maybe his first language is Spanish!" Phil said.

I called my sister-in-law Giulia and asked her to come

and meet Albert. "Speak to him in Spanish," I said. Giulia is Italian, but she is fluent in several languages.

"Hola, mi nombre es Giulia. ¿Cuál es tu nombre?"

"Alberto!" The child beamed.

"¿Te gusta jugar con autitos?"

"Sí!"

"I think he knows more Spanish than English!" I said. "Wait till I tell Juanita."

The next day I took Albert home. After being with the Courters' mellow Cavalier King Charles spaniel, Albert was not as fearful of Loki. Erick gave Albert a treat for the dog and said, "You are the boss of the dog. Tell him to sit." Erick demonstrated and then put the treat in Albert's hand. Loki sat even without a command. Erick unfolded Albert's hand and Loki took the treat gently, then licked his hand. Albert giggled and reached for another one to give the dog. "Good job, Albert. Now you are friends."

"I met the kid's father at the resource center yesterday," Erick said when we were alone. "He brought a bag of soiled clothes, diapers, and some bootleg Disney movies."

"What's he like?"

"Tall, good-looking, but he has strange pointed teeth."

"Did he speak Spanish?"

"The weird thing is he barely spoke, kind of grunted the way Albert did when he first arrived." He shook his head. "I heard that the mother was admitted to a psychiatric facility yesterday." Albert came and stood, reaching his arms up. We gathered him between us for a double hug. His frame was bony, and he smelled like sunshine.

"Poor thing," I said aloud. "What chance does he have?"

The phone rang. Erick took Albert's weight off me while I answered it. "LaJanna? Really?" I glanced at Erick. "No, she isn't here."

"Is LaJanna all right?" Erick asked.

"I sure hope so. The case supervisor thought she was still with us."

"In other words, they've lost her."

I sighed. "They lost me for almost a year—at least on paper. I would have thought they'd have better systems now." Suddenly I started to cry.

"What's wrong?" Erick asked.

"I haven't been a foster child in years, but it's so painful to see the same mistakes being made with these kids more than a decade later." I wiped my tears so Albert wouldn't get upset. "We have an appointment at the health department tomorrow, but let's find a pediatrician who takes Medicaid to look into that cough. Then we have to get him into speech therapy. Oh, and he loves music. If we knew how long he'd be here, we could put him in dance class."

"Whoa," Erick said, "we don't have to do everything at once."

"Oh yes we do! The brain of a baby his age is still elastic and accepting, but the window of opportunity closes around age three. He already has language learning deficits, and we have to make up for lost time."

"Thank you, Dr. Rhodes-Courter Smith," Erick said. "We'll do everything we can."

We were enchanted by Albert, with his heart-shaped face, eyes the color of black olives, skin the copper tone of a surfer.

The head banging stopped after a few weeks. He slowly began to speak—a word at a time and then short sentences. If he pointed his bony finger, I'd say, "Tell me what you want" and not give in—well, most of the time—until he found a word. We dressed him in crisp button-down shirts and trendy pants I'd iron myself. He had an astonishing appetite and relished anything we served. I saw my childhood food issues in his hunger, which went beyond enjoying a meal. People who don't worry where their next meal is coming from can't begin to understand, any more than someone who has not experienced an excruciating migraine can imagine the pain. There's a survival need met with a combination of gratitude for the delicious food combined with the urge to get as much of it as possible while it is available. Now I know that my own drive to overeat stems from those years of deprivation, and darling little Albert had already faced the same hollow ache.

Determined to boost him with the best nutrition, I started reading supermarket labels and rejected anything with sugar in the first few ingredients or too many additives or content I couldn't pronounce.

I filled in Gay when she called one afternoon to ask how we were doing. "Albert's dad has only shown up for one visit since Albert's been with us, and yesterday he brought a bunch of food from a gas station to their visit. When we got home, Albert had a disgusting case of diarrhea."

There was a long pause. I knew Gay wanted to say something about my conversion to healthy foods, but she stopped herself. "How did the visit go?"

"He was hesitant to go to his father, and he separated from him easily. The minute we got home, he leaped into Erick's arms."

"Erick's wonderful with him."

"If Albert's parents don't complete their case plans, Erick wants to adopt him."

"Don't get your hopes up. He may have a relative who would qualify."

"We didn't go into this to adopt. . . ." My voice caught. "It's just that we adore him."

"Even you, Ash?"

"I guess I'm still trying to be realistic," I said, and the truth was that it was so much harder for me to commit myself.

"Right, and you two are newlyweds. You'll be starting a family of your own in a few years."

"Life is what happens when you are making other plans," I said, quoting one of Gay's favorite lines back to her.

Over and over I reminded myself—and Erick—that Albert wasn't ours. He was on loan, temporary, checked out like a library book or a hamster during school vacation. We had to turn him back in the moment we were asked to. We might not even be given notice. The thought of this tender toddler, who had just turned three, receiving the same heartless treatment I had endured petrified me. To guard myself, I had bundled most of my affectionate feelings in reserve. Was that what my former caregivers had done? I had perceived my foster parents as being distant, and I believed they disliked me. Had they just been protecting themselves from becoming too attached? And if their unattachment had made me so distrustful of everyone's motives, how could I knowingly pass my misgivings on to another child? Wasn't the point to do a better job with this child than anyone had ever done with me? So why was I holding back? Here was a little boy who needed love, who demanded love, who deserved love, and yet . . .

We fell into an easy routine. When I asked his caseworker, Juanita, why Albert didn't have a Guardian ad Litem, she said, "Why does he need one? He's going to be reunified no matter what."

"His father hasn't seen him in months, and neither parent has done anything on their case plan. We are also constantly fighting to get him services, so having another set of eyes on the case may be a good idea. No one listens to us in court," I said angrily.

Erick and I had to resign from being guardians when we became foster parents because of conflicts of interest. A guardian, or court-appointed special advocate, had been instrumental in getting me free for adoption, and I knew that one was essential in Albert's situation. Albert's next visit with his father took place at the social services office. This would be the first time I would use the training we'd had in the fostering class. My job was to tell the father all about Albert's progress, then listen to his concerns and address them.

When I arrived, the receptionist took the diaper bag from me and reached for Albert's hand, which was clasping mine tightly. I started to follow her into the visitation room. "You can't go in there," she said in a clipped voice.

"That's not what I was told," I replied. "We're supposed to forge relationships with the parents, tell them about their child."

"Let me get the visitation supervisor."

"I'm sorry you were misinformed," the supervisor said.

"We don't allow foster parents to interfere with visitations," she said. "Besides, this child is too attached to you. He might refuse to go to his father if you are in the room."

Albert's eyes were wide.

I started to let them go, but called, "Wait, I need my cell phone and car keys that are in the bag's pocket."

I hurried toward the elevator, infuriated that nobody knew that foster parents were now being trained to be active parts of the case and interact with siblings and biological families.

"Hey, Ashley!" Annabelle said as she got off the elevator. "What are you doing here?"

"Am I ever glad to see you! I thought you worked in another office."

"I'm here one day a week," she said, and noticing my scowl asked, "What's going on?"

I blasted her with what had just happened. She checked her watch. "I have some time before my meeting, so let's get this sorted out right now." She walked me into the supervisor's office and Juanita was called in as well.

"Didn't we just have a training on this?" Annabelle said.

"She's the first foster parent to have asked for the new rule to be enforced," the director said.

"It's not a new rule," Annabelle said in a conciliatory tone, "it's a new paradigm—a way to integrate foster care and reunification."

"As long as you are here," Juanita said to me, "we had a staffing about Albert."

Staffings bring together as many people as possible who are involved in a child's case to discuss his status, well-being, and plans for his future. Since foster parents spend the most time with the child and thus know him best, we should have been invited to anything involving Albert, but I decided to bring that up another time.

Juanita continued, "So far we've ruled out all biological family on both sides. The parents have failed services provided previously—which is a bad sign. But we're going to give the father another chance and place the child in a foster home closer to him."

"Move Albert?" I gasped.

"When his father is ready for increased visits and overnights, the child will be nearby. You're—what—two hours away from here?"

"I've been transporting with no complaints."

"It's hard on our workers and his guardian."

"He doesn't even have a guardian."

She looked at his file. "Yes, he does."

"Nobody's called or visited us." I forced myself to speak in a calm voice. "Moving him now would be detrimental. He's settled in and making progress." I flushed, feeling panicky for Albert. Hadn't they learned anything since I was a child about the damaging effect of moves? "I spent a month getting him into the developmental preschool, and they're thrilled with his progress."

"We'll consider our options," was Juanita's noncommittal response.

Trying to get Albert all the services he needed took weeks of time. I enjoyed advocating for the little fellow, although it seemed we were the only ones initiating any action on his behalf. Nine months had passed since he was placed with us. Albert's mother was out of the picture, and his father had stopped coming to the monitored visits.

One afternoon Juanita stopped by the house. "The court has granted Albert's father unsupervised visits."

"What?" Erick said, shocked.

"Mr. Sosa requested it at the last staffing, and the court accepted."

"What has he done on his case plan?" I asked.

"He's got a job at Checkers—working sixty hours a week."

"That's impossible," Erick said. "No fast-food place gives that number of hours."

"That's what he told the judge," Juanita replied, her face a mask that concealed what she really thought.

"Have you confirmed it with his manager, or has he provided pay stubs?" Erick asked. "And what about safe housing?"

"He's sleeping on the sofa of a former roommate."

"Someone who lived at the crack house?" Erick said sarcastically.

"Of course we're doing a home study of this apartment."

"Does this other guy have a criminal record too?"

"We don't disclose that information to foster parents."

We were the ones who nurtured and loved this little boy and were the most concerned about his safety. His father hadn't visited him in nearly five months. When he had shown up for a visit, he ignored our advice about appropriate activities, toys, and foods. He barely even spoke to Albert during visits. He would just bring a loud movie to watch. When Albert first came to us, he was practically feral. Now he spoke, laughed, was potty trained, drank from a cup, ate politely, and engaged with the world around him. If his father couldn't entertain Albert for an hour, how was he going to meet his special needs? His dad couldn't even maintain stable housing and had moved several times, living with numerous questionable roommates since the case began.

My phone rang. The number indicated it was from Annabelle. "We're really in a jam," she said. "We have a baby whose foster mother can't take care of him anymore, and he's already been through both sets of grandparents."

"Not a problem," I said, if only to be amenable so Annabelle knew I appreciated her standing up for me regarding Albert.

Two hours later sturdy Lance arrived in a diaper meant for a baby half his size and—as usual—without any clothes or supplies.

10.

becoming the other mother

The love of a foster-mother for her charge
appears absolutely irrational.
—Winston Churchill

"You're Lance's fifth placement," his caseworker, Mike Bigelow, said as he unbuckled the baby from his car seat.

"How's that possible?" I asked. "He isn't even six months old!"

"Mom and dad both have severe mental health issues. He was born in a secure psychiatric ward and given to the maternal grandmother. Then a neighbor reported that she was hallucinating about feeding him to lions, and so he moved to his paternal grandparents. After we discovered a relative living there who had a sex-crime conviction, he went to a shelter home and then his first foster home."

"Why didn't they keep him?"

Mike looked embarrassed. "The foster mother complained he took too much time away from her dogs."

Erick pointed to our dogs, which had been adjusting to life with small children since our first foster child arrived. "Our priorities are different," he said.

"Are there any other relatives who can take him?" I asked.

"Since he's already been through both grandparents and his parents are unstable, this will probably go to TPR." TPR meant this baby would be available for adoption. "His parents are hard to talk to, but we don't think there is any other family."

As soon as Mike closed the door, we prepared the usual welcoming bath. Lance's diaper area was raw, an indication of poor care, but we didn't find any signs of abuse, infestation, or disease.

"I hope he'll be a good sleeper," I said, since I was starting a new internship the following week.

My social work major was Children and Families; however, my initial field placement had to be in a different concentration. After a stint at a local homeless shelter, I was assigned to work in the social work department of a local hospital. Many patients needed additional services upon discharge because they had no family or friends to care for them. All my life I had been worrying about the possibility of having nobody to count on when I was an adult. My connection to the Courters was solid—we talked almost daily and saw each other often—and the large Smith family also enveloped me. I also knew I could ask Josh or Blake for anything, and I even felt that some of my biological relatives would be there in a pinch, including Lorraine, who can be quite responsible and doting when sober—although it was too little too late for me.

Fortunately, this internship had long but flexible hours.

I could schedule my initial 550 hours around my speeches, classes, or foster child emergencies. Best of all, my supervisor, Arlene, was one of the finest mentors I ever had. She let me learn the complicated computer and charting system at my own pace and was always eager to answer my questions. I admired her easy, caring bedside manner. Nurses and other staff told me I was fortunate to be working with "the best in the business."

After the first week I had a better understanding of the local resources, but there were many unusual circumstances and protocols. I still wasn't fully confident three weeks into the job. I could handle most of the routine and less complicated discharges. While I loved working with Arlene, I realized that hospital social work was not going to be my career.

One family was very belligerent. I was trying to arrange for the mother—a stroke victim—to be transferred by stretcher to a nursing home that accepted her insurance. Her son wanted to move her in his car and to a facility closer to his home. When I tried to explain why neither would work, he cussed me out at his mother's bedside.

"This man is not only unreasonable, he's out of control," I said to Arlene.

"I like to remind myself that it's easier to be mad than sad," Arlene said. "People who are grieving often act irritated." She paused. "Try to be sympathetic to his circumstances and see if he calms down. If not, I'll talk to him."

Her suggestion worked, and I scribbled a note to bring up the mad/sad question in class.

I was working on a rainy Friday morning after a week of

travel and classes. My first case was easy: a teenager with a broken leg was going home in his parents' car. I returned to my station and scanned the next patient's file.

Her name was Melissa Flicke, and under next of kin was listed: Chelsea Duffy, daughter. My head throbbed as I tried to focus on her address. Dark spots burned concentric holes in the blurred words. Marjorie Moss, one of my most horrific foster parents, had a daughter-in-law named Melissa who was a regular at the Moss home. My strongest memory of her was that she had once tattled on me—and I always felt she'd done it just so I would be punished. I had been watching her husband doing tricks on his motorcycle and I hadn't come away from a fence when she called. When Melissa told, Mrs. Moss beat me so viciously that my mouth bled. The last name Duffy also sounded familiar. And Melissa's daughter was named Chelsea, who had been a teenager when I was seven. I was fairly certain the address in the file was on the same road as the Moss home. Either way, many of the Moss family members lived in the same area. Eventually, the Mosses were prosecuted on more than forty counts of felony child abuse with torture and were sued by many of their former foster children, including Luke and me.

I forced myself to concentrate on the discharge folder. Melissa Flicke seemed quite young to have terminal brain cancer. I rubbed my eyes, as if that would clear the fog that had descended. I stroked my name tag. The family might recognize my name after everything that happened. I headed to Arlene's station. She was on the phone, working on another difficult case. I tentatively motioned to her for a word when she was finished. Arlene waved me to the chair next to her but kept talking. "So what's the patient's condition?" She rolled her eyes. "She'll have to come back here to be reevaluated. No, no—just stay there. I'll get right back to you."

"Sorry to bother," I said when she got off the call, "but I believe I've had a prior relationship with this patient and—"

Arlene wasn't really listening. "You're a pro, Ashley, I'm sure you will handle it just fine."

"It might make the situation worse emotionally for the family—I can explain later—but maybe you should take lead on this one—"

"Okay, just flip over your name tag, and we can deal with it together."

I felt crushed by absolute dread as I stood in the doorway of the patient's room. It was if I were carrying dive weights—my body heavy and awkward, like I had to remind myself how to walk. Peachy morning light dappled the dim, sad room. A man dozed in a chair while two other relatives or friends guarded the bedside. A large woman lingered by the window and another—gaunt and yellow—lay motionless on the bed.

The patient groaned.

I startled, my heart beating wildly.

"Ma?" The woman by the window turned around. Could this be Chelsea? I searched for the features of the plucky teen inside the unrecognizable body. "Do you want more medicine?"

The man in the chair opened his eyes. "Tell her to squeeze your hand."

"Squeeze my hand," Chelsea said. "Nothin'. I can tell she's hurtin'."

ASHLEY RHODES-COURTER

That voice—both raspy and childlike—was it really hers?
I couldn't be 100 percent sure, but still, like a crack of
lightning, my professional compassion dissolved into a
molten ball of fury. This family had put me through a hell
that still inhabited my dreams and had given me a permanent
layer of distrust . . . of everyone. An even more evil thought
intruded: pull the plug! She wasn't really attached to any
lifesaving machines, and I never could have done it. Still,
how ironic it was to witness someone who once held my
young life in her hands now on her deathbed.

Arlene caught up to me and I walked into the room
behind her. I double-checked to make sure the name on my
ID couldn't be read. Arlene cleared her throat. "I'm your
discharge coordinator," she said. "Who is signing for the
patient?"

"Me," Chelsea said.

The tray table at the foot of the bed was littered with
to-go food and cups, so Arlene led her out to the corridor.
Chelsea signed all the papers while leaning on the nurse's
counter without reading them. The moldy smell of her
sweater caused saliva to rise in my throat. Before we were
finished, my pulse started racing and my forehead became
damp. I took a few deep breaths.

"The transporter will be here in two hours," Arlene
said. Normally I would have interjected something politely
consoling, but I had to keep swallowing.

The daughter lumbered back into the room, her hunched
back like that of a tired bear.

I hurried to the nearest lavatory and gagged into
the sink. I sat on the edge of the toilet until the nausea
passed, then washed my face, rinsed my mouth, and ran

my fingers through my hair to smooth back the loosened tendrils. When I walked into the hallway, Arlene was passing. She steered me by the elbow into the break room on that floor.

"You look like you saw a ghost."

"In a way I did." The whole story tumbled out.

"You handled yourself wonderfully," Arlene said.

"I almost lost it."

"The point is that you didn't—and that's the mark of a professional."

"What were the chances?"

"Yes, quite a coincidence. Are you absolutely sure it was the same family?"

I paused.

"Sometimes our minds play tricks with us." Arlene gave me a meaningful look.

Did she doubt my story, or was she giving me a way to extricate myself emotionally? Her gentle words allowed me to recall the incident as a possibility instead of a probability.

Darling little Lance had been with us for more than four months and was walking. Albert coaxed him and helped him up when he stumbled. We were amazed that he showed no jealousy of the smaller child. Nobody had said anything about moving Lance when we heard that both parents had signed over their parental rights to the state and we were told they were looking for an adoptive home. Erick and I started conversations about being his family.

After three more months, we had not heard anything

from the agency and settled into a "normal family" routine. One afternoon we got a call from a new case manager.

"Hi, I'm Georgina Roy from the adoption division. I'll be handling Lance's case from now on."

"Oh, thanks for calling," I said. "We haven't heard from Mike Bigelow for several months and didn't know what was happening with the case." I took a deep breath. "Since Lance has been with us over six months—half his life, really—we have considered the possibility of adopting him."

"What do you mean? This child is slated to go to Maryland."

"Maryland?"

"He has an aunt there who's willing to adopt."

"Then why did Mr. Bigelow tell us he was free for adoption and that there was no family?" My pitch verged on the hysterical.

"Apparently the mother named this relative just before she signed surrenders. The interstate paperwork got lost on Mike's desk and even so, he got promoted, so I have to start the ICPC process again."

I was infuriated that the incompetent Mr. Bigelow was now in a higher position. My mind was spinning with the implications of this new development. ICPC, or Interstate Compact on the Placement of Children, is a long, tedious process that can take months—even years. In the meantime the aunt would have to take Maryland's adoption classes and undergo a home study and an extensive background check. It was likely that Lance would be well over two years old by the time all this was sorted out. How would it affect this little boy to be moved after being with us for almost his whole life?

I spent the afternoon e-mailing and copying everyone connected to Lance, from his case manager to his Guardian ad Litem to the guardian's supervisor. Each professed to be shocked and would "get right on it." It was useless to contact Mr. Bigelow's boss, because he was now that boss.

Lance woke from his nap with a sloppy grin on his face. His arms reached out for me to lift him out of the crib. I pulled him close and sniffled. We adored Lance, but if his aunt was going to get custody, she needed to be the one seeing him walk and hearing him talk for the first time. The older he was, the harder the transition would be on him—all because someone had carelessly misplaced his paperwork. We had feelings too. If we had known that Lance had other prospects, we might have been slightly more distant emotionally. This little cherub had enchanted us with his smiley spell, and we were as bonded to him as he was to us.

The following week while I was flying to Seattle to give a speech, Jenny, the placement counselor, called Erick to ask us to take another foster son. "Tyson is two—and he should fit in nicely between Albert and Lance," she said. "We are exploring a grandmother as possible placement as well."

"I need to discuss it with my wife," Erick said, "but I can't reach her until after six our time."

"It should only be for about a week," she said.

My flight was delayed, and I didn't return Erick's text—which didn't sound urgent—until he was already in bed. He called me right back. "We can talk about it when I get home on Friday," I said.

"Actually, Tyson is here now."

"What!"

"Last night he stayed in a shelter—and his sister Diamond was just transferred to a girls' group home. They needed to move him today."

"Don't you think three kids is a little much to be taking on?"

"He needs us." Erick is very economical with words. I could not refute him.

"Okay," I said from the other side of the country. "Something tells me that we are going to have to take the lead to get them to do the grandmother's home study promptly."

Two days later when I walked in the door, Tyson was sitting in the corner, partially hidden by draperies. Erick was on the floor, trying to coax him out with a bowl of dry Cheerios. "He won't eat anything! I've made him smoothies, tried formula. Nothing. Not even a bottle!"

Erick was exhausted and worried. "When they found him, he had been eating his own feces."

I joined him on the floor. There was a sippy cup with milk. I passed it to the child and spoke to him in a singsong voice. "Hey, Tyson, my name is Ashley. Peekaboo!"

Tyson kicked his feet and threw his head back, crashing into the window. Oddly, he didn't cry.

"They had been abandoned in a trailer, and his teen sister has practically raised him." Erick's voice was a combination of disbelief and anger. "They didn't have a home for both kids, so Diamond went to a group home for kids aging out of foster care. She's been in the system several times before. His mother never reported Tyson's birth, so he doesn't have a birth certificate. We can't even take him to a doctor yet."

"Is he sick?"

"He's got a wicked cough, his nose is running green slime, and—" He reached under the curtain and drew Tyson out, murmuring gently, "Come on, baby . . . come see Ashley."

I took a deep breath. Tyson had a mullet of long blond hair that had grown past his shoulders and blue eyes the size of marbles. He looked like a Botticelli angel. But his teeth! They were brown nubs, rotting away before they even fully emerged. When I reached for him, he shook his arms in front of him.

I called his case manager. "I need to talk to his sister about food he likes," I explained. She mumbled something about confidentiality. "We are supposed to have access to siblings for visits and to maintain contact," I said. "And in this case we need information to help Tyson that only she might have."

She relented.

"He only eats Cheez-Its and Fig Newtons," his sister Diamond told me.

"He won't drink milk from a cup or a bottle," I said.

"He gets red Gatorade or Coke in his bottle."

"Really? No other food?"

There was a long silence, and then she whispered, "Can I please see him? He used to sleep next to me every night, and he must be scared."

"I'll work it out."

I found an oral rehydration solution that looked like Gatorade. Then we slowly introduced yogurt, peanut butter on crackers, and slices of banana.

As expected, Erick and I had to be the ones to initiate contact between the brother and sister. The group home staff wasn't always helpful or easy to deal with, but we knew what the policies and regulations were, and we weren't afraid to quote them or offer to contact those in charge.

Erick and I tried to be low-key foster parents and separated that role from our public advocacy. But in a case like this, we needed to do whatever it took to be Tyson's champions. We had been told that Diamond was a runner and a very troubled teen. Since I'd had so many labels put on me, I couldn't help but give her the benefit of the doubt. Over the next few months, she opened up to me. Her group home was designed as an independent living facility with a policy of leaving teens to "make their own decisions" in preparation for "the real world." Needless to say, she wasn't getting much guidance or structure from them.

"Have you thought about getting a job?" I asked. She looked at me as if I had asked if she had a bar of gold. "How are you doing in school?"

"I don't really know."

"The group home should have programs to help you with finishing high school and getting into a college or trade school. You can even get help finding an apartment. You will also qualify for some subsidies."

"Really?"

When I was a Guardian ad Litem, I had helped my teen girls with these and other issues—like getting a driver's license and going to prom. So many foster teens miss out on these important milestones and experiences because there is no one who helps them or cares. I knew how to steer her to the right services in our area, but she had a grandmother who was willing to take both kids, so there was no point initiating anything until she was settled in her new town.

When the placement was officially approved, Erick and I talked to the grandmother.

"I'm not worried about taking on the girl," the grandmother said, "but a baby! I don't even know how to work those paper diapers."

"Don't worry," I told her. "Diamond will be a big help, and we're only a phone call away."

On moving day a transporter arrived without Diamond.

"They're supposed to go together," Erick said.

"Diamond wasn't at the home. She went out the night before to say good-bye to some friends, and she never showed back up."

"Does anyone know where she is or how to reach her?" I asked.

"That's not any of my business. I've gotta take this one to the grandmother anyway and don't have time to wait around."

Two hours later their case manager called me back. "Just wanted you to know we found Diamond. She's in the hospital in critical condition. The weekend worker on call is with her."

"What's wrong?" I imagined everything from a hit-and-run to a violent rape to a suicide attempt.

"We're not sure yet."

I dialed the weekend on-call number and spoke to the worker. "Actually, I am sitting next to the young lady right now," she said, "but this is a confidential case, and you have no right to be involved. Only family is allowed. Her mother is on her way."

Her mother? This was a woman who had yet to have a single visit with the children and had abandoned them in the first place. Erick and I had been the only stable, reliable adults in this girl's life during this time, and yet we were being treated like the enemy.

Luckily, we had developed a solid relationship with the grandmother, who kept us in the loop. She explained that Diamond had an ectopic pregnancy that had ruptured.

When we finally got to talk to Diamond, she was more frantic and angry than in pain. She was on the verge of tears because of the access the case manager had given her mother.

"My mom took my best clothes just before she dumped us in that trailer, and now everything I had when I came in the hospital is gone too! She even stole my jewelry while I was in surgery and was gone by the time I woke up."

What a piece of trash! I thought. I called the regular case manager right away and told her what had happened. All she could say was, "The mother has the right of access to her child. And they needed her to sign off on the surgery."

"We're willing to take in Diamond when she's discharged," I said, hoping to protect her from a woman who would steal her child's possessions and not stay long enough to see if she was recovering.

"You'll have to take that up with placement, but it's easier for her to stay at the group home until she's medically cleared to travel."

⁂

Albert had enjoyed having more children in the house. He and Lance were growing up together like brothers. Unlike brothers, however, it was preordained that they each would suffer an inevitable separation. Although many of Albert's skills were delayed, he had a precocious emotional awareness. He also had a knack for making every adult in his life feel important. The first words he learned were everyone's names, including all our extended family and his teachers. We were Mommy and Daddy. Workers, however, would call his birth father Daddy, which just confused Albert. During the rare visits, when someone would say, "there's Daddy" or "go to Daddy," Albert would search for Erick.

After Albert's father missed more weekly visits, Erick brought up the big question with a simple declaration. "I love Albert. I don't want him to ever leave."

How was it that Erick found it so easy to love? Erick had loved me years before I could admit I felt the same way about him. Albert didn't have years. I was the designated mother; so I was the one who had to find a way to feel that fondness and commit to him first. That would be the signal for him to bond to me. Later, if we were separated by official decree, he could carry that emotional memory through other relationships.

"The law says his father should have only had twelve months to complete his case plan," Erick continued, getting more irate. "He rarely visits, even though he was granted all that extra unsupervised time. Isn't he at the put-up-or-shut-up stage?"

"Judges can make as many extensions and exceptions as they wish if they feel parents have made some kind of effort or face other hardships," I responded.

"Yes, but that's not what's happening here. He keeps telling the court that Albert's 'his seed'!"

That evening when I tucked Albert in, I kissed his soft cheek. I remembered being twelve and telling Gay that she could kiss me good night, but that I would never, ever reciprocate. Why had I been so rigid? This darling little boy was overflowing with love for us and almost everyone he met. I could not fail Albert like his parents had, or I might be dooming him to a lifelong attachment disorder.

"Albert, I love you very, very much," I whispered into his ear. As I said these words my heart swelled; it overflowed with the reality that they weren't just spoken, but were true. Maybe it was easier to love than I thought. In parenting him, I realized that I had been parenting myself. By wholeheartedly loving him, I was loving who I had become.

Albert had been living with us over a year when the judge extended the case plan to give his father more time. A few days later, we received a call to bring Albert to a visit for the first time in months. His father shot me what I felt was a hostile stare, as if daring me to hold his son back. Albert went to him easily—however, he did the same with the mailman or the grocery cashier. Yet in this case, someone would write a report saying that he was "bonded" with his father. While his father fed him a fast-food sandwich in a playroom, I met with Juanita, his caseworker, and her supervisor.

"Time is of the essence," the supervisor began. "So we're stepping up the reunification process. Mr. Sosa's car hasn't been reliable, which is why he has missed so many visits. Now Juanita will be arranging for unsupervised visits twice a week."

I was shocked by their change of direction.

Why were they lapping up Albert's father's lame excuses and offering to walk him through his tasks well after the one-year mark?

"We can't transport Albert four hours round trip twice a week," I said. I shot a glance at Erick. Other foster parents had warned us that child protection policies had recently shifted to fast-track reunification as a budget-saving measure, but now the rumors were impacting Albert. The following week his father was granted unsupervised weekends, even though he had seen his son only a handful of times the entire case plan—even after he had been granted unsupervised day visits.

"Where will his father take him?" Erick asked, deeply distressed. "Does he even have a safe place to live, or is he crashing with the same druggies?"

That night I jumped on the computer to do some of my own research. We took out Albert's file and made a list of mentioned names and addresses, and we searched for relatives or roommates his father might have brought up in court or during visits. The social media profiles for Mr. Sosa and his friends were revealing, unflattering—and uncensored.

"Bingo!" I called out, showing Erick what I had found.

"Wow. Now that we have proof of Dad's lifestyle," Erick said, "maybe someone will step in to protect Albert. Be sure to send those to the caseworker."

"I just did," I said, "with copies to her supervisor and to the Guardian ad Litem office."

For months we had been taking Albert to doctors for a cough that seemed to worsen every evening. A specialist finally determined that Albert had asthma and prescribed inhaler therapy. A few weeks later, we found out we were being investigated for medical neglect. We were eventually cleared, since three doctors had seen Albert, we were following all recommendations, and we'd kept meticulous records of visits and prescriptions. We never learned who'd made the bogus claim, although Mr. Sosa could have made it himself out of spite—especially if Juanita showed him the compromising photos and he suspected we were the ones who'd found them. There were so many possibilities. We were upset—not only at the false allegations, but also by getting a blemish on our foster care record that could never be erased.

We made sure to attend the next court date. I introduced myself to Nell Grasso, Albert's court-appointed guardian, in the hall outside the courtroom. A courtesy Guardian ad Litem had visited Albert at our home earlier that month and passed her notes on to Mrs. Grasso, who had never met the child herself. "Before we were foster parents, my husband and I were both guardians," I told Nell. The woman, who looked about Erick's grandmother's age, sniffed as if smelling me for the truth.

"Albert has severe asthma and is getting inhaler treatments three times a day," I said. "Maybe you can bring this up, since both his father and his roommate smoke."

"Tobacco is a legal substance," she said.

"So is a car, but a child needs to wear a seat belt." Nell didn't get the metaphor. I tried another tack. "Do you think Mr. Sosa has the ability to care for Albert on his own?"

"He loves his little boy."

"We're willing to offer him an open adoption."

"Then your motives are obviously clouded."

"Everyone for Sosa," the bailiff called, and we entered the courtroom.

Juanita reported that visits were going "exceptionally well." She painted a picture of a father and son who were very bonded and aching to be reunited.

"Where do you live?" the judge asked Mr. Sosa.

Martin Sosa gave two different addresses in two counties. His lawyer tried to sort out the confusion by explaining that one was an old address and one was his brother's.

"Are you living with your brother?" the judge asked. Albert's father shook his head. "Does anyone else live with you?"

"A guy named Rocky and another . . ." He hesitated. "I think it's"—he scratched his head— "Johnny."

The judge wanted their last names and their places of employment. Martin was stumped, but his lawyer said he would provide the court with the information.

The child welfare agency's lawyer said they were in favor of a reunification with a safety plan. He added that Albert would be sleeping in the father's room. The judge asked the guardian's opinion. "We don't have anything else, Your Honor."

"Your Honor," the father's lawyer chimed back in, "Mr. Sosa was busy fulfilling probation requirements, he worked around the clock, and he got lost trying to find the parenting classes."

When he finished, I stood up from my seat in the audience.

The attorney for the Department of Children and Families waved her hand at me. "Please sit down."

17

"With all due respect, Your Honor, foster parents have a duty to report issues to the court."

"You may continue," the judge said.

"First, there was a period of more than six months where this father did not visit at all, nor has he shown the ability to find stable housing. He's moved four times since his child came into care."

"That's the past, and we are focusing on the future," the father's attorney said.

"Anything else?" the judge asked, as though he were about to shut me down.

I looked to the caseworker's table, waiting for her to stand and say something about what we had discovered online. She refused to meet my gaze. "Yes, we've found recent photos on various websites of the father and his brother partying, looking intoxicated, and using drugs in the home in question. Some of these pictures were taken on dates the child was visiting."

"A picture could have been posted on a date but taken months earlier," the father's lawyer chimed in.

"Mr. Sosa is in the process of moving anyway," Juanita added, proving she was the department's mouthpiece and not looking out for Albert's welfare.

My stomach squirmed, and a wave of heat rushed through me. I sat down and hugged my purse to keep from getting sick. Nobody in this room cared one whit for Albert. Nobody had seen the sunshine in his eyes or the rhythm in his step or been led by his tiny hand to a puzzle he wanted taken down from the shelf. Nobody else had wiped his chin—or his bottom—or soothed him when he cried out at night. They didn't know what it was like to put your lips on his forehead to see if his fever had gone down or to spoon him strawberry yogurt when he was too weak to feed himself. They hadn't seen him grow from being terrified of dogs to teaching them tricks. Nor did they witness how loving he could be to his foster brothers. He used silly faces to coax a smile out of Tyson and made animal sounds to Lance to make him laugh.

None of this mattered. Albert was a liability on the state's balance sheet. They needed to take him off the books and claim yet another success story—a family rehabilitated by their program and reunited to live happily ever after.

11.

safety last

Darkness cannot drive out darkness: only light can do that. Hate cannot drive out hate: only love can do that.
—Dr. Martin Luther King Jr.

Albert disintegrated. We watched, helpless, as he unwound after spending more and more time with his father. At school he had so many wetting accidents they put him back in Pull-Ups. He pinched other students and kicked a teacher when she asked him to pick up a pencil he had thrown. When he returned from unsupervised visits, he ran coughing to his nebulizer, put on his mask, and waited for us to turn it on.

He started pitching from side to side during sleep again and sometimes called out in the night. After school one day he ran into the house and was greeted by Loki. "Bad!" he yelled at his favorite dog, then hit him with his fist between the eyes. Loki put his tail between his legs and left the room.

Albert glared at me, almost defying me to react. "We will always love you, sweet boy," I said to him.

The permanent transfer from our care to his father's was to take place in a park halfway between our homes. As I packed all his possessions, I felt physically ill. He had celebrated two Christmases and a birthday with us; had two sets of doting grandparents, aunts, uncles, cousins, and various foster care and guardian groups that made sure he had clothing, shoes, hats, books, toys, a bike, and—his favorite—a box of tiny cars. I lay down on his bed and sniffed his pillow. I had to close my eyes to quell a surge of dizziness. Everyone said that giving up a foster child could be emotionally brutal. Even though Erick and I had been preparing for this day, it was like surgery—you knew it would hurt, you just couldn't imagine how much.

"If only we believed he was going to a safe situation," Erick said, "I could accept it. Even if someone else was going to adopt him or he was moving in with a stable relative. But not only hasn't this guy made any real progress, he's been enabled by bureaucrats who don't give a damn about Albert." I was helping Erick squeeze everything into our SUV. "Wait!" I ran back inside for Albert's pillow, because I remembered that I had hated leaving mine behind. "I love you," I told him as I buckled him into his car seat. I ruffled his hair and closed the door before he could see me break into sobs.

On the way home, Erick would pick up Lance from day care. Was he too young to understand why his "big brother" suddenly disappeared? I summoned the energy to strip Albert's bed and start a load of laundry before heading to the bathroom to take something for my pounding headache. I opened the medicine cabinet and noticed an old pregnancy test that I had bought when I had a very late period just after we got married. I now stood in the bathroom counting backward, and something didn't add up. I checked the expiration date on the test—it showed only a few months were left, so I decided to use it.

Ten minutes later, I texted Erick: HEY, WE NEED TO TALK WHEN YOU GET HOME.

I felt so drained by losing Albert and yet so buoyed by the idea that the two of us had created a baby. A baby who wouldn't have a caseworker or court dates. A baby who wouldn't be taken from us. There was also an ironic solace in finding out that I was pregnant the same day that Albert left.

Soon I was experiencing all-day—and night—"morning" sickness. When I was in class online, I kept some barf bags by my desk, so I could just bend over and do what I needed to. My computer's camera only showed my torso so when my jeans became tight, I wore comfy pajama bottoms paired with a pretty blouse. One time I was in such a hurry to deal with my nausea that I knocked the camera over, showing the entire class my mismatched outfit.

"Sorry about that," I said to the polite laughter. "The thing is—I'm expecting a baby." The class applauded. After that, if I disappeared briefly, everyone understood.

We hadn't heard a word from Albert's father—and never would.

Albert's bed had barely aired out when Jenny from placement called. "I have two of the most adorable brothers," she said. She went on to explain that they wanted to keep the boys together. We could sympathize after seeing how difficult it was for Tyson and Diamond to be apart. Diamond had finally been reunited with Tyson and was settling in at their grandmother's house. Before Tyson left, we had sent along a letter describing his schedule, the foods he had learned to like, his preference for smooth textures, and the importance of avoiding bottles and sugary drinks. I felt reassured by the grandmother's calls to ask how we handled certain behaviors. We were heartened by her determination to do right by them.

"Marcus is three and just the sweetest thing," Jenny continued. "His half brother Manuel is five."

I knew she had a tough job selling foster parents on taking children they had never met, and often on the spur of the moment. Humor and arm-twisting were two of her job's qualifications—as well as downright lying.

"Where are they now?"

"In an inappropriate home with teens." She sighed. "They're being bullied." I paused too long. "We'll have them there by four," she said, and hung up before I could argue further.

There was nothing adorable about Manuel or Marcus. They looked—and behaved—like mini gangsters. "How old is Manuel again?" I asked the case manager.

"Five?" She checked the paperwork. "I know, he looks ten."

At three Marcus weighed twice as much as Albert, who had been about the same age. While Erick was still carrying in their belongings, they began to irk each other by trying to stomp on each other's feet. "Little" Marcus was the dominant personality, who constantly provoked his brother for attention—and the attention he got was in the form of elbow jabs and a barrage of F-bombs.

"Whoa, buddy," Erick said. "You can't use that word in this house."

"Why the hell can't he?" Manuel asked.

"Because . . . ," Erick said slowly, "it's not polite or good for the baby, who is just learning to speak."

"Oh," Manuel replied, accepting that answer.

Over the next few days they begged for television. With Albert we limited viewing to a few educational programs a week, but I relented with these two because I needed to write a paper.

"We want something with guns," Manuel said.

"Yeah! Bang-bang," his brother replied.

"Sorry, not here," I said.

Marcus pointed to the Nintendo Wii. "Grand Theft Auto!"

"Don't have it." I changed to a children's program on PBS and took the remote with me.

I understood foster children's preoccupation with violent movies. Luke had been obsessed with them, and I remember bragging to one foster home that I had seen *Children of the Corn*. In order to deal with foster care chaos, and with dysfunctional pasts, children like us flattened our feelings. Scary movies awakened senses, if temporarily. I remember both the thrills—as well as the bad dreams. When I had awoken, though, my reality was sometimes even more frightening.

※

"Who told you this was temporary?" the new boys' case manager said. She had come early for a visit and was waiting for Erick to bring the brothers home from school. "We have not been able to locate any suitable family members who could pass a home study, so this is being considered a cold case."

"I don't know how long we can keep them; they're way too rough with Lance, and I'm worried about them hurting me while I'm pregnant."

"But you're amazing parents." She beamed at me.

The front door flew open and Marcus rushed into the room, heading directly to the bookshelf. He pulled out his new favorite book—*Pinocchio*. We were weaning them from TV to books and imaginative toys like trucks and Legos. He hurried over to Erick, who was walking inside. I had to admit that it was encouraging to see these boys beginning to enjoy calmer, more age-appropriate activities in such a short time.

"Just a minute, buddy," Erick said to Marcus, then turned to the caseworker. "I have interesting news. When I went to pick up the boys from school, a girl came running over to me. She told me that the brothers are her cousins and that they share a grandmother named something like Heidi or Hedda."

"Did you get the grandmother's number?"

"Of course!"

The caseworker had an odd smirk on her face. "We should hire you to do our diligent searches."

We didn't trust anyone else to make the first contact, and so we called the grandmother ourselves. She already had custody of another set of related children whose parents were in jail on drug charges.

We passed on the news to the caseworker. "If the grand-mother is agreeable, you can place them immediately," I said. "Her home study is only two months old."

The boys moved in with their grandmother after only a few weeks with us. Our going-away gift to them was a new set of children's fairy-tale books.

As for Lance, his aunt's home study was still "in progress." It had been completed, but then his aunt had moved to a bigger house to accommodate him, which required paperwork on the new residence. We suggested that she Skype with us so Lance would get to know her face and voice. She loved these sessions, and when he blew her kisses, she started to cry.

Before long, our placement counselor Jenny called late on a Friday afternoon. When the agency number showed up on the caller ID, we never knew if it was a worker or a placement, but it was almost always something that would alter our plans—if not our lives.

"We have the most adorable baby boy—an infant really, just five months old and simply gorgeous."

"You don't have to sell me. I'm pregnant and am a big softie this week. What's his story?"

"The usual. Drug affected when he was born, slightly premature, developmental delays."

"His brother is in another foster home, but they didn't feel like they were ready to take on the baby." Jenny paused. "Can we bring him over in the morning?"

Erick's mother Sharon was there when little Dakota arrived. She took the bundle of baby while I signed the paperwork. I asked the caseworker to stay while I went through the medical file to be certain we could handle his care.

"Isn't he awfully small for five months?" I asked my mother-in-law.

She was examining him with the expert eye of the mother of four children. "He can't even hold his head up." He gave a little mewing cry that sounded more like a kitten than a baby. "That's strange too."

"Of course you'll take him to your local pediatrician in the next few days," the worker said. "He can answer your questions. Here's his formula and a few diapers to get you started."

Dakota terrified me. He wasn't normal, and nobody could tell us why. Seeing him so fragile and frail increased my fears about the baby growing inside me. His navy-blue eyes bulged slightly, making them seem otherworldly.

"It might just be sensory deprivation from being in an incubator so long," Sharon suggested, all the while rocking Dakota and gently rubbing his back. "The only cure for this sweetheart is to keep him close so he knows he is loved."

Dakota was lethargic, ate poorly, and had a bluish cast to his skin. The pediatrician thought he might have shaken baby syndrome, a traumatic brain injury that is the result of being handled violently. We had to make the rounds of specialists who looked for bleeding in his retina and brain, damage to his spinal cord or neck, and scanned for other fractures.

I began to dread the waiting rooms. The limp baby in my arms had the complexion of a freshly peeled almond, and the fuzz on his head was wiry. He drooled a lot and didn't respond to my attempts to get him to smile. Other parents, technicians, and personnel gave me disapproving stares, figuring I was the mother who had harmed him—and to make matters worse, my own pregnancy was now showing, so who knows what they were calculating. Even though we tried not to use the "foster" word in relation to any of our children, Erick and I started emphasizing it with Dakota's medical visits to avoid an overzealous health-care worker calling the abuse hotline.

After one appointment, Erick and I only had Dakota with us, and we went to stock up on diapers at the store. I was carrying the baby in a harness on my chest while Erick pushed our purchases in a cart. When Dakota fussed, I replaced the pacifier he had spit out. A woman with silver hair glanced from my bulging tummy to our biracial baby to Erick, trying to figure the relationships.

Erick gave the lady a winsome grin. "I forgave her."

The woman reeled back and moved to a different aisle. When we got outside, we both cracked up. "Did you see her doubletake?"

But the truth was, I felt like I was always being scrutinized, and I hated the stares and comments we would get when we used subsidies for our foster kids. All foster children under five qualify for WIC—the federal supplemental nutrition program for women, infants, and children. If I shopped with my foster kids in tow, clerks would look at the kids and my pregnant belly and roll their eyes.

"Nice purse," a woman behind me in line once said, meaning: *Maybe you should be spending money on your kids and not handbags and a smartphone.*

Erick wasn't spared the rude remarks. Once, when he was buying formula, he gave the cashier his WIC card. Thinking he was pulling a fast one, she called her manager. "We don't see a lot of men," she said later as an apology.

Assumptions are everywhere. Another time I was sorting my grocery items on the belt because the WIC items were checked out separately at this store. In front of me was a tall African-American woman teetering on brightly colored leather high heels. She had paid for her order and had started to move her cart. "Wait till I ring up your welfare items," the clerk said to her.

"Those are not mine!" the high-heeled woman spat back.

I had come from a meeting and was wearing business attire. The cashier hadn't considered that the items could belong to me.

Family friends were fostering three siblings under age three. "I've been called 'white trash,'" the wife said, because she bought formula with the subsidy. "Another time someone said, 'If you can't afford your kids, stop sleeping around and go to work.'" She had been too shocked to answer, but I wished she had been able to point out that her husband is a pilot with a major airline and she is a physical therapist. One of the children in her care had her leg snapped by the mother's boyfriend, and she helped the baby through an arduous recovery.

Fortunately, many of the people in our community have come to know our family and respect what we do. "And what's this fellow's name?" one of our favorite cashiers asks when we bring a new child to the market. I like to think that for every intolerant bigot, there is a bighearted person who would also foster if they were able.

I kept a meticulous diary of the number of bottles, meals, and wet and soiled diapers Dakota had to prove we were doing everything possible to help him gain weight. The doctors ruled out various diseases and syndromes and changed his formula several times. There was no information on what drugs his mother had taken during her pregnancy, and she didn't visit him. She also didn't think she had done anything wrong.

One unintended problem with my pregnancy was that I was losing my lap space, but I still had babies who needed to cuddle closely. Later in my pregnancy, I was told to not lift anything heavier than twenty pounds, so I had to discourage Lance when his little arms went into the "up, up!" position. Dakota was still so light I didn't hesitate to carry him. Sometimes I'd rest on the couch with him lying across my chest. When he'd fall asleep to the beating of my heart, I felt a wave of maternal satisfaction.

To our amazement and joy, Sharon's love cure seemed to be working. After such a long time without any measurable growth, we started to see Dakota gaining strength week by week. Erick—with a lot of help from Lance—coaxed him to giggle. Soon he began to give us shy smiles. The staff at his day care doted on him too. I would have preferred to keep him at home, but Florida's Rilya Wilson Act requires foster children to be in day care. Named after a child in state custody who disappeared for two years without anyone knowing about it, the law makes sure that teachers or child-care workers see the children during the week, and they must report absences. Much sooner than anyone expected, the tiny tot started to crawl, and to our amazement he stood up and began to walk at only ten months! No sooner had we celebrated this milestone than we were told to pack up his belongings. They were moving him to the foster home where his older brother was living.

This time I didn't have so many of the pangs that came

with the other children's farewells or the heartsickness that accompanied Albert's leaving. I realized that part of the grieving for Albert had been my fears for his safety and knowing he was not going to a good, stable situation. We had really helped Dakota, and he was being reunited with family—so that counted for something.

In any case, there was little time to worry about Dakota, because the very next day Bruce replaced him.

"My mommy does pills," the boy said before he had even crossed our threshold. "And Granny does pills too."

"Oh my," said the transporter who brought him for "just a few days."

"He speaks really well for a kid who's two," Erick said.

"He's four," the worker said.

Erick looked at me and we laughed. Once again Jenny had fudged.

"You know what else?" Bruce said in a cute, raspy voice. "My mommy's belly-button baby's gone because she does pills."

Had his mother had a miscarriage, or had the state taken the child from the hospital?

The phone rang. Jenny was breathless. "You have dogs, right?"

"Yes, three."

"Has Bruce arrived?"

"Yes, why?"

"Has he seen the dogs?"

"Not yet. He just—"

Jenny cut me off. "Bruce was mauled by a dog and has a panic attack when he sees one."

"Great." I muted a groan. "What do you expect us to do?"

"It's Friday," Jenny said. "I'll move him by Monday, okay? You seem to be able to cope with anything."

"Look, we don't want to upset the kid. If he freaks, then you'll have to find him an emergency placement."

"Okay," she agreed.

"And one more thing," I said. "This kid is double the age you claimed. We know you're under a lot of pressure, but all we ask is that you tell us the truth."

Jenny hung up with a barrage of apologies.

That night, when it was time for Bruce to get into his pajamas, I helped him out of his shirt. He winced. His torso looked like a road map, with lines from beatings and cuts in varied stages of healing.

"Erick!" I called. I was too shaken to do this alone. "Look here. . . ." There were noticeable teeth marks on the side of his neck and similar ones on the back of his arm, but not everything had been done by an animal, because there were so many old scars. It looked like someone had used a chain with spikes to get the punctures evenly spaced on his back and belly.

This was the worst case of physical abuse I had ever seen—even counting children I knew when I was in foster care. At The Children's Home, older kids sometimes one-upped each other with their histories—some of which were probably exaggerated; many, though, were the gruesome truth. The story that had horrified me the most were siblings whose hands had been superglued to the wall in a closet, and they weren't found for several days.

When I dried Bruce off, Loki started barking at a squirrel. The little boy stiffened ramrod straight and began to shiver. "Don't worry, the dogs will be outside, and we won't let them near you."

The weather was mild, and the two largest dogs slept outside on their beds under the covered back porch. I carried Bella, my Chihuahua, up to our bedroom, and she was content to cuddle on my pillow and only go out when Bruce wasn't around. Because of Bruce's injuries, his diligent Guardian ad Litem insisted that he get priority for a therapeutic placement—a more highly trained foster home with fewer children and more services. I offered to transport Bruce to the new home the following week.

"Why don't you hang around while we settle Bruce in," Dana, his new foster mother, suggested.

"All his clothes are clean, except for last night's laundry." I showed her the separate plastic bag. "His Pull-Ups were dry this morning." I reached over and did a high five with Bruce, who returned it shyly.

Dana lived in an upscale town house that was artistically furnished. She settled Bruce on a beanbag chair and handed him a new stuffed animal. "This is Rusty the rabbit," she said. "He is very lonely and needs lots of hugs. Let me know if he gets hungry. We have carrots and peanut butter crackers if he is."

I immediately liked her approach. "So you are technically a therapeutic foster home?" I asked. "Bruce . . . well, you'll see that he's been severely harmed . . . but his behavior has been very compliant. He was with us less than a week, so we were still getting to know each other, but many of our so-called 'traditional' placements were much needier."

"The squeaky wheel gets the grease," she said, pouring iced tea. "Let's face it, almost every single foster kid has been shocked—if only because they have been removed from their family. They all need therapeutic treatment."

"What are the differences between therapeutic and regular foster care?"

"Well, the board rate is higher and you get fewer kids. Our agency is smaller and much more supportive. The kids get a lot more services and help too." She gave me a warm smile.

"Rusty wants potty," Bruce said.

"Good bunny rabbit," Dana said. "Will you help me take him there?"

I knew this was my exit line. "Bye, Rusty. Bye, Bruce," I said as Bruce went off with Dana and didn't look back.

On the way home, I considered the possibility of being a therapeutic foster home. Erick and I wanted the best services for the children in our care, yet we often felt as though our recommendations were ignored. I was confident we could care for a child like Bruce if we had an agency that helped us rather than blamed us every time something went wrong.

12.

that's the ticket

Never confuse a single defeat with a final defeat.
—F. Scott Fitzgerald

"If you're transferring your license to the therapeutic agency, we'll have to move Lance." The agency placement supervisor told me this as if I were a disagreeable teen having my privileges revoked.

"But he's going to his aunt in less than a month!"

"In the meantime, he'll have to live with one of our agency's families."

"This baby has lived with us for most of his life. He doesn't know any other family."

"You made your choice. We can't mingle our children with those in the therapeutic program," she said in a chilling voice.

"We don't have to accept a therapeutic placement until he leaves."

"We aren't willing to pay the higher board rate."

"We don't care about the subsidy." I paused. "We want what's best for him."

"You don't understand how complex this is. We'll call you when we have a family willing to take Lance for the interim," she said, and hung up.

I phoned Maya, the head of the therapeutic agency. Instead of a parade of new agency workers and placement specialists, we would only be dealing with her, Bonnie, the therapist, and Sheila, the targeted case manager who would integrate all the services each child needed.

"There's no reason to move your little guy," Maya said after I explained all the supervisor's arguments. "We won't give you one of our children until he leaves. The idea that he would be in danger is ridiculous."

"I feel like they're trying to punish us for some reason, but he's the one who will suffer."

"They don't like to lose what was theirs," Maya explained.

"Then maybe they should have been more encouraging. They pushed a reunification and gave a child back to an unsafe, unfit parent. They've pressured us to take children who were not suited for our profile, and they didn't even pay attention to the fact that we had dogs when they placed a child with us who had just been attacked by one. When we speak up for the kids in staffings or court, we're either ignored or asked to sit down. We are tired of being the bad guys when all we're trying to do is help these kids," I grumbled. "But the point is, what can we do about Lance?"

"Let me see if I can work something out between the agencies," Maya said.

I felt like we were going through a divorce and the child was suffering for the decisions of the adults. There was no way I could explain it to Lance—or even his aunt, who tried to get permission to move him a few weeks earlier.

Two days later Jenny called. This time she didn't sound like we had won a free vacation. "Just letting you know that a transporter will be coming for the child today between four and five."

"Today! He's at school till five, and he's not packed. Besides, I thought the agencies were still working on another plan."

"Sorry, that's not what I was told."

"Where's he going?"

"To the Gordon-Becker foster home." She paused to see if I would react.

"Oh, Margot and Carlotta! They're great. I spoke at one of their training sessions. Give me their number and I can transport him for a smoother transition."

When I phoned, Margot answered. "I remember you," she said, "but I didn't realize you were the one who had Lance."

I tried to explain why Lance was being moved without bashing the agency, which would be unprofessional. "Can you maintain Skype contact with the aunt?"

"Of course we can. My wife is in IT."

"I'm glad he'll have two moms for a while," I said. "He's my cuddle buddy."

I typed up Lance's schedule and packed his favorite toys, his clothes, some organic snacks, and his sippy cups.

Erick and I brought him to their home. "Bye-bye!" Lance chirped, and blew kisses, probably expecting us to return shortly.

We smiled and waved and clapped, determined to give him a happy send-off. But when our car was out of sight, I slumped into my seat and sobbed.

That evening Beth, my best foster-mother friend, called to console me. "Do you need any clothes for your little Frankie?" I asked. We had a huge stack that Lance had outgrown.

"How did you guess?" Beth said. "He's turned into the cutest little butterball."

"Great!" I said. "I'll bring them over tomorrow."

I was driving to her house when she called, crying so hard that I could barely understand her. "Don't bother coming. Frankie's gone."

"What!" Beth was even more sensitive than I was when it came to these children, because she hadn't been hardened by so many disappointments. She had a master's degree in child development, had married her college sweetheart, and had grown up surrounded by a loving family. "I'm still coming over."

"Day care called and said a worker took Frankie to a new placement," Beth said when I arrived.

"Without any warning to you?" Beth nodded. "Maybe he was kidnapped by a family member?"

"N-no," she stuttered. "I called the caseworker. She knew about it and acted like this was normal."

"What about all the clothes and toys you bought him?"

"They took our backpack—Brian's, actually—and what-ever he had at day care. I d-don't understand why."

"This is so wrong," I said. "They are desperate to recruit foster parents, but then they pull stunts like this."

"But we brought him home as a preemie from the hospital, and he's only known us for all this time. He has to be terrified."

Supposedly babies are more resilient, but we really don't know how the separation affects them.

"I can remember feeling cold and empty and scared when I was moved without being able to say good-bye. Once I was woken in the night and taken on a plane to live with relatives I had never met."

"I'd thought the system would have changed since then," Beth said.

"Me too," I said after a long pause. "Obviously it hasn't. It may even have gotten worse."

My latest field placement was with a religious group that assisted pregnant women and also ran an adoption division. I could make my own hours, which allowed me to keep my classroom and speech commitments.

Mary Lou Krebs, the program's director, had read my book. "We're thrilled to have you on board," she said. "I'll organize a fund-raiser, and you can be our speaker."

"But—" I started to explain how my bookings work, but she continued without pause.

"The cornerstone of our mission is preventing abortions." Mrs. Krebs handed me the first of several fetal models. "This is twenty weeks, which should be about your baby's size, right? Here, hold it. It helps a woman understand that she is carrying a human child."

The plastic replica looked like a stillborn. I passed it back as though it was a hot potato.

"I can see this makes you uncomfortable. You are keeping your baby, right?"

She didn't wait for my response, and I resented the

implication that at this stage in my pregnancy and life I could consider not having my baby.

"We have an adoption division and a counseling component for those wishing to parent instead," she prattled on.

"We also have a bus that goes to shopping plazas, medical centers, and targeted areas—like across the street from Planned Parenthood—and we encourage women to see their child on ultrasound. It's a very effective deterrent. Would you like to do some shifts on the bus?"

I knitted my fingers together across my baby bump and thought about the ultrasound when I had learned whether my baby would be a girl or a boy. We had invited my parents along for the big moment. I can't say we had a preference, but we *all* thought I was having a girl. When the technician said, "A boy, definitely a boy" and circled the critical part on her monitor, I had to ask her to check again to be sure.

Everyone had laughed and cheered, especially since almost all our foster children had been boys and we felt like we understood them and their care well. I did not want that joyful memory to be diluted by seeing women in different circumstances feeling negatively about their pregnancies.

"I don't think it would be the best use of my skills. . . ."

Mary Lou sensed she had touched a nerve. She handed me a piece of paper. "Our rules are very simple, but there can be absolutely no deviation." Mary Lou's chipper voice became more grating. "Let me know if you can follow them."

I scanned this list that forbid mentioning any sort of contraception or unapproved referrals. "I think I can comply with this," I said. I had already worked at a shelter for pregnant teens run by a church, and they also hadn't let us talk about birth control. I assumed I could bottle my own beliefs and strive to help each client to the best of my ability within their program's framework.

Outside Mrs. Krebs's office, the waiting room was filled with women in various stages of pregnancy. Most had come in from smoking outside. I was warned not to criticize them in any way, because that might scare them off.

I started by observing my immediate supervisor, Priscilla, doing intakes. That afternoon Priscilla asked a woman how many children she had. "Two," she replied.

"How many pregnancies?" Priscilla said as she filled out her sheet.

"Five or six."

"Only two babies!" Priscilla said without hiding the shock in her voice, because she assumed the woman had aborted the rest.

"Oh no, I got more."

Priscilla stopped typing into her computer. "I don't understand. . . ."

I cleared my throat, and Priscilla nodded that I could speak. "Are some of your children living with relatives, or could they be in foster care?"

"Yeah, the state took a bunch. Some are with my mom; the baby's with me."

"So why are you here today?" Priscilla asked, relieved that she wasn't dealing with her version of a serial killer.

"I need more diapers and wipes."

"We'd be happy to help. Anything else we can do?" Priscilla said with a practiced kindly tone. "Do you need a pregnancy test?"

"My man—we're engaged—he's out of prison in a few

months in Georgia. Can you fix me permanent—so we don't make a baby?"

"Don't you want to give him a baby?" Priscilla said to the client. As if reading my mind, she shot me a look that I wasn't to intervene.

Afterward, though, I couldn't understand her flat-out encouragement to bring more babies into this woman's world of poverty and crime.

One of the first clients I saw on my own was N'vasha, who was on disability because of psychiatric problems. I asked about her children.

"I got a nineteen-year-old boy who's living with me, but I know he's gotta leave."

"Why is that?" I asked.

"I caught him having sex"—she paused—"with his half sister."

"How old is she?" I asked, trying to keep censure out of my voice.

"Ten. She's big enough to get a baby."

N'vasha had also come in for the free supplies provided to help women keep their children. She still had two in diapers at home. I checked her file. She had been in several months earlier to ask for free supplies, and I saw a note about the sexual abuse concerns written then.

"Why didn't anyone follow up on this?" I asked one of the supervisors.

"That's not our role," she said. "We can't know the Lord's plan."

"We're talking about child sexual abuse!"

"Don't be hasty to judge."

"As a foster parent I am a mandated reporter," I said, "so no matter what your policies are, they don't trump my sworn responsibilities."

Later, I called the Department of Children and Families' hotline as required.

My strength turned out to be talking to the moms who were considering surrendering their children for adoption. I also made hospital visits to see brand-new mothers. One undecided woman agreed to an open adoption after we spoke. She was comforted by my adoption story and that I am still able to be in touch with my biological mother.

I found it excruciating not to answer direct questions about preventing pregnancy. One woman who was having her *twelfth* baby became angry. "Why won't anybody tell me what to do?" she shouted. I wanted to blurt out for her to just go to the health department, but that was also against the rules.

I thought I could have suspended my personal principles, but this woman's plight had been the last straw. I asked Priscilla to see her.

Afterward Priscilla said, "Are you feeling all right?"

"Actually, her case upset me," I admitted.

"Of course," she said in a syrupy voice. "Everything is more personal when you are pregnant."

"No, this is different," I said. "Did you know most of that woman's other children are in foster care?"

"Really?" Priscilla raised her plucked eyebrows. "Well, what's the big deal about being in foster care?"

My jaw dropped. If I started to reply, I couldn't trust what I would say. "I have a really bad headache. I'd better go and rest for my baby's sake," I said so no other questions would be forthcoming.

The minute I got home I called my fieldwork placement supervisor and insisted on a new position. "We don't have any openings," she said.

"I know several groups that might be taking interns."

She explained the rules for changing a placement, and in a few weeks I had transferred my internship to the juvenile division of the public defender's office.

For a brief moment in our marriage Erick and I were childless, except for the one we were expecting. We had done a major cleaning and tidying, placing all the children's clothes in boxes with the sizes marked and sorting toys by age group.

A few days after Lance left, Erick took me out for dinner. I enjoyed putting an outfit together that wasn't covered in spit-up or peanut butter. We went to our favorite sushi restaurant, even though I couldn't eat raw fish. I did have two servings of miso soup, which appealed to my hormonally-altered palate. My band was also preventing me from overeating during my pregnancy.

I didn't share my worries about how pregnancy would change my body, since it seemed so easy for me to pack on weight under normal circumstances. Some of my friends had gained fifty to a hundred pounds during their pregnancies, and many were still struggling with baby weight. I was concerned about how I could maintain my newly modest portions while still meeting the baby's needs. During the period I was experiencing severe morning sickness, my band was loosened because regurgitation can create slippage. In the second trimester I caught myself eating more voraciously, and so I had my band tightened a little and was extremely careful to select the nutrient-rich foods that would be best for the baby. I would then have my band completely deflated in anticipation of labor. All this loosening and tightening was painless, and we were able to find a "sweet spot" for every situation.

"Ready for another course?" Erick asked at the restaurant.

Instead of ordering everything at the beginning of the meal, I had waited to see how what I ate settled. I knew I couldn't eat more than an appetizer size. "All these years I've been looking for some internal switch—what everyone calls willpower. My band does it for me."

"Whatever works," he said. "You look beautiful tonight. And I love you more than ever."

We beamed at each other like kids with a crush. I had never been happier. Together we had made a lot of tough decisions and had weathered the loss of Albert and now Lance. We had known this came with the fostering territory, but it is hard to anticipate feelings. Privately we referred to our baby as "Keeper." Nobody would ever come and move him from our home.

"I wonder what will be different about our own baby," Erick mused.

"Do you think we'll have first-time jitters?"

Erick laughed. "We're the baby drill team. We can change diapers in the dark, know who's crying and for what reason, and are experts at sleep-training children who come from chaotic situations."

I nodded. One of the best gifts we could give those in our temporary care was to get them on a schedule of naps and regular meal- and bedtimes, heal the inevitable diaper rashes, make sure they were inoculated, and cure their wounds and infections. We were proud of what we had accomplished for eight children so far. "I bet we'll be in for some surprises," I said as I sipped my hot tea and smiled with contentment.

"I'm glad you dropped down to part-time in grad school," Erick said. "You were so exhausted."

The MSW was up to a two-year degree program, which had seemed doable when I enrolled. The stumbling block turned out to be the many internships on top of the foster children, my speeches and traveling—and now our baby, who was due in less than five months. I calculated everything carefully and decided I would be able to get all my research, hours, and papers in before the birth and just have to take my final exams afterward. I figured I could always study in between nursing or naps.

The following Monday we had two phone calls that required quick decisions. Maya wanted us to "consider" Lillian Gentry, a complicated two-year-old. "She also has some medical issues. The short intake form we got on her says she has had herpes," Maya said.

They would e-mail over Lillian's case summary to read, and then we could discuss her care before making a decision.

"This is so much better than having to make a snap decision over the phone," I told Erick. "They're giving us all the facts up front and leaving the choice up to us."

Just as we were discussing the disturbing aspects of the child's case, Phil called. "Hi, hon," he began. "I know you aren't busy or anything, so I thought you might be interested in a new project."

I knew his sarcastic tone and laughed. "Whatever you say, Pops."

"You remember Floyd?" He filled me in about a man who managed campaigns for the state Democratic party. Phil had done commercials for some of his candidates.

"Isn't he the guy who said I should run for office someday?"

"Right. How about this election?"

"In November? That's only a few months away!"

"Yes. A lot of incumbent Republicans are running unopposed. The party is looking for people who are not afraid to run against them."

"I think I'll be busy then. Our baby's due right around Election Day."

"It only takes one day to have a baby," he said with a laugh. "Just keep an open mind and talk to Floyd about your political aspirations."

A few hours later Floyd called. "We'd like you to file," he said. "There are only five days before the qualifying period closes."

He had stirred the part of me that loves a challenge. "But I'm only twenty-six."

"Hey, Debbie Wasserman Schultz was the same age when she was elected to Florida's House of Representatives, and now she's chair of the National Democratic Party. I'd love you two to meet."

"Okay, let me talk to my husband." I'd almost hung up when I thought of another question. "What office do you want me to run for?"

"State senate."

"Really?" My voice went way too high and squeaky.

Erick had questions and major reservations. "But think about all the good we can do for people just by campaigning," I said.

Within a few hours Floyd had e-mailed the paperwork to register my campaign. Erick and I tackled it immediately—if there was anything at which we excelled, it was bureaucratic forms.

The next day we met with Floyd. "Are you sure I should run for the senate? I feel like I'm skipping a few steps."

"It's been done before."

"Is my pregnancy a deterrent?"

"On the contrary, nobody's going to trash a pregnant woman," he said.

I could almost see Floyd's mental gears meshing as he considered the pros and cons of every point. Erick was also analytical, and I would rely on his ability to sort out potential issues. We'd make a superb political team, I thought, hardly believing I was actually running for a state-level office. Floyd promised we would get all the help we needed. By the end of the week I was a registered candidate, and the newspapers started calling it the "David and Goliath" race.

Lillian Gentry and her two older brothers had been living with their grandmother in a rural area of the county. I shouldn't be shocked about the youthful age of grandmothers—my own would have been only thirty-three when I was born if she hadn't died the weekend I was conceived. Here was another one in her early thirties. Lillian had been placed with her due to the usual—drugs and domestic violence—or so we were led to believe. The reason the three children qualified for therapeutic care was that they were on multiple psychotropic medications, including mind-altering drugs used to treat attention-deficit/hyperactivity disorder, anxiety, depression, and psychosis.

"This is ridiculous for a child her age," I said to Erick. "I mean, these are intense drugs, and they could permanently change a young child's brain."

"Why do they give them?" Erick asked.

"Let's face it, every child who is removed from their family is upset, and some freak out more violently—at least on the outside—than others. But in this case, I bet the family just didn't want to deal with three young, hyper kids."

"Did they give them to you?" he asked.

"No. I was able to control my feelings by pretending I didn't have any." I grinned. "Worked for me. But lots of kids at The Children's Home took several pills at 'medication time.'"

"We'd better find out if this little one really needs them," Erick said.

While we were considering accepting Lillian's place-ment, the agency's therapist, Bonnie, called with the latest information. "It's quite the story," she said. "So the grandmother spends Sunday shopping with the three children and a family friend. A couple of times the grandmother runs into a store while the friend remains in the car with the children." She took a long, whistling breath. "When they return home, the grandmother unpacks the car and starts cooking. When she calls everyone for dinner, the friend doesn't show up. The oldest boy says she's still sleeping in the car. Grandma tells him to go get her. He comes back and says, 'She's blue.'"

"Blue?" I asked.

"As in D-E-A-D."

"The kids were driving around all day with a dead lady in the car?"

"Apparently she'd been gone a long time, and Grandma never noticed."

"That's a new one."

"Are you considering Lillian?"

"Tell me more about her medications."

"She has prescriptions for oppositional defiant disorder, attention deficit/hyperactive disorder, and a mood disorder. She's even on a blood pressure medication."

"And she's how old?"

"Two and a half."

"But all two-year-olds are defiant and hyper and moody!"

"We expect to wean her off all the meds to see what she's like on her own."

"Why did they prescribe them for her in the first place?"

Bonnie's voice was calm and soft. "The grandmother was overwhelmed by the three siblings, and so she complained to a doctor."

"It's like a psychiatric leash," I said.

"Exactly. If you turn them into zombies, they behave better."

"Speaking of drugs, I saw a note that said Lillian had overdosed. What is that about?"

"She swallowed some of her parents' pill-mill drugs." I gasped. "She was in a coma for a few days," Bonnie continued. "I think that's what precipitated the original move to her grandmother."

"I have a call in to my midwife to find out if I can care for a child with herpes during my pregnancy," I said. "I'll let you know after I talk to her."

My midwife, Darlean, hedged a bit. "If there is an outbreak, you'll need to wear rubber gloves for diaper changes," she said.

"Hopefully we can potty train her soon." Erick counted on his fingers. "I think we've trained four so far, or is it five?"

"Maybe I should put that on my campaign résumé!"

Within a few days of filing to run for the Florida senate, state-level party representatives scheduled a lunch with me. They talked about my competition. The current senator was Jack Latvala, a moderate Republican. "Have you heard the expression 'All politics is local'?" one of the party reps asked. "Start by making a list of everyone you know in the area, even if they aren't in your district. They will talk to their friends and associates who could vote for you."

"My Boy Scout network is huge," Erick said to them,

"not to mention Ashley is well known for her child welfare advocacy and often appears on television and radio."

Erick took over most of the logistics, while I concentrated on my classes, internship, and prenatal appointments. Erick's research brought some worrisome news. "No wonder nobody would run against Latvala," he said. "He runs a printing company that can turn out posters and political paraphernalia."

"Maybe I should hire him."

We both burst out laughing because of the absurdity of our undertaking. How naive we had been to think I could put together the network and funds needed to run for the mosquito control board, let alone the state senate.

The newspaper reported that Mr. Latvala had raised more than half a million dollars, while we had cobbled together a ludicrously small campaign fund. Since we couldn't compete with my worthy opponent's ability to blanket the district with signs, my friends moved around waving banners at various key locations at rush hour. Others volunteered to go door-to-door and talk me up. We had flyers at various events. Phil, who had made dozens of commercials for candidates from both parties—most of whom won their races—produced one for me.

I spoke at various functions and was solicited by a variety of sources wanting to be paid for their services. The most nerve-racking moment came when I had to be interviewed by the editorial board of the *Tampa Bay Times*. Their questions were tough, but I was prepared. They wrote an article that could have been far less flattering.

"I know what it's like to be impoverished, have lived the child welfare system, felt the impact of budget cuts. I've been able to experience firsthand what happens when we don't have legislative priorities in place," they quoted, and then told more about my background.

In the article Mr. Latvala called me "very bright." He also said that while foster care is "a very important issue . . . we've really got a plate full of big issues." Erick loved the article's last line and read it aloud. "'Asked why she didn't first try for a smaller post like school board, Rhodes-Courter joked that the senate is the natural next step for this former fifth-grade class president: "I wanted to jump in feet first. Go big or go home."'"

A transporter delivered Lillian at the exact time Sheila, our new agency's targeted case manager, had arranged a visit with us. Erick unbuckled Lillian's car seat and lifted her out. When he placed her on the ground, her knees buckled. She couldn't even put her limp arms around his neck, and so he carried her in a cradled position into our home and propped her on the corner of our couch.

"Is she ill?" I asked Sheila.

"No. She'll be fine in a minute."

"Does she have some other impairment?" Erick asked. Lillian was drooling like a much younger child.

"No, that's just her meds. I'll go over the weaning plan with you." Sheila went out to her car and found the child's stuffed kitty and tucked it under her arm. Then she came back and handed me some pharmacy bottles. "Discontinue these two immediately and cut back as per the list. She should be detoxed in two weeks."

"Will she go through any sort of withdrawal?"

"Hard to say. We don't have much experience in children this young on so many drugs."

I caught Erick's look of disgust.

By dinnertime, Lillian started to emerge from her zombie state, but she still needed to be spoon-fed. I bathed her while Erick made notations in a notebook about any marks or bruises. She was a beautiful child, with huge green eyes and straight straw-colored hair and bangs. "Normal bruised knees and a black-and-blue mark near her left elbow." I photographed them for reference. We both wore rubber gloves the first time we diapered her. She had a mild diaper rash—nothing we hadn't seen before—and a few spots that either were normal discoloration or from something that had healed. There were no fluid-filled or healing blisters.

"Doesn't look like she has herpes now," Erick said with relief. "How does a kid her age get herpes anyway?"

"I think babies can get it if their mother has an active case when she gives birth. That's one reason for C-sections," I said, having read about it in one of my pregnancy books.

That night we were too tired to read Lillian's paperwork. The next day, though, our innocence turned to horror.

I had woken up earlier than Erick. I made myself a nutritious smoothie, let the dogs out, and sat on the patio watching them frolic before tackling Lillian's thick file.

Two pages in I started to perspire. I almost woke Erick up but forced myself to get the full picture before I panicked. Besides having herpes, she had been diagnosed with a severe case of HPV—human papillomavirus, which she had acquired through sexual contact. I looked at the top of the page. This had been written by an intake caseworker. Maybe she had misunderstood something. I knew personally how often children were misdiagnosed or falsely labeled. I flipped to her medical paperwork and found a forensic report from the child protection team. There had been indications of sexual abuse at her six-month exam . . . she had been to the doctor for chronic bladder infections . . . sexual abuse noted again at one year. I began to quake. Why hadn't the agency warned us? The therapeutic agency's documents said nothing about sexual abuse, only the shock of the dead body and needing to wean her off her meds.

I hurried upstairs and lay down next to Erick, gasping. "What?" he asked as he roused. "You okay? The baby . . . ?"

"The little girl . . . Lillian . . . they didn't tell us . . . horrible sexual abuse . . . since infancy!"

"What the—?" He sat up abruptly. "We can't keep her."

"I know," I said. Here's the thing: Foster parents worried most about false allegations of sexual abuse. As a stay-at-home dad, Erick was already viewed suspiciously by some people, and as a well-known person in the child welfare field, I could be a target—and even more so now that I was running for office. Brian and Beth had just gone through an inquiry because a disturbed child accused his foster father of hitting him, even though the boy didn't have a bruise and his story kept changing. Eventually Brian was cleared, but he was put on suspension at his job, and the accusation itself remained on his permanent record.

"Her medical report says she had so many genital warts and blisters that her anus was 'unrecognizable.' Also that she had 'significant signs' of penetration."

Erick exhaled through the corner of his mouth. His face

was mottled with rage. "I don't know who could take better care of her than we could."

"You want to take the chance?"

We talked about the risk. "She's two," he said, "and doesn't have much language. I don't think she's going to make up wild stories."

"Yet."

"She probably won't be with us more than a few months anyway."

"We can talk about these issues with the agency," I said, "and then we can decide."

He reached over and kissed me.

"Hiya!" came a singsong voice. Lillian toddled into the room without the previous stumbling walk or flat tone. She reached her hands up for me to lift her onto our bed.

Erick looked over his shoulder at me. He was right. We were keeping her.

Having a little girl was different. Although foster parents were not supposed to cut their charges' hair, hers was so uneven and matted that I took her to the beauty parlor so her bangs were straight and her hair fell in a sleek bob. After so many boys, Gay and I shopped for cute clothes and found bargains at a local consignment boutique. Gay and Phil also treated me to some maternity clothes for my travels and the campaign.

While we were out shopping, I got a call from Luke, who only phoned when he had a problem. "What's wrong?" I asked reflexively.

"I'm in the hospital."

"Oh, Luke! Are you okay?"

"Yeah, sort of. Some asshole hit my motorcycle with his truck and almost got me killed. I broke my leg and my bike is ruined. But I have a lawyer who's going to sue the driver for everything the guy has."

"I'm sorry you're going through this. What hospital are you at?"

"Oh, I'm not sure. I gotta go."

He quickly hung up the phone. I took a long breath and realized I hadn't told him I was pregnant. My fingers hovered, ready to text him back, and then I stopped. Something about his story seemed odd. When I got home, I checked the county website for incarcerations and saw that Luke had been recently arrested for fleeing the scene of an accident, with property damage, driving on a suspended license, and various other charges over the last year. There was always some critical piece missing from Luke's wild stories. I couldn't understand why he was determined to stand in his own way and be his own worst enemy.

When Bonnie came for the first in-home therapy session, Lillian twirled into the room in her watermelon-colored pinafore dress and twinkle-toe sneakers, with Bella, the Chihuahua, following like a shadow.

"Hello, Ms. Bonnie," I said.

"Hello, Ms. Bonnie," Lillian echoed.

"She's a different child!" Bonnie enthused.

"Yes, she doesn't drool or mumble," I said. "Those drugs were poisoning her."

"I love her hair."

"Shampoo works wonders."

I left the therapist to work with Lillian and went outside to help Erick in our all-organic—after all my junk-food binging, Gay had laughed at *that*!—vegetable garden. Lillian knocked on the glass door to alert us to come back inside.

I gave Lillian a puzzle to work on in the playroom, while we joined the therapist to review our concerns. "First of all, we were told she has herpes, but the medical report says she is positive for HPV," I said. "If we had known this, we would have asked a lot more questions before accepting the placement. With the herpes, we were thinking maybe she contracted it at birth if the mother had an outbreak. But this kind of HPV is sexually transmitted."

"A female child with a history of sexual abuse is a problem for us," Erick said, glancing over to Lillian, who was saying "High five!" to Loki and hitting his raised paw.

"Why is that?" the therapist asked smoothly.

"Because it puts our family at risk for a false accusation," Erick responded bluntly.

"I'm on the road several times a month," I said, "which is one reason we've mostly fostered boys."

"Everything will be fine as long as we keep the lines of communication open between us," Bonnie said. "Your family has our full support."

"That's reassuring, but it only goes so far if this kid blames me for something or some doctor gets the wrong idea—" Erick's face blanched.

I reached over and held his hand. "Has there been a thorough investigation? What's happened to the perpetrator?"

Bonnie shrugged. "I honestly don't know, but I can get the rest of the case file, if that would help."

When Bonnie called us back a few days later, she confirmed that the original removal came after Lillian overdosed on her mother's medications. "At that time her two older brothers confirmed that they had been sexually abused and had seen Lillian abused by the same man—a frequent visitor to the mother's home," she said. "One of the brothers said, 'I saw Murph Buckles kissing my sister's privates.'"

"So did they lock him up and throw away the key?" I asked.

"The prosecutor is worried about 'jurisdictional issues,'" Bonnie said.

"Are you kidding me?"

"Also," she said in a whispery voice, "they are talking about revising the case plan from the placement with the grandmother to reunification with the mother."

At first I was too startled to reply. I flipped through Lillian's file on my lap. "Have you read through the report on their living conditions? It says, and I quote, 'All three children had impetigo with major lesions on their skin caused by the filth in the house.' Not only were they neglected, but they were also raped. I'm all for reunification, but does this sound like a place where she'll ever be safe? It's going to take a lot more than a piece of paper and a verbal agreement to protect this little girl—particularly with her perp on the loose!"

The second week Lillian was with us, I was scheduled to give a speech in the Florida Panhandle. It was a three-day weekend, and so we invited Penelope and Jasper to come along. Penelope's Girl Scout troop was going camping, but Jasper wanted to join us. He kept Lillian occupied on the eight-hour car trip with books and a magnetic drawing pad. Thankfully, she also napped for an hour or two.

Gulf Breeze is a small peninsula of land lined with a white beach that sparkles like diamonds. Jasper wanted to explore the Gulf Islands National Seashore. Erick was torn. "I don't think Lillian will last long in the sun," he said.

"I don't want to spend the whole day in the hotel," Jasper complained.

"This conference is filled with social workers," I said. "I'm sure I'll find someone willing to watch Lillian while I'm onstage."

When I went to the conference center for a microphone and audiovisual check, I asked how I could arrange for child care during my speech. One of the conference coordinator's assistants volunteered to watch Lillian.

"I'll be right outside that curtain, and when I stop talking, we'll get to go play for the rest of the day," I promised, handing Lillian a bag of books, toys, and snacks. "See you soon, Silly-Lilly!"

I waited in the wings for my introduction to be over and walked out to the podium. As I was wrapping up my remarks, I could hear Lillian backstage becoming restless. She cried out, "Mommy!" in a frantic voice.

"Mommy's coming right back," the babysitter whispered. She opened the curtain to let Lillian peek at me through the slit, thinking that if she saw me, she would quiet down.

Lillian broke loose. "Mommy!" She rushed toward me, arms reaching out.

I bent to calm her. She sighed with relief, turned slightly away from me, and faced an audience of hundreds of people. Without skipping a beat, she stepped forward, bowed, and said, "Thank you! Thank you!"

The audience erupted with laughter and applause. Lillian responded by clapping right back at them. The babysitter looked on helplessly. I waved her off. Lillian wasn't about to separate from her adoring audience or me. I pulled her back toward me and held her hand through the final words of my speech.

"People with no direct experience with foster youth have preconceived notions about who these children are." I then gave some examples about how many professionals had so few expectations of me. "Youth who have been abused or neglected feel worthless, so they are desperate for someone to believe in them. We just have to find ways to enhance their strengths." I mentioned the advocates who had made a difference in my life—teachers, counselors, and chiefly my volunteer Guardian ad Litem. "We need to make certain that every child is heard. We must encourage and empower the children we know in any capacity.

"I've also been a Guardian ad Litem—so I understand how complex and frustrating the legal system can be. I'm just completing my MSW, thus I have that clinical perspective." I pointed to Lillian.

"We should be working together to help every child like this one become their best selves and let them shine!" I clapped for Lillian. The spotlight on the stage created a halo atop her sleek hairdo; her cheeks were baby-doll pink and her eyes wide with the excitement of it all. It was an electric moment. I felt it. The audience felt it. And Lillian glowed.

13.

ours and theirs

> *It is easier to build strong children*
> *than to repair broken men.*
> —Frederick Douglass

In life you never know what will walk through the door; in foster care the same is true—only the surprises happen more often. We figured that the next two children who entered our home would be with us for a matter of weeks or months. We never imagined one would become ours forever.

Sheila called to say that Denver, age two, and Skyler, age four months, had been with an aunt for a few weeks, but she could not handle them and they needed to be moved quickly. "Only Denver needs therapeutic care," she said, "because his meltdowns are extreme. The baby is recovering from severe injuries but has an easy disposition."

"Any sexual abuse?"

"Thankfully, no."

I said I'd call her back because Lillian was being unusually oppositional that morning. She was trying to put on a dirty blouse that was in the laundry instead of the clean one I had selected.

"If there's anything I'm not in the mood for today," I griped to Erick, "it's two more toddlers!" At this stage of pregnancy, I had many annoying aches.

"What's their situation?" Erick asked.

"There's an injured baby and a freaked-out toddler." I pivoted my hips to take the strain off my back. "You know we're crazy, right? We have this election coming up, I have to finish my internship, get ready for finals"—I pointed to Lillian, who was trying to hide under the bed—"cope with that little gem"—I sucked in a long breath—"and in our spare time have this baby and figure out what to do with a newborn."

"It sounds impossible when you put it like that," Erick said. "But given that we can't change most of those things, what difference will two more kids make?" We cracked up. Lillian peeked out from under the bed and started laughing too.

"Maybe it's just for a few weeks," Erick said. "We can do anything for a few weeks."

The new boys arrived during an afternoon thundershower. Erick ran out with umbrellas to help get the boys inside.

I sat on the couch, and Erick slipped Skyler into my arms. I adjusted him around my baby bump. "He just got his body cast off," the worker said. "A therapist will teach you his stretching exercises."

"Body cast? On this tiny baby?"

Erick took Denver out to be introduced to the dogs so the caseworker and I could talk.

"The respite home was happy to keep the baby, but they thought Denver needed more services," Sheila said. "We didn't want to separate the brothers."

"So they were with their mother, then an aunt, then respite, and now us." I counted on my fingers.

"Really five placements if you include the hospitalization for Skyler."

"What's their legal situation?"

She exhaled a long breath. "The baby's father is in jail. We're hoping there's enough evidence to send him to prison for a long time. We haven't located Denver's father. The mother wasn't present when the guy tried to kill the kids, and so she has a case plan."

"What did he do?" I asked, bracing myself.

She closed her eyes. "It's best if you read the file."

Erick brought Denver inside. "Way to go, Denver!" he said. "This kid is a natural with dogs!" Denver gave a tentative grin and reached up for Erick to lift him again. As soon as he was up, he flailed to get down. "I've got to pick up Lillian from school," Erick said. "She's enjoyed being the queen bee and may not like competition."

"You two are brave," the caseworker said. "But I'm sure you'll be fine."

After she left, I put the drowsy baby into the portable crib in the living room. I tucked a blanket around him—not an easy feat, since my belly got in the way when I bent over. Skyler stirred slightly, then fell asleep with a gentle smile on his face. The idea that anyone, let alone his father, could purposefully injure something this precious was unfathomable.

I turned my attention to Denver, who looked like a wary squirrel caught in the middle of the street. When I moved slightly in his direction, he twitched backward and fell. Just like Tyson, he didn't cry, but slumped over in a heap and covered his face with his hands. I sank to the floor beside him and patted his bowed head. He flinched. Slowly sobs rose from somewhere deep inside. He cried in muted sniffs and gulps.

Interestingly, Lillian paid no attention to newcomers. It was as if they were stuffed animals that she had to negotiate around or over. She rarely spoke to them or commented about them to us. It was so peculiar that we decided to be very observant, because we feared she might try to undermine them in some way. Denver settled into the routine, and smiley Skyler reminded me of Lance and hardly ever cried. By the end of the week, we were a well-oiled machine. I laid out outfits the night before, and Erick did morning diapers and dressing while I made breakfast. Then he delivered all three to different sections of the same day care. We spent the rest of the day campaigning if I didn't have class or my internship. After school Lillian had her snack on a stool by the kitchen counter, Denver went into the high chair, and knowing he needed a strong maternal connection, I cuddled Skyler with his bottle. Amazingly, all three of them slept through the night. We congratulated ourselves on being able to manage this little brood so smoothly.

After the first week, I took out the brothers' stack of files. Erick was downstairs watching a Monty Python movie with Jasper, who was spending the weekend with us. The notes detailed that when Denver had been rescued, his face was bruised and bloody. He had been hit with a hard object, and there were so many wounds on his belly and back that he had received a CT scan for internal organ damage. Skyler's tibia—the strongest weight-bearing bone in the leg—had been snapped on purpose. I felt so queasy I had to lower my head.

From various accounts the story emerged. Tiffany, the boys' mother, was living with Daryl Archer, the man she named as Skyler's father. Daryl hated babysitting the boys. Tiffany had a job at an ice cream store, while he was unemployed. Tiffany's mother had promised to relieve Daryl by noon. It had been a broiling summer day, and their sardine can of a trailer sizzled on its sunny lot. There was no air-conditioning and little food in the house except beer, dry cereal, and the latest craze: Spice, also known as synthetic marijuana, which was legally available in convenience stores and was known to cause psychotic episodes. At some point Daryl flipped out. He beat Denver until he went quiet and went after Skyler when he started crying. Then he left.

Thinking about these boys being abandoned in the steamy trailer, hungry and in excruciating pain, triggered a crying jag. Erick overheard me and came rushing upstairs.

"You okay?" he asked.

I indicated the files strewn on our bed. "The grandmother was supposed to babysit but she was running late, so this—this monster beat the crap out of the kids, broke Skyler's leg, and left them alone to die." I handed him the report that said when Tiffany's mother arrived, the trailer was locked with the two unconscious children inside. By the time the authorities broke in, the air was fetid with garbage and dirty diapers and the temperature was almost 104 degrees. "The baby would definitely have perished in a few more hours," the doctor told Tiffany. Luckily, Denver's injuries were more superficial, although he was old enough to remember, as we would soon discover.

At first Lillian seemed to be free of any symptoms from her sexually transmitted diseases. Then one evening I noticed some odd pearly bumps on her buttocks when I dried her off after her bath, and so I took her to the doctor.

Lillian was sitting on the edge of the examining table, wearing her big-girl panties with ruffles and holding a doll. I spoke rapidly, using a cheerful voice to keep her from feeling anxious. "She's our *foster* daughter," I emphasized. We had never met this nurse, even though we had been in that medical office many times with several children.

"What brings you here today?" the nurse asked in a singsong voice.

"A new rash," I said. "It could be an STD."

The nurse gasped. "I know that's horrifying," I said, and I lowered my voice. "She was molested before she came to us."

The nurse rushed from the room with tears streaking her face.

Dr. Swanson appeared in her wake, and I showed her the bumps. "This is called molluscum," she said. "It will take awhile for this outbreak to clear."

"Is there any ointment or other treatment?"

"Sure," she said, writing out a script. "It won't really do much, but it might make her more comfortable and make her workers feel better."

A few months later Lillian sprouted lesions on her lips and inside her mouth. This time the doctor diagnosed an active case of herpes.

"I wonder if she was contagious before we noticed anything." I shuddered because I had let down my guard during my pregnancy.

"Just use infectious disease precautions," the doctor told me. "Your husband should put the medication on her lips wearing gloves and wash thoroughly afterward. You need to avoid all direct contact due to your advanced stage of pregnancy."

"What about the other children in our home?"

"Make sure they wash their hands regularly and try to keep them from touching each other."

Yeah, right, I thought, although we did our best. We gave Lillian her own "special" dishes, cups, and flatware. The dishwasher worked overtime to sterilize everything, including toys. We encouraged blowing kisses to show affection and say good-bye, and high fives to congratulate or relate happiness.

Lillian's Guardians ad Litem were a husband-and-wife team, Edna and Howard Daugherty, who were in their late seventies and worked in Pasco County, which was where she had originally been removed. We kept her home from preschool on the day of their monthly visit and met in a nearby restaurant. We arrived on time, but by the time the guardians showed up late, she was about to reach her toddler-in-public limit. I pulled some toys out of my purse to add a little time to the meter.

"How are her brothers doing?" I asked Edna.

"We're hoping to get all the kids back to Mom, starting with the brothers."

"Really? We were told they were very disturbed," Erick said.

Lillian stuck out her tongue and started chirping like a wounded bird. "Hi, cutie," Edna said to her. She turned to me. "We are lucky to have such sweet kids on our first case."

"The caseworker told us that her mother is living with a new boyfriend who has three children and a felony domestic violence charge for choking a woman, so how can that be a safe place for Lillian?" I asked.

"We're hoping he learned his lesson," Howard said.

I dropped my fork with a clatter. "So you plan to put all these kids back together and see what happens?"

Lillian had touched my heart in a different way than Albert or Lance. I saw some of myself in her girlish ways—spinning in a dress, making faces in a mirror, and talking to her dolls. As a woman I took the nature of her abuse as a personal assault and had a visceral reaction anytime I thought about her perpetrator. I worried how this would affect the rest of her life. Had she been young enough to forget it entirely, or would it be a dark shadow she couldn't quite shake—or even define? With a few of our foster children, Erick and I had "the moment" when we asked each other, "If they were available, would we keep them?" The answer for Albert had been a resounding "Yes!" For a long time we had come to believe Lance would remain with us until a mystery aunt was presented in the final hour. All the others—until Lillian—were too temporary or had positive placements to move on to. What about her?

First, she had two brothers. We had met them several times during court-ordered sibling visits and realized they were very angry, disturbed, and not only had been abused but acted out on each other; therefore they had to remain in separate foster placements until they had been stabilized. They had also been cruel to Lillian. And yet the long-term plan was for them to be reunited with their dysfunctional mother, who hadn't protected them in the first place.

During a staffing, she admitted that she knew about the sexual abuse but didn't think it was a "big deal." Now the mother had chosen another dangerous partner with a violent felony record who had three kids of his own. Didn't anyone else see the danger behind this twisted *Brady Bunch* scenario?

My old foster child defense system—turning off my feelings—failed me when it came to worrying about children in my care, and my inner mother tiger tensed to pounce if I could identify the target.

It took far too long for the guardians to order their food. Lillian started squirming, and I took her to the bathroom. She refused to get back into her booster seat.

"Would you like some ice cream?" Edna asked. The guardian should have checked with us first, but we let it slide. "I wanted you to know that we're recommending the court reunify with the grandmother first," she said.

I snapped, "This is the same woman who left the children in a car with a *dead* person?"

"That was an isolated incident," Edna answered.

"The long-term goal remains reunification with the mother," Howard added.

"Where's my ice cream?" Lillian cried out.

Edna looked around for the server. "Just a moment, hon."

"You know what?" Lillian blurted.

"What, honey?" Edna asked.

"My daddy hurt me."

My mouth gaped. "Lillian, where did your daddy hurt you?" I asked.

She pointed directly between her legs. Both guardians shot daggers at Erick.

Edna turned to her husband. "We are going to have to call this in as an abuse report to the hotline."

"You do understand her prior history?" I said carefully just as the ice cream arrived.

Lillian had play therapy with Bonnie. Last week Bonnie reported that Lillian had undressed an anatomically correct doll and poked a toy screwdriver between its legs. I had gone to a staffing the next day with Bonnie and Lillian's mother. When the therapist described this behavior, her mother said, "Oh, she's been inserting things in herself since she was a baby." At that, I had to excuse myself from the meeting and get some fresh air.

Lillian started to pitch her ice cream spoon across the table, but Erick was a split second ahead of her and caught it. She kicked. He stood and lifted her from the booster seat. "It might be time for us to be on our way. I'll put her in the car seat."

Later that evening Edna e-mailed me a copy of what she'd sent her case coordinator and what she'd called into the abuse hotline. She had put "Daddy touched me" in quotes without any discussion about which daddy that might be, and she didn't even quote Lillian correctly. All abuse reports go to a central hotline, which prioritizes them before passing them down to local investigators. Panic suffused my body, and even my baby began to kick wildly inside me. Would the next knock on our door be an ignorant bully of a worker who would try to nail my gentle husband for hurting this traumatized child?

Even though it was late, I phoned Edna. "I just got your e-mail," I said in as steady a voice as I could manage. "You need to clarify that Lillian was not referring to Erick."

"Oh, well, I'm sure they'll find that's the case," she said.

"Mrs. Daugherty!" I said shrilly. "This little girl came to us with several sexually transmitted diseases, and she had been living with a child molester who also abused her brothers. You should have made that clear in your report. Someone new to the case isn't going to know these important details and may suspect my husband. You have to call the hotline back and leave no room for speculation."

I took a long breath. "Further, Edna, this is precisely the reason we have been wary of parenting sexually abused children. We agreed to take Lillian before those facts were known. But the minute someone shows up to investigate us because of irresponsible reporting, they will have to find her another placement."

"But why? You are so wonderful with her. We wouldn't want her moved from your home."

My voice was stern. "I realize you are new guardians, but a report like this can ruin someone's life."

"Yes, of course," she backpedaled. "I didn't mean to implicate your husband."

Thankfully, we were not involved in the police investigation that took place after these allegations. Bonnie confirmed that the child had been placed in our home because of prior abuse. The brothers gave the most graphic descriptions of what at least two men—Murph and someone named Roddy—had done to them and Lillian. The boys described pornography tapes they had watched as well as seeing their parents, grandmother, and other adults in sexual situations. The investigators said Lillian couldn't speak well enough to get a solid statement, so they dropped the case in a few days. After that, Erick and I became more insistent that if a foster child wanted to call us "Mommy" or "Daddy" that we were to be "Mommy Ashley" and "Daddy Erick" to separate ourselves from their parents.

When we learned the sexual abuse case was not going to be prosecuted, I tossed a dishcloth across the room and clutched my swollen abdomen. "The boys named the guys who did it, and they get to walk free because the different county departments can't figure out who should take it on. They jail people for possessing pot or for shoplifting, but not for ruining a child's life!" I fumed.

My schedule was busier than ever—balancing school, my trips for speeches, as well as campaign-related events. My friend Nikki was going to babysit one Sunday while Erick and I attended a political forum. She texted us to say she thought Lillian was running a fever. We came right home and found she had a slight temperature. We gave her a dose of a children's fever reducer and she popped up ready for school Monday morning. At noon her school phoned as I was packing for a flight to California the following day. "Something's wrong," her teacher said. "Lillian's doubled over like a little old lady."

I took her directly to the pediatrician's office. The nurse said she needed a urine sample to test for a bladder infection. Lillian refused to pee or drink water or juice. "I'll do it at home where she's more relaxed," I said.

"That won't be acceptable," the nurse said.

I insisted on taking one of their sterile jars anyway, since it was time to get the other children. "I also want to see the doctor before I go."

Dr. Swanson gave me less than a minute of her time. "With little girls that age, she most likely has a bladder infection or constipation, but we can't give her medication without a sample. We can do a swab for strep throat."

"Look at how she's standing." I reached for Lillian's hand and pulled her toward me. She was bent doubled over like a pretzel. "Stand up tall, sweetie," I said.

I pulled her shoulders back gently. "No!" she screeched.

"Could it be something else?" I asked.

"I can't do anything without a urine sample," she said.

We managed to get a trickle of urine at home, which I delivered to the doctor on my way to the airport the next morning. When Erick called for the result, the nurse said there hadn't been enough to test.

I texted Erick for an update as my plane taxied to the gate at my connecting airport. Erick called right back. "She's much worse. She can barely stand up."

"This can't wait until I get home; take her to the hospital!" I shouted when he picked up the phone as I changed gates. The message waiting for me when I landed at my destination read: *Lil needs surgery; ruptured appendix.*

I began to weep. Poor, poor baby! Less than three and she had been through more suffering than most adults I knew. I phoned Erick. "Within an hour of getting to the ER, they diagnosed a perforated appendix," he reported. "She had surgery to clean out the abscesses and infection in her belly."

"Did they take out the appendix?"

"No. They want her to have antibiotics for a few weeks first."

"You mean another surgery?"

"Yes. If Dr. Swanson had done a blood test, she could have had a simple laparoscopic procedure."

"Could she have died?" I asked with a quavering voice.

"I don't know, but she was filled with pus and she was in critical condition."

"I feel like the doctors at that practice treat our foster kids like second-class citizens."

"Oh, that's not even the worst part," Erick added sarcastically. "There was a huge problem about getting permission for surgery. They wouldn't let me sign, and I couldn't reach her case manager. Technically, only a parent or a judge can consent, but this was an emergency."

"So what did you do?"

"I called Maya and they faxed some paperwork back and forth that will cover it for now."

"You should have just said you were the father and asked for forgiveness later."

"I was almost at that point."

As we talked out the issues, we both calmed down. I wished I weren't on the other side of the country, leaving Erick with one child hospitalized and two more at home.

"Got it covered," Erick said, and explained his plan. "I'm going home as soon as I know she's stable. My parents are at the house with the boys. Then Nikki is going to spend the night in case I have to go back to the hospital." He paused. "Thank goodness we have friends who are background-checked babysitters."

Erick was spending all day at Lillian's bedside and taking care of the boys before and after school until I returned from my speaking trip.

Erick had deep bags under his eyes and a scruffy face.

"Can't sleep well when you're not here," he said.

"I'll go to the hospital in the morning," I said, "and you can sleep in."

I brought Lillian a balloon bouquet. After playing with it for a few seconds, she looked around. "Where's Daddy Erick?"

Every nurse who came into her room looked crestfallen to see me instead of Erick. "Your husband has been a saint," the charge nurse said. "He reads to her all day long and will do anything she wants, because she needs to keep that IV in."

"He's the best."

"You have no idea! We figured he was her father, but when we heard he's only the foster dad—well, nobody can get over it. Half the time we don't even see real parents here for more than an hour a day."

She looked at my large belly. "Lillian has done best sitting on your husband's lap, but I don't see how your condition will allow that," she said sympathetically. "Otherwise she has to stay in bed and not jump around or she'll dislodge the IV."

"I'll do my best," I said.

After I read her two books, Lillian kicked the blankets into knots. She pointed to my phone on the bureau. "Call Daddy Erick!" she demanded.

"He's busy," I said, determined to give him a break. But tending Lillian at bedside hurt my back. I had a condition of pregnancy called severe symphysis pubis dysfunction, which gave me chronic pain in my pelvis. After two hours, I knew I had to go home and lie down. I decided that Lillian— and the nurses—would be happier if Erick came back.

14.

losing and winning

Once you bring life into the world, you must protect it.
We must protect it by changing the world.
—*Elie Weisel*

As November approached, I wondered which would come first: the election or the baby. He was due only two days after the election, so we did absentee voting just in case.

"I just don't want to be embarrassed by the election results," I said. "Latvala's last opponent got only thirty-six percent. If do better than that, I'll be happy."

On election night I was transfixed as my numbers jumped from 50,000 votes to 75,000 in an hour. Jack Latvala was still ahead, but the margin wasn't substantial. More worrisome was the cramping in my back. Could this be the start of labor?

When "Final Results" flashed in green on the television, I had 93,296 votes! That was a huge amount considering my opponent's wealth and status. I had a solid 42 percent of the votes—far more than anyone had imagined. Friends and family called in congratulations. Yes, I had lost, but I proved that I could be a contender. The next time I run for office, I could win!

Erick and I both wanted as natural a birth as possible. We found a local medical group with two midwives who work in conjunction with two obstetricians. One of them—Darlean—had studied under our family friend Ruth Wilf at the Frontier Nursing University.

We had done a lot of reading and watched documentaries on birth; however, between my classes, travels, the foster children, and the election, we had not been able to squeeze in childbirth classes. In the last weeks we found a local doula to give us a "crash course" at home. Our plan was to stay home as long as possible, because the hospital was only fifteen minutes away.

I had a scheduled checkup one day after my due date. I had gained only thirty pounds during my pregnancy thanks to my LAP-BAND, but one of the other doctors had worried that my belly was measuring too small. Darlean listened to our little boy's heart. "He sounds fine, but let's get an ultrasound."

Darlean watched the screen carefully. "Is he okay?"

"Yes, but I want Dr. Reyes to check something."

I could see the baby moving; therefore, I tried not to panic. Darlean came back after consulting with Dr. Reyes, and she helped me sit up on the ultrasound table. "You know we've been monitoring the amniotic fluid," he said. "Today there's almost no amniotic fluid in the pockets around the baby."

Darlean rubbed my back. "That means you are going to have your baby today."

"But—" I was taken completely off guard. This was

supposed to be a routine checkup, and Erick wasn't even with me. "I'm not ready. I haven't made plans for my other children."

"I don't want to scare you unnecessarily," she said, "but oligohydramnios—the technical term for this condition—requires immediate delivery. You need to go to the hospital right away."

"Does this mean I'm having a C-section?" I asked with a tremulous voice.

"Not necessarily, but we will need to induce you."

"Do I have time to go home first?" I asked. "I need to pack and make arrangements for our foster children."

"We really would prefer for you to go straight from here to the hospital, and I'll meet you there," Darlean said.

I stayed around for a few more instructions, which I barely heard. I felt like I had come to swim a few laps in a gentle pool but found myself pulled out to sea by an undertow that I couldn't overcome.

The minute I got out of the elevator, I called Gay. "I'm having the baby today!" I started to sob. Gay and Phil had been part of the natural childbirth movement in the 1970s and had produced a series of films on birth and breastfeeding. Gay had attended many births and even delivered a few babies, and so I was counting on having her by my side during labor and delivery.

"Are you in labor?" she asked.

"No! It's low amniotic fluid . . . they said the baby has to be born today . . . or something bad could happen to him!"

"Hold on, honey. If that were true, you would be in an

ambulance. Let me get Ruth's opinion. Meanwhile, go home and get ready to go just in case."

"Really?" I asked timidly. "I haven't even shaved my legs!"

"Do whatever you have to do. Phil and I will meet you at the hospital."

I rushed home and filled Erick in. We contacted his parents and our standby babysitters, who could stay at our house over the next few days. Once we knew our foster kids had coverage and our bags were packed, we headed to the hospital.

"What did Ruth say?" I asked Gay the minute she walked into my birthing suite.

"Not to panic. You don't have any other risk factors and you are full term at forty weeks. It's a more problematic issue when you're overdue."

"I don't know what to do," I muttered just as Darlean arrived.

"We had a meeting after you left," Darlean said. "I told the doctor how much you wanted a natural birth." She told me about a stress test to check on the baby before a final decision, and then left the room to write up the orders.

"I wanted to labor at home," I said mournfully to Erick.

He looked around at the birthing suite. "At least this place is probably quieter than our house."

The room was huge, with a view over the bay. There was a sofa bed and comfortable chairs for family members, and a private bath.

Gay pulled back a curtain. "Ta-da!"

"Oh!" Tears flowed when I saw the baby's station and bassinet.

A nurse came into the room and handed me a gown. "When you are ready, get in bed, and I'll get you prepped."

Showtime, I thought wryly, with the worst case of stage fright I'd ever experienced.

Erick was busy on the phone, organizing his parents to pick up the foster children and the three friends who had volunteered to stay days or nights while I was in the hospital. Luckily, it was a Friday, and everyone was available that weekend.

"You okay, honey?" Phil asked.

"It's weird to be lying in a hospital bed when I feel fine."

"I know you're disappointed," Gay said.

"I feel everything is out of my control—and you know how much I hate that!"

"What else is worrying you?"

"All the books say induction is the slippery slope that leads to cesareans."

Gay was uncharacteristically silent for a few beats. "I know many of your friends have had cesareans after scheduling inductions for convenience, but this situation is different."

Darlean came in and checked that the monitors and IV were in place. "I'm going to give you something to ripen your cervix gradually." The next part was slightly uncomfortable. "You probably won't go into labor for about twelve hours." I looked at the large clock on the opposite wall. It was just past two in the afternoon.

After an hour, I vented. "I hate lying here attached to all these machines. I feel like a corpse waiting to be dissected!"

"Sorry, babe," Erick said.

"Whoa!" I called out. "Is this a contraction?"

"What does it feel like?" Erick asked.

"Like pain!"

"The doula said it would be like a wave that builds up and then tapers off. Is that it?"

I gulped. "No! More like being stabbed with a—"

"Don't hold your breath," Erick said, trying to remember the instructions.

I took a long breath. "That's another one."

"I thought you were supposed to have more of a break," Erick said, more to Gay than to me.

"There's a blip on the monitor," Phil said to prove something was really happening.

The guys watched the screen while Gay tried to get me into a more comfortable position. Another contraction tumbled over me five minutes later.

At four the nurse came to check my progress. I knew my cervix eventually had to dilate to ten centimeters. "You're at four," the nurse reported. "That's really an excellent start. How's the pain?"

"Manageable."

"Good job!" I felt like a teacher had just commended me. Two hours later, though, my tolerable contractions turned into cramps that were so torturous I would have confessed to anything to have them end.

Erick attempted massages and coached my breathing. Gay handed him an orange. "The aroma of citrus is supposed to help with pain," she said.

I knocked it out of his hand. "Shove it up your nose." Erick had the nerve to laugh. "Not funny!" I gasped.

"The contraction's almost over," he said.

"No, it isn't!"

"Does this help?" He rubbed my lower back.

"No, no!"

Darlean arrived. "Let me check you," she said softly.

I panted and clutched the sheet through the exam.

"Good progress. You're already five centimeters."

"I—can't—catch—a—break. Nothing is helping! I want an epidural!" I said as the pain started to crest again.

Erick was rubbing my shoulders. "You said you didn't want one."

"How did I know what it was going to be like?" I murmured.

"But—" I had told him to stand firm if I caved, mostly because I had been terrified of the long needle in my back. I'd never, however, imagined such intense, excruciating, continuous pain.

"So, shall I call for an anesthesiologist?" Darlean asked.

"Yes!" I no longer cared whether anyone thought I had wimped out; I couldn't take this pain, which felt like I was being torn internally and never eased completely.

The prick of the needle—two, actually, because the first did not numb one side of my body—was nothing compared to the searing contractions.

"It's magical," I sighed, when moments later the agony completely subsided.

Darlean turned down the lights. "Okay, Ashley, try to get some rest." She turned to Erick and pointed to the sofa. "There are pillows and blankets in the closet."

Gay and Phil met Erick's parents, Sharon and Rob, in the waiting room. Jasper and Penelope were also standing by. The Smiths tiptoed in to see me. I was just stirring. They wished me well and ducked out again. The hospital had a rule that only two people—not including the father—could be in the room simultaneously, so Gay and Phil came back in.

"You're doing great, hon," Gay said.

"Do you want something cool to sip?" Erick asked.

"Are there any of those ice chips left?"

"I'll get some from the nurse," he said before leaving the room.

Just after he departed, a nurse came in to check on my progress. "Oh goodness, you're ready to push!" she cried.

"Phil, get Erick!" Gay said.

A lot seemed to happen at once. Lights flicked on, the bed was repositioned, and all sorts of equipment—including the baby bassinet—was rolled near me. Darlean made an adjustment to reduce the epidural medication, and suddenly I felt a long, tumbling wave rolling through me.

Phil was stationed at my head to film the birth. Erick was on the other side, supporting me. Gay was helping me keep my legs in position.

"Anyone else you want in the room?" Darlean asked.

"We are already at the limit," Erick said.

"I'm the boss now," she said with a laugh. "You want us to get *your* mother from out there?"

"Ash?" he asked.

I nodded. "That'd be great," I said.

I tried to follow the instructions to push, but apparently I wasn't making enough progress. Darlean insisted I get into various positions to help move the baby down. More people were called, including someone for the baby and Dr. Reyes, who I later learned had been standing by in case I needed an emergency cesarean. A nurse put me on oxygen. Darlean helped me turn on my side and Dr. Reyes used his skill to help the baby get into position. Then Darlean took over for the delivery.

I didn't care who was in the room or that Gay and my mother-in-law were holding my legs up or that Phil was filming or that the machines were pinging. Suddenly Sharon, who is usually reserved and quiet, shouted, "There he is! There he is!"

The baby . . . almost there . . . A wave of energy coursed through my body as I pressed down with all my might.

"Look, Ashley," Darlean said. She lifted our son onto my chest. Erick reached around to steady the baby. Phil filmed his first breaths.

Erick kissed me. "Ethan, right?"

"Yes. Ethan Philip Smith. And he's just perfect."

15.

breaking bonds

There are only two lasting bequests we can hope to give our children. One of these is roots, the other, wings.
—Johann Wolfgang von Goethe

The morning after Ethan was born, Erick texted Lorraine and told her she was welcome to visit that afternoon. Gay and Phil arrived early and spent some time holding Ethan and taking pictures of our new family.

"I didn't expect to still be so sore after the delivery," I confessed to Gay. "I have shooting pains when I move, and I can't sit easily."

"Sounds like you may have broken your tailbone," Gay said. "It happens to some women."

When Darlean came in to check me, she agreed it could be a possibility and prescribed some medication that I could take while breastfeeding.

Then Josh and Giulia arrived to cuddle their first nephew.

"Everything will go better if I'm not here when Lorraine is," Gay said, grabbing the backpack she used as a purse. "I intimidate her."

"You intimidate most people," Josh said with a grin.

I took a nap while Erick called more friends and family. Giulia saw Lorraine and Autumn coming down the hall and stopped them at my door. "Ashley's resting. Let's go have a coffee until she wakes up."

"I can't wait to tell Ashley how well I've been doing," Lorraine said. "I've been sober for a year this month—today's my anniversary, actually—and now I'm a leader in my Alcoholics Anonymous group."

Giulia congratulated her on her achievement.

"When do you think I can see Ashley? We left a new puppy at home."

"I got him for my birthday!" Autumn crowed. "I'll be thirteen next week."

"And now you're also an aunt for the first time, just like me," Giulia replied to her.

Josh cracked open the door to see if I was awake and then signaled for Lorraine and Autumn to come in. Autumn carried a huge stuffed animal that was longer than my hospital bed, and Lorraine gave me a gift bag, which held a Harley-Davidson onesie and matching cap.

"Aw!" I said. "His first biker 'gear.'"

"Aw!" Lorraine mimicked, but more sarcastically. "Is it too redneck for you?"

"No, it's really cute," I said, but she still seemed annoyed. She mistook my physical discomfort for a lack of interest.

Lorraine held Ethan. "He looks like a Rhodes."

"Can I have a turn?" Autumn asked.

"I don't think that's a good—" Lorraine started.

"Just sit in a chair," Erick said kindly. "I'll hand him to you."

Autumn glowed as she stared down at her nephew.

"Well," Lorraine said, "I was worried because she can be clumsy. Besides," she continued, "we have to get back to your puppy."

Autumn handed Ethan to Erick.

Lorraine hovered over the transfer. "He's so beautiful!" Tears welled up in her eyes. "I never thought I would be lucky enough to see this," she said. "I'm sorry I made so many mistakes." She reached for her purse. "Is it okay if I take a few pictures for the family?"

Erick said, "Sure, but please don't post them on any social media sites."

"Whatever you say."

When she left, I said, "That came off better than I expected."

"She looked like she's doing well, don't you think?"

"Hard to know for sure," I said. "I don't see or hear from her enough to tell."

The media thought that the confluence of my due date and Election Day made for good copy, so many articles about me mentioned my pregnancy. Luke might have also seen a post on the Internet that the baby had arrived, and he called while we were still at the hospital.

"Hey, what's new?" he asked.

"You're an uncle."

"Yeah, cool. I'm going to vote for you, and I can pay other people to vote for you."

"That's not legal," I told him, "and the election is over."

I started to tell him the baby's name, but he cut me off. "You should have told me about the election sooner, because I could have paid for your whole campaign." Then he said, "Oh, gotta go!" and hung up.

When I got off the phone, I told Erick about the disappointing conversation. "Well, don't worry," Erick said. "Our son has plenty of family on all sides to balance the scales."

Ethan Philip was both our first and our thirteenth child. We had briefly provided respite for other foster children, and we thought we knew everything about babies—but discovered we knew nothing. Plus, we had underestimated how much more time this "homemade" baby would take. We had parented three infants—Lance, Dakota, and Skyler—but we were able to get them sleeping through most of the night shortly after they arrived. Ethan was up every two hours and sometimes more frequently. Nursing didn't come naturally to either of us, and so I ended up with an exhaustive pumping schedule. All the complaints doctors said would go away after birth still remained. My fractured tailbone hurt whether I was sitting or lying down, and my postpartum hormones allowed me to indulge in a pity party. Still, while I bemoaned my physical aches and pains, I was also thrilled at Ethan's every burp or smile.

Breastfeeding was important to me. Gay had breastfed both her sons, and Erick's mother also nursed her four children. I knew this was the healthiest, most natural food and that it held endless benefits for the baby and me.

Ethan, though, had not read the memo on what he was supposed to do and refused—and I do mean adamantly refused—to latch on. Was it possible my baby was rejecting me, or was I doing something wrong? Early on, nurses came in and out of my postpartum room, each with their own set of instructions. The lactation specialist was called, but Ethan didn't appreciate her prodding. I was hooked up to a breast pump, because the sooner my real milk arrived, the more interested the baby would be. In the meantime, he was given a bottle with what little I did produce.

Just after a late dinner, a nurse came in and claimed our insurance was only giving us a few more hours before we had to be discharged. Since Ethan wasn't "feeding," they said I would have to give him a bottle of formula or face leaving my baby behind. I begged the lactation specialist to rent us the hospital-grade breast pump, but she said she didn't want to do the paperwork. I called Erick's mother, and Sharon somehow found a place to buy a good pump at that late hour. I was overcome with gratefulness for having his parents in my life. Most people don't know the feeling of thinking you are never going to have anyone to permanently love or support you. It is because of this that I appreciate the tiniest gestures.

Gay told me that Blake, her older son, refused to nurse for the first five days. Her pediatrician sister, Robin, reminded me that her first son also was a slow starter. Plus, she talked about the myriad of patients she counsels on breastfeeding and encouraged me to continue. I called La Leche League, but nothing they suggested worked. I found a private lactation specialist, who also could not get the youngest member of our team to do his part.

There were times when I had two or three women manipulating my baby and breasts at the same time. I remember once when Erick came into the room, he wasn't sure where he should or shouldn't look. All the massaging and pressing was embarrassing for someone like me, who is very private about her body. Growing up with so many strangers in foster care made me very modest. I also realized one reason why I didn't know a single other former foster child who had breastfed their babies: You don't end up in placement unless you've been severely abused or neglected, and some of those women had endured sexual abuse. Now I saw how exposed you feel during childbirth, postpartum, and breastfeeding and could understand that any of these situations could cause these women post-traumatic stress.

"Erick," I shouted one afternoon. He came running at the sound of my terrified voice. "My breasts are bleeding!" The pump was not as gentle as a baby, and I have the classic redhead's fragile skin.

He brought ice packs and sympathy. "Babe, you don't have to put yourself through this," he said. "We've given formula to all the other babies and they've thrived."

"I want to do this for Ethan. I need to."

"Then how can I help?"

I never stopped trying to interest Ethan in the breast, and I will never know exactly why he rejected my attempts adamantly each time.

Still, I determined he would only have my milk for as long as possible, and it turned out I was an excellent source of dairy. I produced so much milk that we had to buy an extra freezer just to store it all. With the excess, I contemplated sharing it with babies who needed milk, but I found that many milk-sharing programs are complicated and controversial. Ethan was also consuming more and more, and I did not want to deprive him of a single precious drop that I worked so hard to produce.

Trying to breastfeed was one of the most emotionally painful and anxiety-producing experiences of my life. Travel made my commitment to nursing even harder. I had to go through additional security lines to have my stored milk and pumping equipment examined. Delays in the air or in traffic that ruined my pumping schedule caused physical pain and embarrassing leaks. Airport and hotel bathrooms are not set up for pumping or nursing women, but I had no other choice. And those after-speech huggers! I couldn't push them away, but I cringed when they pressed against my hard, swollen chest and I prayed that I—and they—would stay dry.

Because I still couldn't sit comfortably enough to drive, Erick did the transporting. Ethan was home with us, and the boys went to one day care near our house. After Lillian was expelled for biting, she had to be taken to a therapeutic in-home provider twenty minutes away.

The school also threatened to expel Denver, who didn't hurt other children, but was sometimes impossible to soothe. One moment he would be playing happily, and then darkness descended like an eclipse and his features crumpled. Overwhelmed by whatever memories or feelings flashed through his mind, he would fall to the floor in a heap. This was not a tantrum brought on because he wasn't getting his way, and no amount of cajoling or kindness helped. I thought it was more like an emotional seizure that had to take its course.

"I think he remembers the day he was hurt," I said to his therapist, who had never witnessed the meltdowns. "You can see the fear in his face."

Tiffany didn't know who had fathered Denver. There were many men tested, but Jude—who never even knew Tiffany had had a baby—won the DNA lottery.

"I was already with someone else when I found out I was pregnant," Tiffany complained. "I assumed the baby wasn't his."

Jude turned out to be a nice guy with a clean record. "I want to do the right thing," he told the agency. He lived with his parents and was caring for an eight-year-old son from another relationship.

After a few visits, he asked us about Denver's bizarre behavior. "It's like one minute he's happy and the next someone Tasered him. Why does he fall and cry and act like a monster's attacking him?" Jude asked. "I don't know what to do."

"What have you tried so far?" I asked.

"I just sit down next to him so he knows he isn't alone."

"That's what we do. You can't force him to stop, but eventually he does."

"I guess that's just what happens during the terrible twos. My mother says he'll outgrow it."

Because Jude and his older son lived with his parents, and all the supervising workers said they were supportive, we encouraged Denver's case manager to let him move in with his father as soon as possible. State law requires six months of follow-up; so we knew they both would get additional counseling. We were sorry to split the brothers and agreed to facilitate visits, since Denver's father did not feel like he could handle both boys on top of his other son.

November had been a momentous month. First came the election, then Ethan's arrival, followed by Erick's thirty-first birthday a few days later. We introduced Ethan to everyone at a large Thanksgiving feast with the Smiths and the Courters in Crystal River. I also had to finish all the coursework and papers for my MSW. I officially graduated in December but was asked to give a speech to my graduating class in Los Angeles in May. By New Year's, Denver had moved in full-time with his father.

We had been concerned about Lillian's reaction to Ethan, but she was never curious about where this baby came from, and she never approached him, talked about him, or wanted to touch him—which was just as well. Because we were never sure when or if she was going to have an infectious outbreak, we considered her disinterest a blessing.

Lillian always returned from day care ravenous. She couldn't wait to jump on the stool at our kitchen counter and munch the treats I had waiting. One afternoon she was chewing cheese and whole-wheat crackers. When she finished, I removed her bowl to exchange it for her dinner plate. This set her off like a screaming firework. She manically kicked her legs and went flying off the stool onto the tile floor. Erick had heard the crash and came running. "Is everyone okay?"

"Whoa!" Lillian said. Erick kissed her head. I came out from the kitchen and brushed her off. She was laughing because Loki was licking crumbs of cracker off her fingers. She climbed back onto the stool, and I handed her another slice of cheese. Though she was acting fine, as a precaution I called my aunt Robin to ask for a concussion checklist just to be safe.

The next morning she woke up with a huge bump over her left eyebrow. I followed procedure and photographed her from several angles and then wrote up an incident report to all parties to the case. When we took her to school, we told them what had happened.

"It was just a matter of time before she hurt herself with one of those tantrums," her teacher said.

By the following day, the bump had drained, resulting in a black eye. The day after that the bruising blossomed across her nose and darkened the other eye as well. We kept everyone informed, and the workers simply said they appreciated the updates.

But then, later in the week, police and our agency director, Maya, were waiting for us in our driveway as we returned from picking up all the kids from their various schools. Two patrol cars idled with lights twirling at the end of our short street. I wondered what our neighbors—one a pastor and one a retired teacher—would think was going on.

"Lillian had a visit with her mother and grandmother today," Erick said, rolling his eyes as we got out of the car. "They are so hostile. I almost expected something like this."

"Hi, Erick and Ashley," Maya said with false cheer. "I wanted to be here for you, since we were notified that an abuse report had been called in for Lillian."

"We sent everyone documentation and photos days ago, and no one has said anything to us," I said stiffly.

"I know, but the reporter claims that when Lillian was asked what happened, she said, 'Mommy Ashley pushed me.'"

After the questioning by forensics, the police, and child protection investigators, my anxiety went from zero to a hundred, as if someone had hit a strongman tester at a carnival. When the house finally cleared, I fell backward on our bed. Ethan was snoozing in the mini-crib nearby. If they believed I was guilty of child abuse, they could remove not only Lillian and Skyler but Ethan as well.

My head pounded with the possibilities. I knew how the system worked. The more I protested, the more they would believe the child. I tried to calm down and think my way out of this web.

"I should take Ethan to my parents' house," Erick said.

"They claimed Lillian walked them through the incident and pretended to fall off the stool and bounce right up. She didn't mention my name once. So unless someone wants to blow this up, it should fade away. The investigator said we didn't have anything to worry about."

I tried to believe my own words, but my anxiety continued to escalate. I felt my face flushing with nervous heat as I recalled being awoken in foster care and questioned by a policeman. How could the Mosses get away with obvious child abuse while Erick and I were being put through hell when we were utterly innocent?

I had a flash of clarity and doubt: Was I dooming myself to relive my life over and over by staying in the system one way or another? Maybe it was time to close that door and lead a nice, normal life with my husband and baby.

When Maya called it was as if she had read my mind. "There have been changes to Lillian's case plan," she said. "The judge wants all the children reunified with the mother."

"But she didn't protect any of them," I said in shock.

"The oldest boy is already with her, and Lillian is going to be placed with her younger brother."

"B-but," I sputtered, "I thought the brother was even more severely disturbed than she is."

Even though I felt the weight of responsibility for her was being lifted, I was appalled about her being back with the same parent who let her get molested. "Isn't there another solution?" I asked weakly.

"I know how you feel," Maya said, "but it's out of my hands."

I spent the next few days putting Lillian's lifebook and photo album in order, amazed how much she had changed from the zonked-out lump to the chatty child. There was so much more we could do for her—but having Ethan altered the stakes. Just the thought of his name being included in any kind of police report made my skin crawl.

Lillian still weighs heavily on my heart. How could the state reunite her with her troubled brothers and then her neglectful mother? Maybe the mother had allowed men to have sex with her children for drugs. Why didn't someone investigate and prosecute that? It felt like protecting Lillian was never the true priority. Despite how much Maya and Bonnie fought, no one listened to their professional recommendations. The day we kissed Lillian good-bye, I tried hard to banish those nightmarish thoughts, but they continue to this day.

16.

blowin' in the wind

Our siblings push buttons that cast us in roles we felt sure we had let go of long ago—the baby, the peacekeeper, the caretaker, the avoider. . . . It doesn't seem to matter how much time has elapsed or how far we've traveled.
—Jane Mersky Leder

A few weeks later Phil called me with a bizarre story. "Guess who was just here?"

"Blake?" I said, because he sometimes surprises the family when he is in the area on business.

"Close. Another brother."

"Josh is already in Crystal River, but it couldn't be—Luke?"

"Yes! You should have seen him! He was dressed in a black suit, black shirt, spit-polished patent leather shoes. At first I thought he was a Jehovah's Witness. He claims the suit was Armani."

"Did you take a photo?"

"Sure, I'll send you one in a second," Phil said. "He asked if I recognized him, and after a double take, I knew him at once. He still has that crooked grin. He was dressed nicely, but there was still something off about his whole look."

"Why was he there? He hasn't been to our house since he was first adopted by Ed."

"He said he was in the area to see an orthopedic surgeon. He'd been hit by a car while driving his motorcycle and had already had several surgeries on his leg. He showed us his scars."

"How recently?" Over the past few years I'd received infrequent texts and calls from Luke—usually in the middle of the night. He was in the hospital; he was in an accident; he was getting married; he was breaking up with someone; he had been arrested; he was out of jail. Each time I felt compelled to stop what I was doing and rush to his aid—but only for about thirty seconds. Then common sense kicked in and reminded me that I couldn't keep responding to his crisis-of-the-week.

"He claims to have won more than a million dollars in an injury settlement. He bragged he bought three houses and is investing in the stock market. Also, he's engaged."

"Do you think he was telling the truth?"

"He put his fiancée, Paige, on FaceTime, and she showed off the rock on her finger. She said she's in college."

"Luke could use a smart woman," I said, "but what smart woman would want to be with him?"

The question hung in the air as we each silently filled in: money.

"Luke bragged about giving a lady at the mall ten thousand in cash for a charity for hungry children."

"Really?" I scoffed.

"I told him he shouldn't be giving his money away without knowing more about where it was going. At that point we were standing in our driveway, and he asked what we were working on. Just making conversation, I mentioned the film we're doing about hunger in Africa. And—you're not going to believe this—Luke reached into his jacket and brought out a wad of hundred-dollar bills and handed it to me for the film."

"You're kidding!"

"I told him that it was a nice gesture, but that wasn't the way to go about investing in projects." Phil started to laugh. "Then he tried to force me to take the money. I pushed the roll of bills back at him, but it was windy, and loose bills began to fly around. You should have seen me running around the driveway picking up hundreds, while he stood there laughing."

"He's literally trying to buy love with cash."

"He gave Paige a Lexus convertible and paid off her parents' mortgage—or so he said."

"So why did he visit?"

"It's all about you, of course. He asked why you avoid him. Gay said it's because every time you try to reach out, it ends up being a painful experience for you."

"That's true." I laughed. "Maybe he should be spending a little of that money in therapy."

Autumn had friended me on social media. I enjoyed her selfies with her dog, friends, and even Lorraine. One day she wrote: *Going to see my brother in the hospital.*

I texted Lorraine: WHAT'S UP WITH LUKE?

She replied that he had been run over by a car and mentioned where he was. HE'S OKAY, she wrote, BUT HE'S LONELY. HE NEEDS US.

I was surprised by Lorraine's empathy and that they were even in touch. My brother still blamed her for everything and anything. A cloak of guilt also settled on my shoulders. "Maybe we should go. It sounds like he's at rock bottom," I said to Erick. "And he's never met Ethan."

When we walked into Luke's hospital room, he began to sob as though he were grieving over a freshly covered grave. "I've lost everything I've ever loved," he wailed. "Paige left . . . taking the car, the ring—cost twenty Gs—when I chased after her, she ran me over!" He gritted his teeth in pain. "Broke my bad leg again—serious bone infection— could lose my leg."

"I'm so sorry," I said, carrying Ethan to his bedside.

"Is that my nephew?" he asked.

Ethan was only a few months old and giggled when I tickled his belly, but Luke changed the subject back to himself. "The bitch still has my power of attorney."

"You had better call your lawyer," I said.

"Did Phil tell you I have money?"

"Yes, I'm happy for you."

"Do you want me to buy you a house?"

"Luke, I don't want your money. I came because I wanted you to meet Ethan and to see how you're doing."

He really looked at the baby for the first time. "Ew, are all babies that ugly?"

It was just like Luke to say something unpleasant and hurtful. "That was rude."

"I don't have anyone, just a ton of money."

"What about Ed?" Erick asked.

"He only cared about the money. He still gets monthly checks for me."

"But you're over eighteen!" I said, although I didn't trust anything he said to be true.

"He claims I live there, and so my trust fund checks go to him."

"Where will you live when you're discharged?" Erick asked.

"I'm staying with Angel, the lady who runs the stables where I used to take riding lessons."

"Does she ask for rent?" I asked.

"I take care of anything they need, because she's done so much for me."

"Luke! She wants a piece of your pie, just like Paige and anyone else who knows what you have."

"Well, Angel did hit on me once!" he bragged.

"She's married!"

"She's always complaining that her husband is a jerk."

Ethan started to fuss. I took him to the window to let him see the rain making interesting streaks on the window. I wasn't sure how much of my brother's story was true, but it seemed like he needed some guidance from someone who didn't want anything from him. Maybe I could help him become less dependent on the leeches who were sucking him dry. Ethan, who had calmed for a few minutes, now let out a wail, which was our signal to leave.

"See you soon," I said at Luke's bedside.

"Yeah," he said, and mumbled something that indicated he didn't believe me.

Lorraine called a few days later. "I figured out something about your brother," she said. "He needs a purpose in life. I could get him an apprenticeship with some Harley guys.

Do you think he might go for that? He's gotta get out of that situation and away from those people."

"Sure, why not try it?"

Luke called me later that day. "Lorraine said I can go to her place when I get out."

"That might be a good idea." After a long pause I said, "I'll go with her to pick you up."

The next day Lorraine met me at a shopping center not far from where I lived, which happened to be the halfway point in her trip. Erick and I were very private about our address, for fostering and other reasons.

"Hi," Lorraine said as I got into her front seat. "Pretty weird, huh?"

I nodded. This was the first time I had been alone with her since I was three years old. I plugged in my GPS to help find Angel's home. Lorraine was driving a friend's car, because hers was having "tranny trouble." It started to drizzle, and I had to help her find the windshield-wiper controls.

"How's the baby?" she asked.

I started to say something about Skyler's first words before realizing she didn't know about him. "Ethan's teething," I said.

"Poor baby." She was thoughtful. "You ran a fever but never cried."

Just like Ethan, I thought, reveling in the genetic information, the first I'd ever had linking Lorraine to my baby. I was about to say, *What about Luke?* when I realized he had not lived with her long enough for her to see his first tooth.

Angel's driveway was jammed with two new pickup

trucks and three motorcycles. I wondered whether any—or all—had been purchased by Luke.

The interior was filled with the most expensive Rooms To Go furniture, which also spilled into the garage and back patio. "I've moved all my stuff here," Luke explained. "I've got a pool table and a hot tub and two more TVs and nowhere to put them. Want 'em?"

I wasn't going to accept anything that put me on Luke's list of takers.

Angel was dressed in too-tight black jeans and a low-cut blouse. She wore elaborately tooled cowboy boots.

Luke shifted his feet. "Come see my room."

A huge carved bed frame took up almost all the floor space. He lifted a stack of files and threw them on the bed. "This is my legal pile. I want you to read it." He grabbed a shopping bag in the closet, dumped out some sneakers, and started to load it with the paperwork.

Angel stood in the doorway. "Leave that here, hon."

"I want Ashley's advice."

"I'll go over them with you again when you get back." Luke's eyes shifted from me to Angel. If I moved in to take the bag, I would have been marking a line in the sand. Angel shot a warning look at Lorraine that said, *Where the hell have you been, lady, when I've been picking up the pieces?*

"Here's my card," Angel said to me. "Call or text if you have any questions—or problems." She gave me a sly smile that indicated she would be needed sooner rather than later.

We drove out to the main road. "Stop at the 7-Eleven!" Luke shouted.

Lorraine pulled in. "Need a drink," he said.

I went inside to the restroom and Lorraine got out to smoke a cigarette. When I returned, mother and son were standing in front of the soda cooler, discussing the merits of Mountain Dew versus Monster for a quick caffeine buzz. "What do you want?" Lorraine asked me. I chose a bottle of water, and she paid for all three drinks. To an outsider this looked like just another family outing, not the first reunion in Luke's life.

When we got back in the car, Luke stumbled from one topic to another, hardly taking a breath. "My leg—three antibiotics . . . another lawsuit—the tires . . . my lawyer can't get the electronic part for his BMW . . . Ed sent me a bill for painting my room because he had to replace the drywall—I mean, how can you ask your son to pay for repairs to a house he bought with his money?—Yum, barbecue ribs . . . could go for some now—I'd rather have a Bud Light—cool blue lighting under that rice burner . . ."

I listened as if I were the social worker trying to make clinical sense of his manic mouth. This felt more like supervising a family visit than being with relatives.

"I'm hungry," Lorraine said when we got back to my car.

I pointed to the restaurant Erick and I frequented, hoping I wouldn't run into anyone we knew. Luke asked for a triple burger, fries, and a Caesar salad. My stomach was in knots, so I just ordered soup. Lorraine wanted fried chicken.

After a few bites, Luke said, "That car trip made me sick." He took a teaspoon and started to taste my soup without asking. "Gross!" He gagged and headed for the restroom. He returned and inhaled his sandwich. "Better," he said, looking droopy-eyed. "My leg . . . the pain . . ." He took out a tiny aluminum tube that was attached to a key ring.

"I'm sorry," Lorraine said. "We'll get you feeling better and back on your feet."

Luke's eyes locked with hers. *They're connecting!* I thought happily. *Maybe something good might come out of this after all.*

"You coming to Lorraine's house?" Luke asked me.

"Well . . ." I felt as if I was a good buffer between the two. "I have to check with Erick and would need to go home and pack a bag. I'll be a few hours behind you." I paid the tab and stood up.

"I'm leading AA tonight," Lorraine said when we got outside. "Why don't you just come straight to the meeting?"

Luke spun around and started vomiting in the bushes alongside the restaurant. People dining on the patio looked on with disgust.

Lorraine pulled me aside. "He's detoxing from something. He was chain-smoking at the gas station, but he tried to hide it from you and told me not to say anything."

I thought, but didn't say, *You would know.*

"Also, Angel is an addict too. I think he scores for her and she's dependent on him, which is why he's there. She said she couldn't work right now because she's had shoulder surgery. They're probably all just sharing their pain meds."

Whoa, I thought, *what den of vipers am I walking into?* "Those people are just using him like everyone else, and probably none of them are clean," Lorraine said. "We need to get him into treatment."

When I went home to pack, Erick said, "While you were having a family reunion, I decided to see what your brother has been up to." He handed me a printout of Luke's recent criminal record.

"I know he's been in trouble a few times as a juvenile— like that knife incident on the Fourth of July— "

"It's much worse than that. He's had several felony arrests every year since he turned eighteen, six years ago." Erick read aloud, "Leaving the scene of a crash involving damage, criminal mischief, domestic battery, aggravated battery, strong-arm robbery, possession of carisoprodol—"

"What's that?"

"Soma, a powerful muscle relaxant. Druggies mix it with Vicodin and sell it as a Las Vegas Cocktail. When mixed with codeine, it's a Soma Coma."

He scanned the sheet again. "There's a burglary of an occupied structure and resisting an officer without violence." Erick whistled. "Operating an unregistered motor vehicle plus fleeing or eluding at high speed with wanton disregard. He has over a dozen felony charges and nearly twenty misdemeanors . . . and counting!"

"Why isn't he locked up?"

"He can probably afford good lawyers."

The rest seemed to all be serious traffic violations, including no license to operate a motorcycle, leaving the scene of yet another accident, driving while license suspended or revoked, and last—but not least—another domestic violence that seemed to coincide with his breakup with Paige.

"Okay, the kid's a mess, which is why I'm offering to help. Lorraine says he has a substance abuse problem.

Maybe we can get him into treatment. He can afford to pay for one of these country-club places." I kissed him. "Sorry to leave you with the kids."

"No worries. Only two kids seems like a vacation."

We hugged good-bye far longer than usual. "Gotta run," I said. "I have an AA meeting to get to."

I met Luke in a church parking lot. He was talking to a guy in a wife-beater shirt who had used half a tube of gel on his hair. "That's my sister," Luke said.

"Your mom is the greatest," the guy said. "She's talked me off the ledge a few times." He pointed to where people crowded around.

Lorraine was holding a cell phone. "Anyone able to go pick up some guys?" She handed her phone to the volunteer. "Okay, people, meeting's starting in five."

We filed into a church classroom. I took a seat toward the front and made Luke sit by me.

Lorraine opened the meeting. "Good evening. My name is Lorraine and I'm an alcoholic."

I thought the whole purpose of AA was to be completely anonymous, so I was surprised that she gave her name. "Welcome to Alcoholics Anonymous, a worldwide fellowship of men and women who help each other to stay sober." After reading some general information, she said, "If there's anyone who is here for their first meeting, please introduce yourself by your first name—or made-up name—only."

A few people spoke. "Anyone else?" she directed her glance to Luke.

Luke shifted in his seat. "Yeah well, I'm only here because that lady is my mom."

"Give a name," another woman coaxed.

"Oh, yeah," he coughed. "My name is Luke, but I'm not an alcoholic or anything like that. I don't really belong here. I make good money and do investments and real estate."

A man on the aisle reached over and touched his arm. "Don't worry, son," he said, "you are in the right place."

I was riveted by the way Lorraine commanded the room like a presenter. She projected her voice, fielded questions smartly, tuned into each person's need, reflected back their feelings, and had that inner glow that couldn't be bottled and sold. Then it hit me: This was the genesis of my talent. What people called my charisma had come from her.

Autumn was away for the weekend, so Luke took her room. I was only planning to stay the night, so I camped out on the couch and would share the guest bath with Luke down the hall. Lorraine had bought some hot dogs and hamburgers to grill outside and handed me a bag of chips to put in a bowl.

Luke grabbed some from the bag and smashed them into his mouth. "Starving."

Once the food was on the table, Lorraine sat down but did not eat. "My dad—your grandfather Rhodes—passed on last week."

"Oh, I'm so sorry," I said.

"In the end he died from booze and drugs and hard living," she said. "Runs in our family—and your dad's, too." She nodded toward Luke. "There's another way, a healthier way. I know I'm not one to talk, but I'm trying—finally—

but I can only do it one day at a time with the support of my family and friends."

"I'm doing fine on my own," Luke said.

"Except for all your arrests." I stared at him.

"People are always trying to get me in trouble. Like Paige. She runs me over and calls it domestic violence on her!"

"Addicts find it hard to admit they're at fault for anything," Lorraine said patiently. "We bury our self-hatred in our drug of choice."

I fell asleep on the couch while they were still going at it. As I dozed off, I thought, *Maybe she can get through to him . . . maybe she is the only one who can.*

"I don't give a crap that it's four on a Sunday morning. Tell him to call me. I've got to talk about my investments today," I heard Luke saying. His voice was coming from the bathroom.

I stumbled off the couch and stood outside the open door. "I know, but my cash is tied up in those damn houses, and I think Paige has the paperwork. Right, they're in her name. I did that after the accident so nobody could come after me. Yeah, I know, I know . . . I'll get it fixed." He saw me and said, "Gotta go."

"Luke, it's the middle of the night. Who are you talking to at this hour?"

"My lawyer. I have court on the twenty-fifth and there are some complications." He popped open the top of a prescription drug bottle and shook several into his mouth, swallowing them without water.

"What's that?"

"My antibiotic."

"How many are you supposed to take at a time?"

"I need an extra dose, because only seventeen percent stays in your body."

"I've never heard anything like that."

He opened a second bottle and took one pill out. Then he looked at me defiantly and took another and downed them both.

I wasn't in the mood to argue with him, so I went back to the couch. Luke sat in the chair opposite me and started playing a game on his phone that went *plink, plink, ding, ding!*

"Luke! Do that in your room and close the door!"

I fell into the hard sleep of a parent who hadn't slept more than three hours in a row for what seemed like forever. The smell of breakfast was my alarm clock.

"This looks great," I said, and took a crisp piece of toast off a paper towel. I told Lorraine about the pills in the middle of the night.

She became alarmed. "I'll check on him."

"He's out cold, and there's puke all over the toilet seat," she reported. "He'll need a medical detox because of his leg."

"I'm going to have to head home. It's not fair to leave Erick much longer."

"I've got this, Ashley," she said.

That night Lorraine texted me that Angel and her husband were on their way to take Luke back.

I called Luke. "Think about the rehab. You need it," I pleaded.

"I'm a grown man, and I can make my own damn decisions."

"Yes, and you're doing a great job so far." My tone was sarcastic.

"Angel has always been there for me. She does whatever I want." He started laughing. "I got Dusty's phone number, and I called him and told him where I was at."

Dusty was his birth father, who had been in prison for as long as I could remember. "He's out?"

"Some halfway place. He's going to buy me a phone. Like I need him to buy me crap, but it was fun to get his hopes up."

"What did Lorraine say about this?"

"She's pissed. She doesn't want anything to do with him."

My cheek began to twitch with a long-forgotten childhood tic. Erick had been right. I was wading in a pond so murky and polluted that I had better get out before I absorbed any more poison. I hung up abruptly.

I called Angel. "You know that my brother is taking a lot more than just some antibiotics," I said. "He needs professional help."

"We're working on it from our end too. We've always cared deeply about him."

"What about this mess with Paige? Does she really control his money?"

"Not now. We've got all his powers of attorney, and he's putting some of his property in our name."

"Why doesn't he just own it outright?"

"He needs to clear up some other legal matters first."

"What's the court date that he has coming up all about?"

She coughed. "That's his business."

A week later Lorraine called. "Good news! All our efforts paid off. Luke checked himself into one of the rehabs I recommended."

"Really?"

"Our intervention was successful. Angel took him yesterday and he signed himself in. I think he's going to work the program."

"I hope so."

Three days after that I wrote a check and noticed it was the twenty-fifth of the month. Two days after that Lorraine called. "He busted out of rehab. It was all a scam to get out of a court date."

"I'm sorry," I said to Lorraine. "You gave it your best shot."

"One day he'll go back and it will work. Look at me. I'm finally sober, although every day is a struggle."

"You've been through a lot of hardship," I said, which was the closest I had ever come to giving her a break.

"What AA has taught me is that no matter how far I have fallen, I know my experience can benefit others." She cleared her throat. "Hey . . . maybe I should write a book."

the white flag of surrender

There are no unwanted children . . .
just unfound families.
—The National Adoption Center

Now our little family consisted of Ethan and Skyler, and everything hummed along as if it were meant to be. "I'd be happy if Skyler never left," Erick said, skirting the forbidden words about love and adoption.

Skyler had come to us with a plan to be reunited with his mother. We had to be prepared to relinquish him at any moment. Friends asked us all the time, though, whether we would keep him—as if that was our decision. They also asked the secret to adopting a baby from a child welfare agency.

"If you ask," I would explain, "they will tell you—and rightly so—that none are available." Then I'd go on to explain how one of our friends adopted a sibling group of three under age three and another has two boys—one raised from four weeks and the other from nine months. Each had been a foster child like Skyler who was destined to return to his reformed parent or, like Lance, find a home with a relative. When neither works out, the long-term foster parents then have the first opportunity to adopt.

Until the moment it is decided that both biological parents cannot care for their children, they have ownership. When a child is in state custody, the parents are still in control of medical decisions and grooming, and they have the right to visit. Social service agencies are required to assist the parents with drug treatment, counseling, and parenting classes to help rehabilitate them over the course of approximately a year.

A year sounds fair, but to a baby like Skyler, a year was his whole life. Except for brief visits with Tiffany, his world consisted of Erick and me, his baby brother Ethan, all his foster grandparents, aunts, and uncles, and our many friends who visited and babysat. He had a second universe at his day-care center, where his sunshiny smile lit up his classroom.

As I cared for Ethan and Skyler, I tried to imagine each one's future. Ethan would never leave us—he'd be ours for the rest of our lives. Nevertheless, a tiny corner of my mind imagined how he would feel if removed from us—even for a few months. I could hear his every cell screaming for us, and that thought alone made me crazy. Yet I was supposed to find this fate acceptable for Skyler, who had lived with us even longer. *This is how it has to be,* I told myself. *You knew what you signed up for,* I told myself. *They took Albert back and eventually the pain receded,* I told myself.

But Skyler! Would he ever "get over it"? Would being wrenched from us scar him in some profound way? I knew I would pull him from a fire or leap in the surf to rescue him, but I was powerless to fight the court process.

There were three power players who would determine Skyler's fate: Bennett, his Guardian ad Litem; Gwen, his case manager; and Maya, our placement agency director. Also on the chessboard was Skyler, who could be moved around by any of those three. Erick and I were bystanders entrusted with his day-to-day welfare but not in control of his destiny. His father, charged with attempted murder, was in jail and barred from the game. The queen, who had retained a lot of power—but not all of it—was his mother, Tiffany.

When Tiffany went to court, a public attorney represented her. In a typical deal with the state, she agreed to work on the tasks in a case plan, and if she successfully completed them, her children would be returned to her. Nobody could prove that Tiffany, who wasn't home when the boys were injured, had done anything to put them at risk—other than selecting the wrong boyfriend. Under similar circumstances, some mothers would have been able to keep their children, but Skyler's and Denver's injuries were so severe that every precaution was taken.

"You don't have to worry about Tiffany," Gwen assured us. "She's going to be reunited with her boys."

On the surface Tiffany had a lot going for her: She was barely into her twenties, attractive, and well spoken. "Gwen's really pushing for reunification," I said to Erick. "She has yet to understand the serious issues beyond that pretty face."

During a visit with Denver, Tiffany told us that she'd been sexually abused as a child. She had listed seven men as possible fathers for the two boys. Denver's father had been a wild card; Skyler's dad was the one who'd tried to kill him. Would her next boyfriend also be unstable?

Gwen was supposed to be an advocate for the whole family—not just the parent. Erick and I initially agreed that she was one of the best case managers we had met and was one of the few who had an MSW. At first she was willing to do the grunt work of transporting and supervising visits. Her offices in Pasco County were an hour and a half from our home in St. Petersburg. Other Pasco workers—like Albert's—asked local workers to do their monthly visits, but Gwen personally transported Skyler and Denver for visits to see their mother. For a change, here was someone hands-on and positive.

While Gwen didn't see us as part of the reunification team, we were willing to do whatever it took to help this young mother get her children back. We believed this was one parent who had the potential to progress. However, when we pointed out something odd about Tiffany's behavior with one of her children, Gwen dismissed it as inconsequential. She also said our fears about Tiffany's new boyfriend were "theoretical" and "unfounded." Soon Gwen delayed responding to our calls and e-mails, and when we did speak, she was very curt.

Since there was such a shortage of volunteers, a Guardian ad Litem supervisor was in charge of the case until a seasoned guardian, Bennett, was appointed eventually.

"I know Gwen is sympathetic to Tiffany," Bennett said, "but I've seen many mothers side with their boyfriends over the child, and Tiffany can't handle both kids at visitation."

"We worry that Gwen has almost done too much for Tiffany," Erick said. "At this stage, Tiffany should be able to transport herself and deal with her kids on her own. She always asks for help during diaper changes and feedings. I don't see her learning to be independent."

"No question about it," Bennett replied. "Not to mention we just confirmed she's pregnant again and has been for months. She's been lying about it in court."

Fortunately, Bennett was only concerned with the best interests of the child. In Denver's case, he was to be reunited with at least one parent as quickly as possible, and that had been accomplished as soon as paternity was proven. "Tiffany talks a good game," he said, "but left to her own devices, she starts falling apart."

As time went on, staffings and court hearings became more divisive.

When a supervisor asked what she was learning in her parenting classes, Tiffany regurgitated memorized lines like: "I believe in positive parenting" and "Redirection and praising work better than punishment" and "A time-out can only last two minutes for a two-year-old."

Though she had "completed" her parenting classes, to the professional observers at the visitation center it became clear that she wasn't applying the information. She was also overheard coaching another mother on how to tell the professionals what they want to hear.

"We're trying to help her get her son back," I told Bennett. "We think she's still making poor choices that could put both Skyler and the new baby in danger."

"Thanks for the information," Bennett said. "Who else knows about this?"

"We told Gwen about our concerns, but it wouldn't hurt for you to pass them along as well," Erick said.

"I had planned to," Bennett said. "Tiffany is very two-faced and can be manipulative. She has already tried to play me against Gwen, so I have been communicating with Gwen more often."

Erick and I shot each other worried looks, because we weren't sure where he stood in terms of us. We knew Bennett was squarely for the child's best interests, but how did he interpret Skyler's needs?

Bennett took a long breath before saying, "We've all seen instances where Tiffany twists people's words. I recommend that you don't have any direct contact with her at this stage. She already thinks you're trying to keep Skyler from her, so there's no reason to give her ammunition against you."

After that meeting, we both had hearts so heavy we couldn't comfort each other. Erick and I had raised Skyler expecting that he would never be ours. Loving Skyler was risky. It was like falling for a married man. Even though you know that statistically the relationship is doomed, you kid yourself into believing you are exceptional enough to beat the odds. Loving Ethan without restraint also made it easy to realize that I had loved Skyler long before I admitted it.

"Maybe we should figure out what to do if Tiffany doesn't regain custody," Erick said the next day.

"Nobody sees the same red flags we do. Skyler's case is going just the way Albert's did. In fact, Albert's father completed fewer of his case plan tasks than Tiffany has."

"Still, I want to ask our families how they would feel if we actively tried to adopt Skyler."

"Erick, why get their hopes up?"

"I need to know how they feel just in case. . . ."

"Okay, you ask your parents and I'll ask mine."

Erick's parents, who lived close by and did the most babysitting, wholeheartedly supported us.

Phil said, "He's our grandchild as long as he's here, and he'll be in our hearts forever."

Gay, who understood the legal situation best, was pragmatic. "The mom is technically complying with the tasks."

"She did all her parenting classes, but she falls apart during visits when Gwen or another worker isn't there to help her with Skyler."

"Legally, though, she hasn't done anything bad enough for them to terminate her rights," Gay said. "I don't want to raise your hopes, sweetie. We all love Sky, but he's probably going home."

"But—" I didn't want to hear the facts; I just wanted her support.

"I know, honey." Gay was so quiet I could almost hear her thinking. "Let's assume Skyler is available for adoption. You and Erick have just started your own family. Maybe he should go to an infertile couple."

"To strangers? Why would they be more entitled or qualified than us?"

"Okay, then I have to ask: Will you be able to love him as much as you love Ethan?"

"We loved Skyler first," I answered, "and we are so freaked about letting him go back. Tiffany means well, but she really doesn't have what it takes—especially with another baby on the way!" I started to cry.

Gay was silent for a long time. "There's one possible way," she said. "Tiffany has to want you to be Skyler's parents." She thought for a minute. "Tiffany lost Denver to his father and hasn't lived with Sky for more than a year. She admitted early on that she isn't very bonded to him, but she may be very motivated to keep a new baby out of the system."

"What are you getting at?"

"Everything in life is about relationships. I've worked on at least ten open adoptions where the parents surrendered voluntarily because they had some type of contact. However, for this to work, you have to build trust with the mother."

"The guardian doesn't want us to interact with Tiffany because she's so deceitful."

"He's wrong," Gay—who is very blunt—said. "You used to talk with her a lot, so I would start that again. You need to show her that you're different from the workers and guardian and that you're not in the enemy camp. Worst case, she'll have more access to information about Skyler and feel more connected to her child, which will help if they reunify. In the best case, she'll realize the stability you can offer Skyler."

Erick and I discussed the problem while supervising Ethan in a bouncy chair. "If we tell the professionals that we are interested in adoption, they'll say we're undermining the reunification goal," Erick said.

Ethan started winding up for a cry, so I handed him a rattle that made a cute noise when he shook it. "I can't see any situation where it's helpful for Tiffany to hate us," I added. "Being friendly would also help if we had to work with her for . . . a transition."

I was nervous as I dialed her phone number. Tiffany picked up the phone after a few rings. "Who is this?"

"Hey, Tiffany, this is Ashley, Skyler's foster mom."

"Oh, hi!" she said a bit hesitantly.

"I know the last staffing was a little intense, and we wanted to reach out and discuss something with you."

"I really appreciate you calling. I was beginning to think the visitation center was right."

"What do you mean?" I said, turning the question.

"You know that lady at the front desk? Well, she said I'd better watch out, because you could cause a lot of trouble for me. She said you're a real bitch."

I reeled back and went to find Erick, who was watering the garden. I put the phone on speaker.

"I'm not sure what you have heard from other workers or staff, but we wanted to be in direct contact with you ourselves to avoid any misunderstandings." I took a deep breath. "The first day we met, we told you that we weren't fostering to adopt. We have helped many children return home."

"I thought I was doing all right, but the people at the place where I'm doing my parenting classes said they will not be recommending reunification."

"Why?"

"They said I'm not internalizing the lessons, whatever that means."

Albert's father had hardly "internalized any lessons" either. Maybe they needed to see more progress in a case where a child had almost lost his life. Or maybe this was all because Bennett made someone pay close attention.

"Can I ask you something?" Tiffany said with a choked voice.

"Sure."

"If they won't give Skyler back to me, would you want to adopt him?"

I felt like a rubber band had snapped in my mind. This was it—or maybe not. While I was trying to overthink how to respond, Erick jumped in.

"We absolutely would, if that were an option," he said softly and simply.

I got my voice back and added, "He's been with us over a year. We're the only family he knows—except his visits with you, of course."

"I appreciate your honesty," Tiffany said. "Someone told me that if I stay in Florida, they could take my new baby—it's a girl." She started crying. "I don't know what to do! If I go, at least I'll have my baby and Lamar—that's her daddy. He's got a job out of state and wants us to come live with him. But I'm also thinking that Lamar's mom could take Skyler while I'm gone."

Erick was gesturing wildly, and I tried to decode his message. "Let's get together and talk about it," I said. Erick nodded. "We can have lunch somewhere."

"Please bring Skyler."

I glanced at Erick. He nodded. "Okay."

Now we were floating free from the foster care bureaucracy, which was as scary as it was empowering. Tiffany picked a fast-food restaurant, and we didn't complain. At least they had high chairs. Tiffany already had a table. She introduced us to Lamar's mother, Marla, who we hadn't expected to be there. Erick positioned Skyler's high chair next to Tiffany, and we took the other side of the table with Ethan's high chair.

For the first time Tiffany and I talked freely. She was amazed to find out that I was only four years older than she was. "You've already gone to college," she said. "That's what I'm going to do next."

"A lot of young parents go part-time," I said, thinking how easily I could have been in her shoes.

"I discussed it with Marla, and I think it's a good idea for you to adopt Skyler. But when I talked to Gwen, she said that I would have no control over what family he went to if I signed over my rights."

"I took Tiffany to see a different lawyer." Marla's voice crackled like a two-pack-a-day smoker.

Erick reached for my hand under the table and squeezed it. "So, what did they say?" I managed without sounding too alarmed.

"I still have the right to work with a private adoption agency," Tiffany said.

"R-really?" I felt bile rising in my throat. There were thousands of families who would pay big bucks for this poster-child toddler.

"Don't worry," Tiffany said, "we still want you to be his parents, don't we, Marla?"

"Yep, he should stay with the folks who's been caring for him." Marla fiddled with a plastic lighter.

"How does the private agency work?" Erick asked.

"I sign Skyler over to their agency, and then you would adopt him through them. I get to set the terms of an open adoption, and their people write out the papers that say I can see him and all that. I know other people who have done adoptions, and the family never let them see their kids again."

"Private agencies usually charge a fee," Erick said.

"There's no charge to anyone if you surrender to the state," I chimed in. "Plus, they cover the legal fees of the adoption. If he is adopted privately and not as a foster child, he would lose his health insurance and Florida college tuition waiver."

Tiffany's eyes widened. "I didn't think about that."

Marla cleared her throat. "Yeah, but that caseworker still said the state can place him with anyone they want—not the family Tiffany picks."

Erick sighed. "Yes, that's true, theoretically, but that isn't what happens. Since Skyler's been in our home for well over a year, they will first ask us if we want him. He won't go anywhere else."

Tiffany was now weeping.

"Tiffany," I began, "I know this is terribly hard and I don't want to put any additional pressure on you, but if Skyler stays with us, you will always be in his life. I'm adopted and I still see my biological family. We believe in open adoption and would be happy to stay in touch as long as it's safe for Skyler."

"I believe you, Ashley." She swallowed hard. "Won't his dad have to agree too?"

The idea that this monster had any power over Skyler was so unsettling, I didn't know what to say. Anything and everything could still go wrong.

A week after Easter, Erick stayed home through Ethan's nap and I caught up on some shopping. I stopped by a display of half-off Easter baskets in the clearance aisle and admired two matching, but slightly different wooden baskets—one was decorated with trains, the other with planes. Perfect for Ethan and Skyler, who were eight months apart and would both be old enough to enjoy them next year. I wanted to buy the baskets, but would I be jinxing the adoption? What if the father refused to sign? What if Tiffany changed her mind? If Tiffany insisted on some relative or nonrelative who could pass a home study, the twin baskets would be a horrible reminder of our lost son. But what if Skyler was with us and I only had one basket? They were two for the price of one. I could donate the extra if it came to that. My thrifty side told me to take the chance.

During the last court hearing, Skyler's father was taken aside by his lawyer, who convinced him that it would be in his best interests not to drag the dependency case out further, because it could have negative implications for his pending criminal trial. He agreed to sign.

None of the officials knew that Tiffany was planning to leave the state when the termination-of-rights hearing was over. We would keep our promises for an open adoption, but we would not be sorry if she became distracted with her new baby or distance made visits less frequent.

18.

three more words

The best is yet to come.
—William Shakespeare

For once everyone is happy to be in court. Children carrying balloons run through the halls. Judges hand out teddy bears. November is National Adoption Month. Thousands of adoptions are finalized in a few short weeks. It's always a busy time for me as I crisscross the country giving speeches—which are often booked a year in advance—at child welfare events.

The call came from a director at the Pinellas County Guardian ad Litem office. "Hi, Ashley," she said. "Sorry to contact you so late, but we were hoping you would be available to speak at the adoption day in Pasco."

Both Erick and I had worked as guardians with her. "Nice to hear from you!" I said, "but—"

She interrupted me. "The event is on Thursday, November eighth, this year."

"I know," I said, laughing to myself.

"Is it possible you'll be available?"

"Well," I said, "I'll be very busy, although I think I could squeeze it in." This time I chuckled aloud. "Erick and I are adopting our son that same day in that court!"

"I can't believe it!" she said, and we happily confirmed that I would speak as part of the ceremonies.

☀

Five months passed between Tiffany surrendering Skyler and his adoption. Despite her fears, nobody snatched him from our home to place him with another family waiting to adopt. If Tiffany had been assured he would have remained with us, her stress would have been minimized. Yet there are no guarantees. I'd heard of instances where an adoption was canceled at the last minute because one of the prospective parents was arrested, so adoption agencies generally do a final background check. Even families that seem squeaky clean on the surface have had unpleasant secrets come to light at the last moment.

In the meantime, we were still a therapeutic foster care family. Maya called one morning. "I need a really huge favor," she said. "We have two brothers ages eighteen months and four who need a placement until they can find a preadoptive home."

"What's their behavior profile?" I asked. With Skyler and Ethan, we couldn't have a hitter, a biter, or a sexually abused child who acted out on others.

"I can assure you they are lovely boys, but nobody in regular foster care will take them."

"I don't understand—"

"They're African-American."

"What! Do you mean to tell me that they rejected these kids because of their skin color?"

"Nobody is forced to take any child for any reason, and apparently they don't have an available family with an open bed and the right profile," Maya said without confirming my comment. "Does this mean you'll accept them?"

"Of course!" I said, shocked that such prejudice still existed.

Their caseworker, Lindsay, delivered Micah and Zachariah in less than two hours. "I am so grateful," she said effusively. "We've been trying to place them for a week."

I sized up the two handsome boys for clothing size. We had plenty to fit little Zachariah, but Micah would need a new wardrobe. I made them a welcome lunch and added a lesson in "please" and "thank you." They caught on quickly.

Then I called Gay, who was coming to Erick's father's birthday party the next day. I gave her the children's sizes, and she went to the nearby children's upscale consignment store—where she got an additional discount for foster children—to outfit Micah.

At the party, Micah played doctor, asking people to open their mouths. He used a belt as a pretend blood pressure cuff and acted very solemn as he went around the room, checking everyone.

"He's had a lot of medical care," I said. "I think he's working out some trauma."

"Shanice—that's their mom—has been homeless for years," I told Erick. "She has mental health issues and sometimes left the children alone for days in the shelters. Anything could have happened to them in that environment."

Gay went online and ordered a child's doctor kit. When Micah came home from school three days later, the package was there. We let him unwrap it. I expected he'd jump up and down with excitement. Instead, his face turned serious. "Let's begin," he said, turning to Erick.

He gave Erick a full exam, checking his ears, his nose, and his throat. He took his blood pressure with the realistic cuff and listened to his heart with the stethoscope, which had a small amplifier. When he was finished, he came over to Erick and took his hand. "I see what the problem is," he said with a concerned tone.

"What?" Erick asked, pretending to be alarmed.

"You have chickens in your ears."

Erick couldn't suppress a smile. "Oh no! What do I do?"

"I'll take them out for you."

Zachariah was close in age to Skyler, but he had some developmental delays. We were grateful that Skyler had arrived when he was so young. In his day-care class he was the most advanced in physical development and speech. Zachariah joined my cuddle-bunny club, and I tried to give him plenty of lap time, because he craved close contact. Micah enjoyed playing independently with cars and building toys. If I took the sofa, I would have one boy on each side. Interestingly, the child who was the most independent was Ethan. I wasn't sure whether it was due to his personality or because somehow he knew there had never been the slightest possibility of going anywhere else.

"Mrs. Smith," the caller said, "Don't forget that picture day is tomorrow for Micah and Zachariah."

"Right. Thanks. I'll be sure to pack an extra outfit."

It had been the most ordinary of calls, yet I reacted with a racing pulse. How I had loved picture day at school! I always wore my best dress, brushed my hair, and even cleaned under my fingernails. When I was adopted, we found a few school pictures in my files—but I had never seen them before. Often I had already changed schools when the photos came back, or I had started the school after picture day had taken place. Of course we ordered each a photo package for their albums, as well as a plaque with Micah's preschool graduation picture on it. Even if they weren't with us when these came back, we would be sure the boys got them.

After a few months, we asked Lindsay about their case. "Any progress on finding them an adoptive family?"

"There are a few issues," Lindsay said. "Both fathers have agreed to surrender. However, their mom said she just can't bring herself to sign the documents."

"Now what?"

"We'll have to file for a termination hearing."

"How long are we talking about?"

"Six months, maybe a year."

"By then these boys will consider us their family. What about a preadoptive family?" I glanced around our living room, which looked like we'd left a window opening during a tornado of toys and blocks.

"There aren't many who will accept the risk knowing the mom hasn't surrendered yet."

"There's no way these children are being reunified, right?" I had heard the mom had added more prostitution charges to her long record.

"Of course not."

"They'll be so much easier to place while they're still young. Zachariah is in diapers, and Micah's developing an amazing vocabulary. He's very interested in science and medicine."

I woke Erick up in the middle of the night. "What? Who?" he asked, figuring it was his turn with one of the kids.

"I just need to talk about the Oliver boys." He groaned and sat up next to me in bed. "Let's look at it from their mother's point of view. She's homeless, mentally ill, and a prostitute, but she still has a last vestige of dignity. She doesn't want to give away her children to people she doesn't know. Remember, Tiffany felt the same way."

"You're right." Erick held his hand up like a traffic cop. "Wait, maybe we should contact that private agency Tiffany told us about."

"They do work much faster. The state could drag the case out for a year or more. Shanice could surrender her rights to their agency and may feel empowered by getting to choose their new parents."

"But the agency charges a fee."

"It wouldn't cost the mother anything. And the families she would be choosing from would already be aware of the costs."

Neither of us could see a downside. I phoned the agency the next day. "Based on the information you were able to provide," the agency head said, "we could help this mom. The last time we took a foster care case, we found the child an adoptive home in two weeks."

"That fast?" I pressed the phone closer to my ear.

"We work nationally," she said. "I want to make a few

calls first. And then I'll get in touch with their caseworker."

Shanice was thrilled with the idea of picking her children's new family. Their caseworker Lindsay was also excited. She was working another case where a little girl had been in her pre-adoptive home for two years and there were still technicalities holding up the final adoption. These young boys needed a forever home as soon as possible.

The adoption agency sent a cab to pick up Shanice at her shelter, and she spent day after day poring through the albums that families make to introduce themselves to birth mothers. The process was slowed by the fact that Shanice kept disappearing. Micah and Zachariah were eventually adopted by a biracial couple in Oregon. Though there were some unforeseen delays, the state could never have offered these children more efficient permanency.

I like to imagine Micah walking along the shore, showing shells to his adoptive father, a science teacher, who might help Micah work on the cure for chickens in the ear.

We adopted twenty-month-old Skyler the day before Ethan's first birthday. All the Smiths and the Courters were there, as well as many of the people we had worked with as guardians and foster parents for several years. I'm also on the board of the Heart Gallery—a group that uses photography to promote children waiting to be adopted—and many children who had found families from their portraits were also being adopted. After my speech, we filed into the judge's chambers for Skyler's proceedings.

"I like to ask children if they want to be adopted," the judge said.

My stomach flipped as I recalled this very moment fifteen years earlier, when I'd spoken my ambivalent three little words so churlishly. I glanced at my parents apologetically, but they were busy grinning at Skyler, who was waving his hands. Then he gave the judge a huge smile.

The judge grinned back. "I'll take that as a yes!" Everyone applauded.

It was done. It had come full circle. I was now the adoptive mother.

Outside the courtroom, our local television station interviewed me. "What do you think of these events?" the reporter asked.

"We all know about the tragic cycle of abuse—where abused children grow up to become abusive parents. I like to think we've changed it to the cycle of adoption."

After the celebration at the courthouse, we went to a waterfront resort for a festive lunch and took family photos around their gardens. We ended the day with the family back at our house for a barbecue. The following weekend we had a "One + 1 Party" to celebrate Ethan's first birthday and the new addition to our family. We rented space at a children's museum in St. Petersburg, which was the perfect place for our friends with children. I loved hearing the squealing sounds of excited children and the murmurings of parents scurrying after them. Skyler discovered the tube slide and giggled all the way down. Then he wanted to climb back up the way he came. Erick had to carry him off and put him back on the ladder. As I watched, I felt infused with a floating lightness—as if helium was filling my veins and I was looking down on the father of my children swinging and lifting and laughing. He was happy. Skyler was happy.

Ethan, who was tucked into his grandfather Phil's arms, was smiling too. Gay was at my side, and the Smith family was at the bottom of the slide, cheering Skyler on.

I guess so.... That young girl, who said those words at her own adoption because she had felt her ties to other people would always be tenuous and ephemeral, didn't exist any longer. I caught a glimpse of myself in the mirrored surface of a nearby exhibit. Although Ethan had rumpled my hair and sticky fingers had mauled my dress, I saw a lucky—and contented—woman.

After the Oliver boys left, we decided that we wanted time to enjoy both Skyler and Ethan without too many children coming and going. We told Maya that we would not accept any long-term placements for the time being. "I know there is still a huge need for respite homes," I said. "We would be happy to help out for short periods."

We had used respite for family trips or when I was going somewhere interesting for a speech and Erick was able to accompany me. Some families have foster children who are so challenging that their foster parents need a breather to reset. We didn't expect Maya to call so soon with a favor.

"Millie is eight," she began, "and her current foster home is closing."

"I've met Millie," I said, recalling a girl with lustrous black hair who tried to hide her missing teeth by smiling behind her hand. Foster parents serving this small agency knew one another well since we regularly came together for trainings and activities. "We'd be happy to have her," I said, because something about her had already touched my heart.

"This should only be for a very short time," Maya admitted. "She is supposed to be free for adoption soon, and we have identified an adoptive family for her."

"I'm a good helper," Millie said when I showed her around our home. "I clean, too! Just tell me what to do."

"That's great," I said, "but here, we all help each other."

I remembered back more than fifteen years ago, trying to sell myself to a new foster parent, hoping this would be the one who would keep me. Millie reminded me of myself in many ways, most poignantly because she too had buried her fears and sadness and was trying so hard to make a good first impression.

Millie was patient while I tended the younger children, who were demanding food or a diaper change. To keep her from being bored, I bought her some jewelry-making kits she could work on, and she used little rubber bands to make everyone in the house their own bracelets. She loved crafts, dressing up, nail polish, and the same girly activities I had enjoyed. After so many little men in my life, I loved doting on her.

Just like me, she had very definite food preferences. I understood her need to control as much as she could, and allowed her to help pick menus that she would enjoy. Often, people are reluctant to foster older children, but they can sometimes be more satisfying than uncommunicative little ones.

One night I went to tuck Millie in. Without prompting, she had taken my book, *Three Little Words*, to bed and had fallen asleep reading it. Erick tiptoed in and snapped a picture. I stood there awhile longer. It was surreal to think that this was *my* foster daughter and realize how far my life had come. I wondered whether she was able to imagine a happy ending for her own story.

After the first week, she said, "I wish you would adopt me."

My heart melted. "It's complicated," I began with a sigh. I remembered kids at The Children's Home asking virtual strangers to adopt them. We just wanted a family—any family. "That's not the plan, sweetheart," I said. "You're going to a wonderful couple in a few days."

Two months later, we learned that just after she left our home, the goals in Millie's case had changed. Because of this, her preadoptive parents had not been permitted to keep her. After that, the veil of confidentiality descended over Millie, and we had no idea where she was. The secrecy that surrounds the children in the system is supposed to "protect" them—as if there were a way to shield them from their pasts. As I know all too well, the memories cannot be erased; they course through our bodies like blood. They are always there and not so far from the surface. I envy children whose recollections are all positive and delightful, and I empathize with those, like me, who had a rougher go. No matter how much happiness I have—and I now have more than my fair share—my own past is a part of my present and will be a part of my future. One of my goals as a foster parent has been to add a layer of joyful times to a child's life while trying to minimize their stress. While we can't escape or erase the past hurts these children experience, we can fill them with positive experiences in a loving home— and maybe even give them some hope. Still, Erick and I have continued to worry about the children who left our home and were returned to what we believed were unsafe conditions. I expected Millie would be one of the lucky ones—like me—who would find loving parents eager to give her whatever she needed.

This is how Millie's story was supposed to end in this book—on a positive note, remembering a child who had every potential, and might still do well despite her early struggles. This was not what happened. I have had to edit this chapter at the last minute and will live with so many regrets and questions for the rest of my days.

This is why: Just over a year after Millie was with us, I was sent a link to a newspaper article, and scanned the headline. "Some guy went crazy and killed his disabled mother," I said to Erick. "And then went after his young nieces."

Erick shook his head. Sadly, these headlines are not uncommon in Florida. A few weeks before, a father flipped out and threw his five-year-old daughter, Phoebe Jonchuck, off a bridge approaching the Sunshine Skyway in St. Petersburg. It was revealed that Phoebe's death could have been prevented because several people had called the state abuse hotline, warning that the father was unstable and a danger to his young daughter. But the workers at the hotline screened the calls and deemed there was no reason to investigate further.

I gasped as I read the article further. "Oh! Oh no!" An icy wave passed from me to Erick. Our worst nightmare as foster parents was coming true! "It's Millie," I cried out.

"Is she . . . going to be okay?" he asked, his eyes instantly welling with tears.

"They just said that she's in critical condition."

I picked up the phone, called the agency, and reminded

them that we had fostered Millie. "We can take her again," I said first thing. They said they would consider us "if she survived."

A few hours later, the television news reported that Millie had died from her extensive injuries. "There are no words," I sobbed to Erick.

The gruesome details unraveled over the next few days. Their uncle, a diagnosed schizophrenic who lived in the home, had first murdered Millie's grandmother—a wheelchair-bound double-amputee with severe medical issues. While Millie's aging grandfather was in the shower, her uncle used the same tire iron to brutalize Millie and her younger sister. Two other children were spared when the grandfather stopped the massacre. The younger sister survived.

"I can't believe they were placed back with those grandparents! Weren't we told there was no suitable family?" Erick said.

"The kids were removed from that home in the first place!" I shouted.

"Their agency probably sent them to relatives just to get them off the books and make their numbers look better," Erick seethed.

My grief galvanized me. I clicked on Facebook and eulogized Millie. I found some of my favorite photos of her on my computer, and I posted them to show the healthy, joyful child whose ending was violent, painful, and senseless.

We were quickly warned by foster care officials not to publically speak about Millie and to take down her photo. "I don't know what to do," I said to Erick. "The lead agency and the Department of Children and Families are going to try to discredit us and find a way to spin this so they're not at fault."

"We know that professionals had good reason to oppose placement with the grandparents, and stated so in court," Erick said, pacing back and forth in the living room.

I went upstairs to put Ethan's laundry away but felt as if I were walking through molasses. I sat on our bed with tears streaming. Then I remembered a drawing on our refrigerator. Running downstairs, I pulled down the picture decorated with hearts. Our names, Erick and Ashley, were written on the back. It was signed: "From Millie." Pain flooded through me as I thought of her grin when we found the art that she taped to the refrigerator as a surprise for us. And I knew in that instant that if we didn't speak up for her, they would bury her story along with her body.

My attorney reminded me that I did not give up my first amendment rights when I became a foster parent, and that once a child dies, the confidentiality rules change.

A week after Millie's death, the agency opened her files to the press and the public, and issued a formal statement saying, "After assessing all the documents in the case file, we've come to the conclusion there were no indications that we could prevent this type of thing from happening with this family . . ."

"How can anyone believe that?" I asked Erick. "We can read page after page of red flags, objections by professionals, and details about the many serious issues this family has."

Millie's brief life may be over, but I am determined her story will live on. In Florida, a Critical Incident Rapid Response Team is convened to study the evidence and make a timely report that supposedly will lead to changes.

Unfortunately, the examination is done by the Department of Children and Families, which may not do the most impartial investigation. However, according to the state, Millie's case—and dozens of other recent child deaths—does not meet the narrow criteria for further investigation. My website (rhodes-courter.com) will include updates on her case, and even though her name here is fictitious, it will be easy to find the real story and links to press coverage.

There was a time when I thought I always had to be wary, because nothing was as it seemed. Millie's story thrust me back into that dark corner. Lorraine was supposed to protect me, but she was never there to pull me out of the swamp that threatened to suck me in. Charming foster mothers could turn into vicious monsters after the case-worker dropped me off. Gay and Phil slowly introduced me to the *L* word with brief "love yous" at bedtime or at the end of phone calls. Erick had told me he loved me *years* before I could admit even a minuscule affection for him. Years! Would any other man have been as patient? In the end, I discovered that to love him, I had to learn to love myself.

Together, we both parented Millie, and together, we will grieve and find a way to make her life count for something. I am a passionate person. I throw myself into projects, whether it is graduate school, running for election, or getting a service for one of my children. I thrive accomplishing things for others.

Yet I cannot take sole credit for my own happiness. To my great fortune, many people have prevented me from falling into the abyss of loneliness and despair. A few

wise counselors at The Children's Home helped me see my potential and showed me how much they cared. My Guardian ad Litem, Mary Miller, worked diligently to free me for adoption. Then Gay and Phil took an enormous risk by adopting a surly preteen who behaved abominably and acted ungrateful. I laugh about it now because I have fostered so many kids who have given me more than a taste of my own medicine. The Courters also showed me something even more meaningful: the example of their own marriage. They never shout, there is rarely anger, and problems are discussed openly and fairly. Their mutual respect and cooperation allowed us to have remarkable family adventures.

Phil is my model for the nurturing man. He made me feel safe coming to him with my conflicted feelings and quietly counseled me. Gay and I collided, probably because we are more alike than we admit. I can see how my marriage mirrors that of my parents. I tend to be strong willed and a detail-oriented planner. Like Phil, Erick is more mellow, supportive, empathetic, and funny. He knows when to step back and wait until I calm down. I had dated enough boisterous, selfish guys who were focused on money, possessions, power, and success to know that I clashed with these types; yet I thought they were the sort that others would approve of.

Eventually I got over the notion of whom I "should be attracted to" or "should be dating" and looked to what made me feel safe and happy. And there was Erick, who provided a lifeline whenever I felt I was being swept into a stormy sea.

From the moment I walked into their home, my parents

have been there. If they are not directly helping me by building new garage doors (Phil) or advising me about my taxes (Gay), they are the stars I steer by as I chart my own course. When I was putting myself through grad school, I remembered how Gay taught me about financial aid and grants during my undergraduate studies. She helped me balance my first checkbook, showed me how to budget money and buy a car, and also gave me a businesslike voice that stands me in good stead when I work on my own projects.

The Courters also instilled a sense of civic responsibility in me. Gay has been a guardian for more than twenty-five years, and Phil has been influential on state and local child welfare boards. Erick also feels a moral and philanthropic duty to the community. We did not go into fostering to adopt a child, but to give back to children when they are at the most stressful moment in their lives.

Every parent is always learning. Erick and I have come a long way—together. We are a polished team and know how to soothe lonely babies, love them while they are ours, kiss their hurts, cuddle and rock them, keep them clean and fresh, help them fall asleep gently, bolster them with good nutrition, get them up to speed developmentally, find them the best services and educational programs, then let them go with grace.

They arrive half-naked and filthy, bruised, and sad. They bring with them tragic revelations of how twisted and cruel people can be to those they should be treating the most lovingly. They depart with suitcases of toys and clothes, clean and healthy. Yes, it hurt when Albert left. Erick and I comforted each other. It worried us even more when we heard Lillian and her brothers were back with their mother, who had let perverts prey on them. We are angered by Florida's policies that still endanger children. A recent exposé of Florida's child welfare system by the *Miami Herald* showed that in the last six years, 535 children, whose parents or caregivers had a history with the Department of Children and Families, died from abuse. Yes, more than five hundred children who supposedly were under the state's watchful eye. As we follow Millie's story and the details behind other similar headlines, we are learning that this number is likely much higher. And now one of our foster children will be a part of that count. But Millie—and all these children—deserved so much more. While the majority of our kids were placed with competent relatives, several went back to such dangerous situations that there didn't seem to be a point to the original removal. Plus, that number of *deaths* is the tip of the iceberg. It takes a lot to murder a child. For every one that is killed, there may be dozens or hundreds who are tortured, sexually abused, beaten, or starved. Many other cases will never be reported, even more are already a part of the system with no action being taken, and there are so many potential outcomes in each situation. If Skyler's grandmother had arrived on time, he might never have been injured; if she had come later, he would have died. If Tiffany had wanted to be less cooperative, she could have insisted on Marla being the one to take Skyler—even though Marla was a nonrelative Skyler had never met.

Even if all the hurt children were removed from their violent families, there aren't enough decent foster homes. While we are connected in a network of exceptional parents and volunteers who inspire us to keep serving, we've dealt with many other foster parents who do not have the same standards of cleanliness, community service, or nutrition that we do. Two respite siblings came to us with lice and bags of clothes and supplies saturated with cigarette smoke—something we expect from a removal, but not a licensed foster home. Other foster parents relied on the schools to provide most of the children's food. The funds that subsidize foster children are meant to support the children, not to be "salaries" for the parents. Since all foster children are severely upset by their situation, every home should have therapeutic training, and all children should have access to counseling, not just a lucky few.

In Florida and other parts of the country, the money-saving trick of avoiding removals or reunifying prematurely puts children's lives at risk. After a report of abuse, some parents defer the complicated court process by signing a "safety plan"—which is nothing more than a promise not to be violent or neglectful or to use drugs in front of the children. While I know the local laws and statistics best, the problem is endemic nationwide. This misguided penny-pinching has resulted in tragic consequences through the child welfare system. When I was a foster child, biological parents were not given the services and resources they needed to take care of their own children, and kids were removed for the smallest of slights. Today the pendulum has swung too far in the other direction, and it has resulted in many avoidable tragedies, like Millie's murder.

When dedicated workers and professionals come together, the system can help struggling families and save children. There are countless policies and laws in place that expedite case plans, allow for prosecution of offenders, and even punish those who do not report abuse. Many of these rules are ignored. Had we not been diligent, many of our kids would have had no other advocate. When we were frustrated, Erick and I reminded ourselves that we were doing this for the children who can't comprehend bureaucracy. Children do understand a gentle smile, a soothing hug, a full belly, and a cozy bed.

We look at Skyler every day and think of what could have been. He lights up with every kind word, funny noise, or any offer to play with him. He gobbles delicious food, sleeps in a clean bed, hugs his little brothers and his pets, and is adored by his loving parents. He is as safe as any child anywhere in the world, and we will do anything to make sure he has a happy, healthy life.

People are always asking us how we dare foster. "We couldn't fall in love with a child and then let him go," they say.

"Yes, you could, if it were best for the child," we reply. "In the meantime you can enjoy their growth and mastery. A teacher who has a class for a year is able to let her students go, knowing she contributed as much as she could during that time."

Our friend Beth said it best: "We're the adults in the situation, and these children deserve to have someone who cares enough to cry for them when they leave."

I try to inspire people to contribute what they can—primarily their time and skills. Fostering is a serious commitment, yet so many more foster families are needed. Being a Guardian ad Litem or CASA volunteer is a powerful way to contribute and influence a child's case in court. Without Bennett's advocacy, Skyler might not have had such a secure outcome. There are many other opportunities to donate and mentor. Many groups that serve children are nonprofits that rely on donations, grants, and volunteers. Adoption can save a child's life. There are more than 100,000 American children of all ages and backgrounds who already have had their parental rights terminated, and they are waiting for forever families. Some are the age I was when the Courters took a chance on me—and a good number are older. Tragically, over 20,000 youths leave the foster care system or "age out" every year. They don't have someone like Phil to call when they have a flat tire or Gay to ask a cooking question.

Two weeks after we finalized Skyler's adoption, I was on the road for a multi-city speaking engagement. My body ached, and I couldn't hold down any food. When I got home, I went to the doctor, assuming I had picked up a stomach bug. Much to my surprise, the doctor came back with a different diagnosis.

I called Erick from the parking lot. "I know we said we weren't going to take any long-term placements for a while. . . ."

"Are we getting another kid?"

"Sort of."

"We can't take in someone tonight with you feeling so sick."

"I think we have a little bit of time before this one arrives."

After a long pause he put the pieces together, and we both laughed.

I no longer question the meaning of life or wonder whether I am happy. I've been hungry enough times without any ability to get more food that I am grateful for plentitude. I have known what it is like to believe that nobody will ever adore me, and now I am thankful for all the affection in my life. I would be bereft without those who offer me unwavering understanding, encouraging compliments, and both honest and critical love. Being loved and allowing myself to feel it finally empowered me to trust. The next step was the hardest. It took me two decades to learn to freely reciprocate and utter the words.

There is no more guessing. The three *more* words are: I love you.

I love you, Ethan and Skyler. I love you, Erick. I love you, Gay and Phil. I love you, Josh and Giulia, Blake and Amber. I love you, Sharon and Rob and Jasper and Penelope. I love you, Lorraine, because we can't escape our past, and Autumn, because you are a part of my future. And I love you, Luke, unconditionally, and I hope someday you can find some peace in this world.

Though it seems like we've only just met, I have loved you, Andrew Lewis Smith, since I could feel your kicks and somersaults under my heart. You will be loved forever. I promise.

19.

postscript

*It is better to conquer yourself than
to win a thousand battles.*
—Buddha

Lorraine and Autumn have had some rocky times during Autumn's early teen years. My half sister has tried living with our aunt Leanne in South Carolina but lasted only a few weeks. After an altercation with her mother, Autumn claimed she was being abused. I talked to the investigator, who didn't feel the report was substantiated. They seem to have a roller coaster of a relationship, worse than I had with Gay as a teen. I see small updates on social media that paint a picture-perfect situation. I recently read that Autumn made the cheer squad and is doing well in her school. Hopefully Lorraine really is still sober and the two will emerge from this phase stronger and closer than ever, because—as I have learned—a girl needs a mom forever.

Luke is back in jail due to his latest felony charge. I fear that one day he'll end up in prison for a long time.

We ran into Albert's old caseworker almost two years after Albert left and asked if she had heard anything about him. "Oh, I see him all the time at a day care I visit for another one of my cases. He's doing so well," she said, trying to placate me. His father should have started him in elementary school by now.

Lance is doing wonderfully with his aunt in Maryland.

Lillian and her brothers are back with their mother. I worry about them every day.

Micah and Zachariah are living happily with their adoptive family in Oregon.

Tiffany left Florida and had a baby girl, but left the baby's father and went to live with relatives in another state. She eventually returned to Florida to live with Lamar's mother, even though she had become pregnant with another man's child a few weeks after delivering her daughter. This is Tiffany's fourth pregnancy in four years.

Erick and I started the Foundation for Sustainable Families as a way to combine our mutual interests and bridge service gaps in our community and globally. Our non-profit will allow us to provide families access to everything from family therapy, parenting and breastfeeding classes, early childhood education and nutrition, to foster and adoption resources—and even their own organic gardens (SustainableFamiliesFoundation.org).

My first memoir, *Three Little Words*, chronicled my life as a foster child up until my graduation from high school. After spending almost ten years in state care, I had few expectations for my future. I never believed that I was destined to be happy.

Today child welfare, foster care, and adoption issues have become the cornerstone of my professional and personal life. As an adult, I felt a strong pull to be a part of the very system that had failed me, and I was determined to prevent other children from being exposed to my miserable experiences. As a motivational speaker, I promote organizations that strive to protect children and I thank parents, volunteers, and professionals who work tirelessly for the same goals.

Once I was called a troublemaker and was removed from a foster home for exposing their cruel abuse. Not only I am still "causing trouble," but my voice is finally being heard. There is so much more to be said and done—and this book is part of my effort.

I graduated college, received a master's degree in social work, and also became a Guardian ad Litem (or CASA) volunteer advocating for children in court—just as someone had done for me and changed my life. Along the way I've also become a wife, a foster parent, an adoptive parent, and a biological mother.

Nationally I am exposed to service providers, social workers, agencies, and groups who use best practices to transform the system to benefit children and families. Today's innovative laws and policies could have helped reunite me with my family and prevented years of heartache. Yet the same misguided case management that damaged me has endangered many of our foster children, and as a result, one of them was killed. There is a bizarre disconnect between my professional advocacy and my role as a foster parent. While many audiences have been inspired by my speeches, at home, my expertise was often completely ignored, or I was bullied by the very workers, professionals—and even other foster parents—I spend my career defending and supporting. Now we are being chastised by our agency for eulogizing Millie and speaking up on behalf of her and other children who have lost their lives under preventable circumstances. Our agency tried to have us sign new documents that accused us of breaking the law, outlined our media involvement, and would have acted as a gag order. We chose to give back our foster license to the state rather than have it revoked, which would have a negative impact on our future plans to foster or adopt.

I wish this book was more of an homage to the exceptional parents and providers who positively change the lives of children and families. However, I can only tell the story we lived. While some of the people are composites, and certain names and situations have been changed to protect identities, every incident detailed in this book happened. Aside from the Courter and Smith families, almost all names and identifying characteristics of the youths and adults have been changed. Children do not end up in foster care for insignificant reasons, so the specifics about their abuse might be difficult to read. It's even harder to comprehend how people can be so brutal to the little ones who depend on them.

I hope my readers will be inspired to take action. We need so many more good foster parents, adoptive parents, volunteers, mentors, and community support to create positive change. Agencies need to be financially equipped to provide the best training and resources to their workers, and they must operate with child-centered practices. Powerful stakeholders—chiefly the legislators who control budgets and the judges who run our family courts—need to understand the daily sorrows and long-term costs of these tragic cases.

No other child should have to live in deplorable foster homes. No other child should be returned to unsafe conditions. No more children have to die—especially those already under the "watchful eye" of a child welfare agency. Every child deserves a happy ending—like mine.

"Ashley, I don't know how you do it all" is something I hear all the time. I couldn't do any of it without the unwavering love and support of my husband, family, and loyal friends.

I am thankful to still be so close to many friends, some who have traveled long distances to be there when I needed assistance. A few went through an invasive background check to become official babysitters for our foster children. Others simply put up with my venting. There was a time in my life that my only relationships lasted a few months. It feels amazing to still have these people in my life after so long.

Graduating from college shows that you have mastered the academic standards set forth by your school. It also means that you survived campus life, classes, clashes with professors, inspirational turning points, failed projects, exasperating group assignments, and life-changing discoveries about yourself and the world. I never could have navigated the waters of my seaside college without the patience, tough love, and forgiveness of my Eckerd friends and faculty—particularly in my early years, when I made classically stupid mistakes. So many Eckerd College faculty members and administrators influenced and steered my academic direction, but I want to specifically thank President Donald R. Eastman III, Dean James J. Annarelli, Assistant Dean Marti Newbold, and professors Anthony Brunello, Cynthia Totten, Eric Haak, Jeff Howard, James Janack, Mark Davis, Julienne H. Empric, and William (Bill) Felice.

The University of Southern California allowed me to complete a graduate degree when my schedule and home life would have prevented me from succeeding in a traditional program. I am grateful for their pioneer work in virtual academics, which allowed me to connect with fellow social-work students and professionals worldwide. During my MSW program, I was challenged, engaged, and stretched to my limits. I could not have asked for a stronger graduate experience.

As I stepped into the world as a professional, I still needed much guidance and advice. Lou and Jonellen Heckler have been invaluable mentors and supporters of my speaking career. Agents Joëlle Delbourgo, Irene Webb, and Donna Buttice have developed so many opportunities and had faith in me. Special thanks to Simon & Schuster and my editor, Caitlyn Dlouhy, for giving me the opportunity to inspire others again through my writing.

I am constantly motivated by the creative professionals who dedicate themselves to healing children in their schools, courtrooms, communities, and homes, especially the honorable Karen Gievers, Andrea Moore, and Robin Rosenberg. I am grateful to the struggling youth and families who reach out and share their concerns and stories with me.

Thousands of children turn eighteen and age out of foster care each year and are expected to take on the world alone. Although I am in my late twenties, I need family more than ever. Both the Courter and Smith relatives surround us with the kind of love and support that we need to thrive as a family.

Erick's team of family and friends has been welcoming and supportive since the beginning. His mother, Sharon, has a calm grace about her that puts everyone at ease. She can soothe the most frightened child, and our sons can't wait to crawl on her lap the minute they see her. Erick's dad, Rob, is always on hand to help with house repairs or babysit when we are in a bind. Nothing seems to rattle either of them, and they are—literally—just around the corner if we need them. Mostly, I thank them for raising such an incredible son for me to marry.

I thought Gay and Phil took their role as my parents seriously—but then I saw them in grandparent mode. Because of them, I have always had a place to go home; someone to call for advice, guidance, reassurance; a father to walk me down the aisle; and a mother to hold my hand as I welcomed my first child into the world. Knowing they are in my life gives me the greatest sense of serenity.

With Phil, Gay, Rob, and Sharon, our children will never be without love, security, and encouragement. Erick's nephew and niece, Austin and Breanna, are two very special young people who are always quick to lend a hand, and they have been superb role models for our many children. Special thanks goes to Aunt Robin and Uncle Josh Madden, both skilled pediatricians, who have fielded many medical calls and texts and have always been there for us and our foster children with loving advice and support.

During the fostering and adoption process, we've made lifelong friends and received help from dedicated professionals. Their stories and passions remind us what we're all fighting for. Our respect and admiration go to Nate and Caroline Wagner, Claudia and Mike Bachmann, Graham and Becky Myers, Robyn and Kyle Matthews, Tammy Curtis, Ashley Capps, Martha Cothron, and Carrie and David Wildes. I must also thank the Pinellas County Foster and Adoptive Parent Association, and fellow foster parent, Marc Silver, for the hilarious, "I forgave her" line and other funny foster-parent coping strategies and resources. Having support from other foster parents has been essential.

I will always be grateful for so many fine mentors, professionals, and workers—particularly Darlene Averill, Kelly Brenner, Ron Anderson, Jesse Miller, Jillian DeMarco, Rebecca Day, Connie Going, Shannon Albert, Brandice Corriveau, Terri Chirstensen, Elaine Hollingsworth, Desiree Crounse, Lisa Jayson, and Laurallyn Segur. Many of them touched our lives, influenced our decisions, or positively affected the outcome for one of our kids. These— and so many more—family, professionals, and friends have been the real secret to our success and sanity.

In some ways recounting the last ten years of my life has been more emotionally draining than reliving my childhood. Special thanks once again go to my mother, Gay Courter, for helping me to create cohesion and make sense of my endless notes, panicked phone calls, stories, accounts, memories, and impassioned ramblings—both on and off the page.

Additionally, I'd like to thank Phil Courter, Erick Smith, Sharon Smith, and Esther Mandel for their painstaking proofreading. I have a great relationship with my older brothers, Blake and Josh. Their wives, Amber and Giulia, are some of the most creative and passionate women I know. It's an incredible feeling knowing that we'll always be there for one another and that my children have such awesome aunts and uncles. A very special welcome also goes out to the littlest Courter, Josh and Giulia's newborn son, Zephyr. How exciting it is to be an aunt!

Finally, I must expose the wizard behind the curtain: my brilliant husband, Erick. I have tested and pushed you away so many times. Thank you for not giving up on me. We have spent the last ten years growing together as individuals, friends, partners, and now parents. I hope our sons grow up with your integrity, honesty, patience, thoughtfulness, and commitment to all that is right and good with the world. You are my best friend and my number one fan. You have given me everything I could have hoped for—even if it took me a while to realize what a treasure you are.

Like my brand-new baby, Andrew, my story is growing and changing every day. I no longer fear the unexpected. I was once the motherless child, lost and alone. Now I know for certain that I always will have people in my life to help me with any hardship I may face.

It is my wish that all children grow up to one day know such security, love, and happiness.

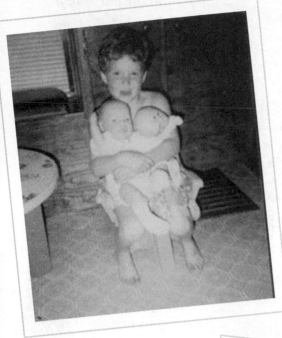

Me hugging my dolls while in foster care.

I was very active as a child and played on a local softball team while living at a group home.

My adpotive parents took me on many amazing trips. This picture was taken at a festival in California.

Ever since I was a teen, I have been speaking about child welfare issues all over the world.

Onstage at Eckerd College. I majored in theater and communications, with minors in political science and psychology.

Graduation day at Eckerd College. I went on to earn my master's degree in social work at the University of Southern California.

Erick and I spent a weekend with my biological family "muddin'" in the Carolinas.

After college, my speaking calendar grew . . . as did I. This picture shows me at my very heavy stage.

With Erick, at our wedding. We had no idea how many waves our cruise wedding would create.

Albert, our foster son, loved his first visit to Disney World.

Erick, with Dakota, one of our most frail foster children.

Often we had children that were close in age. Here are two of our "twins."

Our foster children Lillian and Denver playing piano.

Skyler was four months old when he came into our foster home. He had been nearly killed by his father.

Friends and volunteers waved signs on street corners during my run for Florida's state senate.

A photo of me with Erick taken during my first pregnancy. (Photo by Nathaniel Wagner)

We took our firsborn son, Ethan (four months), to a friend's wedding in St. Augustine, Florida.

Brothers Micah and Zachariah heading to preschool.

Me with our foster son, Zachariah.

Skyler, Erick, me, and Ethan at a local park. *(Photo by Andrea Walls, Off the Walls Photography)*

Left to right: Erick, Skyler, Gay, Phil, Ethan, and me on Skyler's adoption day. (Photo by Susanne Ravn)

Baby Andrew, our second biological son.

Our foster daughter, Millie, had fallen asleep reading my first book. Almost a year and a half later, we learned she was returned to relatives she had been removed from. Millie, age nine, was brutally murdered by her mentally-ill uncle, who was also living in the home.